Praise for *Drawn int*

Walter Berry has a way with words, a way with art, and a wondrous way with dreams. In Drawn into the Dream, *he opens the portals of inspiration and awe and leads readers to vital and creative ways of working with dreams and learning the language of their souls.*

Michael Meade
bestselling author of *Awakening the Soul* and *Fate and Destiny*

Walter Berry has a lot of fun in his dreams and in bringing their energy into the world, and he want to rouse us to do the same. In this engaging and often wildly funny book, drawn from his Hollywood life as well as his private night cinema, Walter plays the magician who is willing to show us what he has up his sleeve and let us borrow a trick or two, including the habit of drawing from dreams. He aims to help us open windows into a deeper world of wonder, and he succeeds. Don't buckle your seat belt for a ride with Walter Berry; it will do you no good at all!

Robert Moss, bestselling author of *Conscious Dreaming, The Secret History of Dreaming*, and *Growing Big Dreams*

This phenomenal book will not only get you whipped up into a frenzy about your dreams, like a kid at the gates of Disneyland, but Walter's expertise in this colorful realm will elevate your awareness and appreciation of your nighttime slumber party to the level of awe. In addition to the wonderful writing, Berry's spirit and genuine amazement at the blessing of our dreams are infectious. I highly recommend that you read this book at bedtime to provoke vivid, inspiring dreams.

Kelly Sullivan Walden, bestselling author of *It's All in Your Dreams*

The author is a great storyteller and his charm comes through distinctively in the book as well as in his unique approach to dreams. This is an entertaining, clever read, full of colorful stories.

Deirdre Barrett, Ph.D., Professor of Psychology, Harvard University, author of *The Committee of Sleep* and *Pandemic Dreams*

Walter Berry has written a truly "hands-on" guide to understanding your dreams. He shows how easy practices of drawing and mapping the content of dreams can lead to amazing "aha!" insights. Drawn into the Dream is filled with fascinating stories about dreams, including many from Berry's colorful life working in the entertainment business. Well grounded in current psychological research, the book explores the farthest reaches of dream experience, including dreams about sex, death, precognition, and spirituality. Especially for people with an interest in art and creativity, Drawn into the Dream *is a wonderful resource.*

Kelly Bulkeley, Ph.D.

Director, the Sleep and Dream Database, author of *Spiritual Dreaming: A Cross-Cultural and Historical Journey* and *Dreaming in the World's Religions*

Walter Berry is an artist of the dreamtime. With compelling storytelling and artistic flair, he evokes stories and images that guide us deep into the labyrinth of dreams to awaken that most mystical and wondrous state: awe. Drawn into the Dream *is packed with powerful dreams that will make your hair stand on end, fill your heart with compassion, and catapult you into the glorious riches of the dreaming mind. This is a wonderful book!*

Dr. Clare Johnson

author of *The Art of Transforming Nightmares* and *The Art of Lucid Dreaming*

WOW, words cannot do this book justice—it masterfully unravels the awesome mysteries of dreams by taking you on a deeply personal journey into their depths and their relation to the life of the dreamer as well as life itself. It unravels the essence of a dream from the inside looking out, in a wealth of deeply moving stories, where you will find yourself captivated yet emerging having absorbed a solid understanding for working with your own dreams. A must read.

Bob Hoss

Past President of IASD, Director of the DreamScience Foundation, author of *Dream Language: Self-understanding Through Imagery and Color*

Drawn into the Dream

DRAWN INTO THE DREAM

How Drawing Your Dreams Can Take You to the Land of Awes

WALTER BERRY

Published by Precocity Press, Los Angeles, CA
Developmental Consultant and Editor: Deborah K. Steinberg
Copyeditor: Julie Simpson
Cover and Book Designer: Susan Shankin
Cover Image: Walter Berry

ISBN: 978-1-7362174-9-8
Library of Congress Control Number: 2021911167
First edition. Printed and bound in the United States of America

THE GUEST HOUSE

This being human is a guest house.
Every morning a new arrival.
A joy, a depression, a meanness,
some momentary awareness comes
as an unexpected visitor.
Welcome and entertain them all!
Even if they are a crowd of sorrows,
who violently sweep your house
empty of its furniture,
still, treat each guest honorably.
He may be clearing you out
for some new delight.
The dark thought, the shame, the malice.
meet them at the door laughing and invite them in.
Be grateful for whatever comes.
because each has been sent
as a guide from beyond.

Rumi
Translation by Coleman Barks

CONTENTS

PART 2. THE DREAM DRAWINGS

A Technique that Allows the Dream to Enter the Room and Speak

PART 3. DREAMS AND THE MIND

The Delicate Dance of Dreamer and Dream

PART 6. MYSTERIOUS WISDOM

When Dreams Reveal Our Inner Knowing

PART 7. SEX, DEATH, AND OTHER FACTS OF LIFE

When Dreams Speak to Life's Big Themes

PREFACE

The most beautiful thing we can experience is the mysterious. It is the source of all true art and science. He to whom this emotion is a stranger, who can no longer pause to wonder and stand rapt in awe, is as good as dead: his eyes are closed. . . . To know that what is impenetrable to us really exists, manifesting itself as the highest wisdom and the most radiant beauty which our dull faculties can comprehend only in their most primitive forms—this knowledge, this feeling, is at the center of true religiousness. In this sense, and in this sense only, I belong in the ranks of devoutly religious men.

ALBERT EINSTEIN
Living Philosophies (1931)

PORTALS TO THE LAND OF AWES

This is a book about dreams, and their ability to inspire an awe-filled life.

There are lots of books on dreams. Some of them take a very scientific approach, some are psychological tomes steeped in Jungian or Freudian psychology, some take a metaphysical approach, many are methodologies of how to interpret or work a dream, and some are dictionaries—of which there are very few good ones.

My approach to dreams is based partially on my studies and reading, including in Jungian psychology, but more importantly on my years of experience working with people's dreams. I am a certified dreamworker, a graduate of the Marin Institute for Projective Dream Work, and I have incorporated the teachings of Jeremy Taylor, Robert Moss, Michael Meade, Robert Bosnak, Monte Ullman, and others into what I do.

My unique contribution to this world of dreamwork is centered in the drawings people do of their own dreams. In my workshops, we use these drawings as maps to the symbolic territory that dreams represent. When we draw a dream, things appear from the unconscious and end up on the paper in front of us. Our consciousness has no idea why we drew them (or left something out), but there they are, marks brought up from the deep interior staring back at us from the page. When this happens, I get the sense that the unconscious chuckles, having put one over on us—not only on our fragile egos but also on our consciousness—and steers us to where we actually need to go. When a dream is drawn, the unconscious has given us a roadmap to the place of understanding and the Land of Awes, as I call it.

There are many ways to talk about dreams, but I think you will find in these pages a unique and refreshing way to see yourself in a new light through your dreams. I am interested in the interpretation of dreams, but that takes a back seat to my vital fascination with the *experience* of a dream. How does the dream resonate with the dreamer and with others? When a dream is allowed to open its arms and invite us into its deep presence, something astounding happens. Something is experienced, feelings appear, our bodies respond, our poetic natures are activated, and we are alive and present. My life is a better place when I am experiencing a dream, whether it be my own or someone else's.

When people find out I'm a dream expert, they usually ask what something means in a dream. "What does it mean when you see a dead mouse in a dream?" "How about raisins in a dream? What does that mean? Am I going to get all wrinkly soon?"

My response is usually something along the lines of: "It depends—on the context of the dream, on you, on many other factors." I think the important part of working a dream is the *exposing* that happens. Dreams are these incomparable phenomena that come lurching up out of the unconscious, perching on the edge of our souls to be experienced. And that is my work. I listen with my ears, my eyes, and my soul as I encourage a dreamer to tell the dream, to draw the dream, to tell the dream again, to tell the dream from the raisin's perspective, to make up something about how the mouse died. The most important thing here is not my ego or the dreamer's ego. We do not even have to know what this missive from the underworld is about. If we can bring the dream up into consciousness, give it form, dance with it, play with it, and silently respect its presence, it will have an effect on our souls. It is like a Zen koan. In the search for the meaning of "the sound of one hand clapping," great work happens.

Dreams ask questions that do not always want answers; they seek to join us with an experience, usually an emotional experience. We need not know what the dead mouse "means" in the dream. Rather, let's ask: "How do I feel in the dream as I look at this dead mouse? Since the mouse is dead, where is he? Where is his presence now? What was the mouse's last thought? Where was he going?" If we posit and respond to questions like these, it doesn't really nail down what the mouse means, but we have brought a dream alive and brought to light something happening inside the dreamer's soul, even if it cannot be articulated.

What I do is a bit of a Zen approach that works to maintain a balance between two sides of existence that are seemingly incompatible—what Michael Meade calls the world of logos and the world of mythos—with the drawing serving as the fulcrum for that equilibrium.

During our seemingly short spiral of existence, we have to eat, clothe ourselves, "make" money, deal with other beautiful messy humans, and do other things that comprise the world of physical, logical existence—logos. But there is another side—mythos, where we are connected to deeper forces like the unconscious. It is the place of intuition and inspiration, where fairies fly and we soar with them, where we learn the secrets of inner peace. It is where trees speak in an ever-so-quiet voice, assuring us of our own beauty.

Mythos is a place of awe that reaches far beyond logic and reason, a place that makes little sense but feels right as you experience it. We all have this illogical resource at our command—if we only reach for it.

Don't tell me you haven't sat at a tree and, when no one was around, had a conversation with her. And then there was the time you imagined the tiny wiggling streaks of light on the ceiling in your childhood bedroom were friendly fairies that you could fly away with on an adventure. These are examples of tiny parts of the world of mythos, experiences that everyone can resonate with.

I believe in having one foot perfectly grounded in reality and another piece of me drifting among clouds of poetry, enveloped in music that forces my body to move to a rhythm I have no control of—all at the exact same time. The important thing in this life is to maintain both connections. If I live in a world where I think every move is guided by the stars, or every image has a message—such as the twigs that form an arrow pointing towards the liquor store mean I should end my years of sobriety—I am in trouble. I'm also in trouble if I live strictly by a logic that insists that when my recently deceased father comes to me in a dream and tells me he's fine and that he loves me, it's just my desire to be okay with his passing, that it's nothing more than my emotions getting the better of me.

If you can balance these two worlds of logos and mythos long enough, and quiet your monkey mind, a door will appear between them that demands to be opened, a magical door made of layer upon layer of thick threads and angel wings. This liminal space is the entrance into the experience of awe that the soul so passionately desires. It is not an easy place to find, but drawing your dream and allowing that drawing to be a portal will land you there if you allow it. It is up to you to open the door and enter the Land of Awes. That is where healing can begin, and joy and enlightenment dance like the dew on a spider web lit by the morning sun.

In my experience as a dreamworker, I have the privilege of plunging into this place of unending wonder time after time, as dream after dream unreels in front of me. As people share their dreams, that heavy, rusty door to the deep interior of the soul creaks open, dropping not only the dreamer but also everyone privileged enough to hear this magical tale into a wonderful place of awe and mystery. I have cried and felt waves of pain sweep my soul as I have worked dreams. I have felt the ecstasy of love and caring, deep compassion and joy as I have become one with the dream that floats and twists and sparkles in the room as the dreamer pours out the astounding mythic tale honed by the Dream Gods the night before.

In this book we will take a journey together. In the course of this journey we will encounter dreams that allowed people to move out of abusive relationships, solved problems, saved the dreamer's life, and dreams that dealt with childhood traumas. We will also experience dreams that gave people much needed self-confidence, and even dreams that sometimes just made us laugh and bond to others. We will appreciate the appearance in a dream of someone who has crossed into that world we all fear and revere—death, the other side, the great beyond, whatever you may call it. Listening and working with your dreams can deeply affect what you do and how you feel for your entire life.

The dreams you will encounter in this book are culled from many years of listening to and working with these breathtaking tales from the soul. I have changed names and other defining characteristics in order to protect the dreamer's identity, except in cases where I have explicit permission to include those details. I have also included many of my own dreams, which I hope you will find no less interesting and insightful.

Each of these dreams is unique and each has a feel and energy different from any other. There are, of course, themes and recurring images in many dreams, such as teeth falling out, being chased, being naked in public, not being prepared for a test, being back in high school or college, meeting a celebrity, falling—and my favorite, death (which encompasses such themes as being shot, stabbed, poisoned, or dismembered, or killing others). But even though the same image shows up in myriad dreams, the circumstances and the "feel" surrounding each one create a unique field, offering another opportunity for understanding or healing.

Almost all of the drawings included here are simple, quick sketches of the dream content done by non-professionals attempting to just get down the essence of what the dream was about. As such, they can seem crude, but are often quite telling. The rawness of the drawings, and at times what is missing from them, can lead down all sorts of paths. I prefer having this rawness to finished artwork, where the pesky ego ofttimes will pave over the "mistakes" that can be signposts to deeper work.

This is my world, and I open my soul to you here, hoping that something sticks to your soul in the process. Let's get started on our journey.

INTRODUCTION

The biographies of great artists make it abundantly clear that the creative urge is often so imperious that it battens on their humanity and yokes everything to the service of the work, even at the cost of health and ordinary human happiness. The unborn work in the psyche of the artist is a force of nature that achieves its end either with tyrannical might or with the subtle cunning of nature herself, quite regardless of the personal fate of the man who is its vehicle.

Carl Jung
The Spirit in Man, Art, and Literature (1930)

MEETING JUDY GARLAND

The Succubus Inside the Angel of Life

Long before I ever got into dreamwork, I had an experience that rocked me to my core, changed me forever, and opened my soul to awe.

In my high school years, I picked up a summer job at a local summer stock theater, The Camden County Music Fair. I worked for a guy named Vic, who had been Johnny Weissmuller's diving double in his Tarzan movies. It was our crew's job to erect the enormous tent that seated 1,800 patrons. This was a theater–in-the-round affair, with a stage and an orchestra pit. The guys who owned it were Broadway producers, so it had first-rate talent passing through during the summer: Jayne Mansfield,

Victor Borge, John Raitt, Gig Young, Julie Newmar, Jack Benny, and bands and musicians like The Dave Clark Five, Ray Charles, Duke Ellington, and Cream.

We were paid almost nothing—I think a buck and a half each night—but what a cool job!

So, in July 1967—July 10–15, 1967 to be exact—along came this broken-down old lady named Judy Garland, who was scheduled to sing. What a bore, thought I. I had never liked *The Wizard of Oz,* and as a 17-year-old kid, The Rolling Stones were more my cup of tea. But this was my job, and I could live through a week of maudlin crap.

Opening night was a zoo. Every red canvas-backed chair was filled. I held my position by the backstage entrance where the cranky old woman would appear, wondering how long this whole thing was going to take.

It was hot and sticky in there, and bugs flitted about everywhere. I found that ironic, because when Judy Garland had shown up to see the space during the day, she had insisted that someone (who turned out to be me) go out and buy a hundred Shell pest strips and hang them in the lighting and sound rig because she hated bugs, just hated them.

"Go get them now, young man. Go! Leave!" she'd said to me, and her manager echoed that. "Go! Go now!"

I spent hours driving to every Shell gas station in Southern New Jersey, gathering as many of the pest strips as I could find. As I was waiting for Lady Maudlin Grumpy to appear to begin this old fogey evening of bore-snore entertainment, I stared up into the lighting grid where I had hung dozens of the pest strips and to my malicious delight there were hundreds of bugs flitting around my strips. They seemed to like them. I guess they worked by actually attracting the bugs.

The lights went down, and that was my cue to make sure Madam Finicky got to the stage. I led her down the dark aisle and onto the round stage, making sure she didn't fall. The music had started, and the crowd roared. The lights came up as I dashed back up the aisle, unseen.

There she was, in her hideous sequined paisley pantsuit, holding court in the center of a ring of adoring fans. She smiled and waved, music vamping in the background, as she took control of the room.

This is going to be a long night, I thought. *She's milking this Wizard of Oz celebrity thing to the max.*

And then it happened.

She opened her mouth and started singing. Maybe singing isn't quite the word. I have no succinct words for what happened at that moment when the angry, dour woman I had met before the show suddenly tore open the heavens. When she stretched her hand out as she sang, sweeping it across the entire circle of the theater, it reached inside everyone's body and grabbed their soul and shook it to life. I was thunderstruck. I mean, she was mesmerizing. And all this happened in the very first note that came out of her. Resistance was futile. She was the queen of everything at that moment, and she knew it. You could feel the immense waves of energy pouring out across the crowd from her diminutive frame.

It was a brand new experience for me, so new that I was utterly confused. Why did my body feel this way? It was as though a switch deep inside me that I had no idea was there had magically been activated.

And it didn't stop. For the next two hours or so, she held 2,000 people in the palm of her hand. I was in sync with something for the first time in my life, which was totally unexpected and a huge shock to my system. It was my introduction to life, really. Everything I do with dreamwork, the way I now listen to people's hearts and souls, results from that moment. It changed me forever. Forever.

I have been employed for more than 30 years in the motion picture, television, and music industries and have worked with or been associated with tons of legends. I have observed and had conversations with Prince, Madonna, B.B. King, Paul McCartney, and so many more, witnessing up-close the magic they make. But absolutely no one in all these years has ever exhibited the charisma, the draw, the magic of that strange little woman.

So, there I was, having some sort of spiritual experience. Every damn one of us in the audience was swimming in the pool of awe she created. We hung on every vibration, we flowed like one, and thunderous applause followed each song. Everyone was cheering, and I mean cheering. People were on their feet for most of the night. The response to her performance was so loud, my buddies who worked out in the parking lot told me later that the tent was shaking like it was going to explode. It felt like the entire place was transported to some place not on this planet.

At the end of the show, I almost forgot that I had a job to do: get Judy Garland off the stage and escort her to her dressing room. Two other guys would help with the escorting, but it was my job to make sure she made it off stage safely.

The final song in the encore was "Somewhere Over the Rainbow," her signature song from *The Wizard of Oz.* Near the end of the song, we were to go down onto the stage, and then walk her up the main aisle to the dressing room.

Well, you can imagine the scene. She started into the song, and the place erupted. In all my life I have never witnessed anything like it. By the end of the song people were crying—no, bawling. Middle-aged guys in suits had tears pouring from their eyes; women's faces were smeared with makeup. The screams and applause were deafening.

And then my worst nightmare happened. They mobbed the stage! People pushed into the aisles, then down onto the stage from all directions. Some bold souls actually climbed over the chairs to get to her. It wasn't mean or pushy, but the entire stage was suddenly filled with adoring fans.

So, the three of us workers sliced through the sea of taffeta, pinstripe suits, and deafening cheers to reach the stage. Oddly, there was a slight clearing around her as she shook hands and embraced people. We stepped into the circle, and my buddies formed a wedge pointing up the main aisle towards the black curtains, behind which were the dressing rooms. I was tall and thin in those days, weighing only 128 pounds, but I was strong. So

I slipped my right arm under her knees, put my left arm around her back, and picked her up. She was small, so she fit nicely into my embrace. She leaned into me, her right arm over my left shoulder waving at people and her left arm grabbing me around my chest for stability.

I guess on some level I understood the theatricality of the moment. I lifted her enough that she was higher than I was, so the crowd could see her, and a cheer went up.

I yelled "Go! Go! Go!" to my guys, and we slowly moved up the aisle, cutting through the sea of people that enveloped us and then filled in behind as we moved. I could feel people tugging at me, grabbing for Judy's hand, but we managed to creep up towards the backstage area.

And here is where things got just weird. Now that we were on the move, and the panic of getting things under control was over, suddenly I became more aware of my own feelings. How do I put this? Well, frankly, I *became* Judy Garland at that moment, as embarrassingly odd as that sounds. Somehow, I was completely aware that that thing Judy Garland possessed was pouring from her body into and through mine. I felt like I was connected to everyone in the room and feeling love from them, making love to them. I guess you can say my mirror neurons, those pesky things that are the source of empathy, were firing on all cylinders. This was weird. Somehow by having Judy Garland in my arms while she was in this moment of blazing glory made me a conduit of feeling—of awesome love and empathy. And what a feeling!

It was the most electric transference of energy from another human I have ever felt to this date. Well, hell, this was fun. I would lift her up in the air, people would cheer, and she would wave and blow kisses, saying, "Thank you! Thank you!" over and over.

We finally got to the top of the aisle, and I had enough sense to turn around so my back was to the curtains that led backstage, giving her a last wave to the crowd. She let out a final *whoop!* and the people went crazy again. My guys opened the curtains and I backed into the dark passageway to the dressing rooms. As they dropped the curtains behind us, we were enveloped in the dark. And then the second strangest thing of my life happened.

Judy Garland slumped in my arms. I don't mean relaxed, I mean slumped, as in a sack-of-potatoes slump. The woman was totally spent, but holy damn, it was more than that. In an instant, she seemed to gain 30 pounds and it was all I could do to keep her in my arms. And that electric current that had been coursing through my body just a second ago? Gone, totally gone. Even stranger, it was replaced by something else, something so dark it's hard to describe. I buckled under the weight of it. All that joy and love that had flowed through me was reversed now, and my very soul was being sucked out of me by a darkness and despair I had never experienced. This wasn't the Judy Garland from out there in the light of adoration, this was the Judy Garland of pain, sadness, despair, and death. For a second, I thought she might *be* dying, but I looked into her face, and she just snarled. Yikes. It was about 20 feet to the dressing room, and every step was painful. I felt like *I* was dying.

And as if that were not bad enough, when I crossed the threshold of her dressing room, the bad feeling pouring out of her and through me filled up the room. I was suddenly surrounded with soul-sucking darkness from every direction. I could imagine Death over in the corner sucking the life out of everything, like the Death that plays chess with the knight in Ingmar Bergman's film *The Seventh Seal.* I know it sounds a bit crazy, but these were the real feelings that coursed through my soul in that moment.

I carefully laid her on a divan, and she collapsed like a rag doll. As I left, I noticed small rolling table, on which was a tray holding medications and a large hypodermic needle, the kind with the three round circles of metal at the top. It was all covered in a diaphanous paisley scarf. I took one more look at her limp body and left. A number of Judy's entourage, including her daughter Lorna, soon went into the dressing room, so I knew I hadn't killed her or anything. She was alive and chatting with her people, thank god.

I stood backstage for quite a while, retreating into my protective closet of solitude that no one knew about, trying to understand what had just happened. I was completely confused. This didn't fit into any box I knew of. The closest thing I could think of was that it had to be a religious experience—like Joseph Smith's meeting God, or Moses getting the tablets, or, well, nothing else fit. I had no language for this, but I had deeply experienced something, and it wouldn't be dismissed, no matter how hard I tried.

That night, I kept waking up from dreams with voices and images; it all made the sleep spasmodic at best. I have no recollection of the dreams, only the feeling that I had been visited by ghosts. Yuck. I was a bit cranky the next day, and guess what? It was only Tuesday, and the show ran until Saturday, so I had to do the same damn thing over again five more times.

I loved the idea of carrying her through the audience—doing that was better than what I imagined sex would be like (being a good Mormon, I failed to succumb to the delightful rigors of transcendent intercourse until I was 25)—but that last part, where the succubus appeared and sucked my soul as she slumped, was just downright scary. Well, perhaps tonight would be better. Maybe I had made up the entire experience.

Well, I hadn't made it all up, because the same thing happened Tuesday night. I mean exactly. I guess we had established a routine, because I carried her off the stage again, and she wriggled in such a way that I knew to lift her for those moments of adulation as we plowed slowly up the aisle to deafening roars and outstretched hands. That weird, unexplainable transference of high energy through my body was there again, in full force. I was expecting it this time, and so instead of being so overwhelmed by it, I let it just pass through my body, and listened to it, or let myself fall into it—oh hell, I was having an experience that I was acutely determined to remember the feeling of, and yet it really defies explanation. Something deep and powerful was being etched into my soul. I was soaring and completely overwhelmed by the greatest sense of awe I have ever, ever encountered.

But there was no escaping the crushing blackness of this glorious, disturbed soul. After we backed through the black curtains, once again she slumped and became heavy as lead. I could feel my soul, or spirit, or something inside me being drained like a radiator. I rushed her to the divan and got her out of my grasp as fast as I could.

Something weird happened then. As I was about to turn and leave, she gently reached out and touched my arm. "Thank you, young man, thank you," she said. And she squeezed my arm a bit and forced a smile. Then she dropped her grip, fell back into the cushions, closed her eyes, and exhaled heavily.

I quietly left a moment before the entourage arrived again.

In that short span of time, in that brief five-second interchange, everything changed for me, permanently. At that moment, long before dreams would teach me this lesson, I began to understand something about the juxtaposition of pain and joy. In the midst of the darkest moment I had ever experienced, this bright ray of light reached out and beamed into me. How was it possible for both feelings to be there at the same time?

A smiling, happy Mormon at the time, I lived an insular life, not really looking at the dark side. One of the teachings drummed into me was not to mention or give any time to thoughts of Satan. In so doing, I was told, you gave him space in your life, and he or one of his followers would influence or possibly possess you and take over your thoughts and life.

But this Judy Garland thing wouldn't and won't leave me alone. It haunted me. If someone could feel that extreme ecstasy standing onstage—communing with something so deep and unseen, sucking the nectar of the gods from the primal source of life and spreading it through an audience of 2,000 people, transfixing them—and then a moment later lie crumpled in pain and despair, life must be more complex than I had ever imagined.

I still contemplate this. How do two things so diametrically opposed live in a single being at the same time? I still don't know the answer, but I do know that like many of us here under this mortal coil, I live with deep pain and ecstasy at the same time. The difference between what I do and what Judy Garland did might be in how I face, accept, and deal with the pain and anger and injustices of life. However, I think it is also about volume. The greater the capacity for feeling, the greater the highs and lows. When Judy Garland opened her heart, it was so large, and she opened it so far, that she became susceptible to both the rush of angels and the stampede of self-doubt.

During her four remaining performances that summer, the intensity of the pattern we had established remained high, searing into my soul the sensations of cold and hot, Dorothy and the Wicked Witch, angels and devils.

On night five I even ran a little test. When we got to the black curtains, and she did her big wave to the roaring cheers, I stepped through the curtains, and she turned into an incarnated black hole as usual. Then, I accidently-on-purpose stumbled back out into the theatre. A cheer arose, and the bright, cheery Judy reappeared instantly, whereupon I immediately crossed back into the backstage—and oh, did I get a look. Yikes. I had almost exposed the dark side of the icon to the masses, and Judy Garland was not at all happy. I swiftly deposited her and escaped, for I was afraid that the evil queen would cast a spell on me. But luckily she reached for her medications as I was leaving, and I was off the hook.

On the last night, just before we stepped through the curtain, she shot me a look that said, "Don't you pull that stunt again tonight, young man." And I didn't. We had developed some sort of strange symbiotic relationship that I relished, and I truly missed her when it was over. What an awe-filled experience it was during that sultry week in 1967.

Judy Garland died two years later of a barbiturate overdose. She was 47. I was shocked by her death but, with all that I had seen, not surprised. She had had a rocky life, becoming addicted to drugs early on. The minions at MGM would give her "pep pills" so she could get up in the morning and work a 16-hour day filming with Mickey Rooney and others, and then they would administer sleeping pills at night. When I met her, she was still living in the fame of her 1961 Carnegie Hall comeback performance, a performance that stands in history as one of the greatest of the twentieth century. The descriptions of it echo all that I witnessed that 1967 summer in New Jersey.

How does this have bearing on dreamwork? The main thought—really an unanswered question about the Judy Garland experience—is about that strange, volatile mix of glorious, euphoric love and the dark ache of despair and utter loss of soul. We humans are a paradox of feelings, a crossing of energy streams, and sometimes we need to let our focus drop and live fully in joy and despair at the same time. As close as I can get to the answer is that it is important to not use love to hide despair or despair to hide love. We must try to the best of our ability to stand in the presence of all that is inside us and let it play out, always adjusting the balance and moving forward.

I believe that Judy Garland ended up crossing over to the other side because a balance was never achieved. She tried to continue the euphoria she experienced onstage by attempting to medicate herself into the same state, and thereby avoid facing the monsters and demons. They were there every night, the unmasked versions of those monsters, literally waiting just beyond the black curtain. And I felt them, heard their gnashing teeth, smelled their bad breath—but just for the time it took to go 20 feet. After that they were hers, until she numbed the experience, turning it into an ecstasy of evasion.

We all have to face monsters, whether they are called addiction, compulsion, fear, denial, self-loathing, indifference, or a thousand other names. We all have brilliant monsters to face, and I do mean *all* of us. And when we do tame or slay or befriend a monster, there is usually another waiting around the corner by the water fountain. The escape into drug-induced states keeps the monsters at bay, but they are still there, and they become larger as they feed on fears that radiate out through the porous walls of our souls. They wait for that moment when we open the door, and they rise up in all their splendor and horror and demand our attention. And what do we do at that moment? Do we face them and possibly get eaten alive? Do we run to our god and ask him to face the monster for us? Do we pretend they are not there, denying they exist altogether?

The answer I am pushing here—what radiates in the core of dreamwork—is to face the monster, and either conquer it or get eaten. Because even in getting eaten, a transformation will occur. Sometimes it is the right thing to seek outside help from divinity. Sometimes it is the right thing to ignore or postpone a confrontation with these things. Sometimes you have to dig a hole and hide from the smelly monster. But often the best plan is to pull out that long sharp sword and slay the monster—or even better, befriend it.

The other piece of the Judy Garland experience that changed me and has stayed with me all these years is feeling the presence of people. I realized that if you sit next to someone, if you are quiet and stop all the chatter in your head, you can feel a bit of what that person is about. My experience over a lifetime is that empathy and compassion are two of the greatest tools to have as we brave these cataclysmic cycles known as the human condition.

Because of the Judy Garland experience, I started *listening* to people. Listening not only to what they said, but to the accompanying emotion, and if I was lucky, I would get a sense of that thing called soul—the dark part of our being that reaches down into the earth—as well as the soaring spirit that gives hope to us all.

What's the difference between soul and spirit? Well, in this book, I use the word *spirit* to mean that part of us that wants to soar, that reaches for a connection to a god thing, that yearns to visit the upper realm via Pegasus (in Greek mythology) or Garuda (whom Vishnu rides, in the Hindu) or Baraq (which Mohammad rode to the heavens). When I experience spirit, it is upward, light-filled, joyous, and soaring. I leap from the branches of the tree of life and fly without falling.

Soul, on the other hand, is the connection to things deep within. Soul has earthiness. It has darkness and wetness and pondering and poetry. Soul has connections to the hidden roots of the tree of life, and in the caves of forgotten dreams.

I've lost touch at times with this skill of listening and really hearing, but it is a skill that has been instrumental in working with people's dreams. Whatever sensitivity to others I bring to bear as I work ardently in the field of dreamwork stems from this one week in 1967 and that awareness I gained with Judy Garland.

I have one last story about the Judy Garland experience. It came full circle for me a few years ago in an unexpected way. I had been a serial dater, going on countless coffee dates, hikes, and dinners, looking for someone with a certain inexplicable magic. I had almost given up on the idea of finding a compatible person I could dance and play with through this difficult and wondrous life. And then it happened. I was sitting in an Indian restaurant in Santa Monica, having a lengthy and wonderful conversation with a beautiful woman on a first date. After 200 or so dates with others, I was done with cuteness and pat questions and answers, and so I let my crazy real self pour out in torrents, consequences be damned. I talked about dreams and became emotional. In turn, I listened to her without any agenda. She was fascinating, completely gorgeous—with the thickest hair I have ever encountered—and damn smart, which I find sexy. But I was pretty sure my enthusiasm had violated every rule of dating protocol. I was headed for the polite handshake at the end of the date.

And then something bizarre happened. She extended her hands slightly across the table. I wasn't sure if she was indicating I should touch her hands or just stretching after this powerful, three-hour conversation. But I took a chance, looked into her eyes, and touched her hands. Oh, my god. I was catapulted into unexpected awe. The same current that had passed through me so many years ago as I carried Judy Garland appeared again and shocked the hell out of me. This woman had magic, real magic emanating from her and it was coursing through my body—I was not really sure if she was aware of it or not.

Well, that was it for me. Done searching. Luckily, she found a bit of magic in me also. And, yes, she and I are still together, and she still carries that magic. Some nights, when she is fast asleep, I ever so gently touch her hand—just to see if that mysterious electric current is still flowing, and sure enough, I flash back on July 1967, as I am launched quietly into the Land of Awes.

Now I have something fascinating to show you. It turns out that there are photographs of the Judy Garland experience, which I stumbled upon. That is me in my maroon jacket with my back to the camera in the first one. The caption reads, "Employees of the Camden County Music Fair prepare to escort Judy Garland off the stage." This is seconds before I picked her up and carried her up the aisle to her dressing room. The second picture is Judy Garland coming down the aisle at the top of the show. You can see the black curtains at the back where I carried her through into her dressing room.

Photos by Bill David

Thank you, Judy.

PART 1

AN EXPLORER IN THE LAND OF AWES

Forging the Tools of Dreamwork

CHAPTER 1

STUMBLING TOWARDS DREAM ECSTASY

A Personal Journey into Dreamwork

If I had influence with the good fairy who is supposed to preside over the christening of all children I should ask that her gift to each child in the world be a sense of wonder so indestructible that it would last throughout life, as an unfailing antidote against the boredom and disenchantments of later years, the sterile preoccupation with things artificial, the alienation from the sources of our strength.

RACHEL CARSON
The Sense of Wonder

THE SCREAMING PTERODACTYLS

The question undoubtedly arises: How did I end up as a dream facilitator? How did all this extreme fascination with dreams start for me?

It all began with a dream, of course.

It was the 1980s and I was deep in therapy, attempting to find my footing after leaving a failed marriage and escaping the gravitational pull of the black hole known as the Mormon Church. How I left all of that is the subject for another time (my friend Deirdre Barrett has suggested more than once that I should write a musical about it).

Suffice it to say that on Sunday, January 1, 1984 I woke up—literally and figuratively—and left Mormonism behind forever.

But, Holy Mother of Moroni, this did not make life any easier; it only made it harder. Having been immersed in a cult-like religion, truly believing it, and then discovering you are living a lie is painful and life shattering. To my amazement, I instantly became the outcast and the personification of evil. I was that guy who had abandoned truth and God and a sacred marriage. I lost many friendships and connections as I climbed out into a world totally unfamiliar to me, stumbling around like a drunken fool. It was a lonely, tumultuous, and depressing time, but I began to love myself for the first time.

I found a way to survive, moving forward one day at a time and promising myself never to fall into such madness again.

So, here I was, five years later in therapy with a small- to medium-sized chip on my over-tight shoulders, and my therapist suggested that I write down my dreams. She thought it might help somehow, and since my recovery had been tremendous under her tutelage, I agreed.

I had been keeping a journal with all manner of musings about dating and self-confidence, dialoguing with my inner self and generating raw, stream-of-consciousness insights that seemed to help. I kept the indulgent journal by my bed, just in case I thought of something profound in the middle of the night. I woke up often in those days, because the young couple next door perpetually yelled and threw things that would slam against the wall. If it wasn't the parade of projectiles from such altercations, it would be their similarly volatile love-making, with its ear-piercing moans and groans and the thuds of naked bodies being pounded up against the wall just above my head.

So, when the book, boot, bottle of booze, or bare-naked body smacked the wall at 2 AM, shattering the dark night and my sleep, one of those pesky dreams would be sitting right there to write down as I waited for the tumult to end. There I was, quietly writing down a dream as the cavalcade of random objects and body parts pummeled the wall in a cacophony of love and hate, finally climaxing in groans and screams that sounded like two pterodactyls in heat. I don't know if I would have recorded any dreams at all if these two didn't have a wild and funky sex life. Thank you, my screaming pterodactyl lovers.

I had written down hundreds of dreams, right along with all my musings about learning to meditate and various poems and quotes. So I began reporting my mental meanderings to my therapist. The dreams would launch a discussion about something I was working on in my soul, and *voila!* Now we were doing dreamwork. Although I was still wounded and afraid I might fall into another black hole of belief in some other cult-like adventure, I started embracing the ideas and passions I found through therapy.

THE HAND IN THE TILL

One night—don't ask me how—both screaming pterodactyls slammed up against the wall at the same time. For a second I thought the wall would break and I would suddenly be involved in the most raucous three-way sexual encounter in history. (I guess their crazy-mad sex acts jostled more than a few fantasies in my soul.) In reality I was perfectly aware of what would come next. There would be a temporary silence, soon shattered by orgasmic thunderbolts of shrieking rapture. As another dream was waiting to be recorded, I seized the opportunity of the momentary quiet.

This is exactly what I wrote down that night, except I must admit I did change one name here to protect the not so innocent.

THE HAND IN THE TILL

My mom calls, and my dad and Jim get on the phone too—

Dad, "Your brother Jim . . ." (they hem and haw) "has been caught with his hand in the till."

I say, "We're talking embezzlement here aren't we?" I am turning off the stereo and TV, catching snatches of conversation.

"How much are we talking about here?" I say.

Dad, "$4,000."

Me, "So, what's going to happen?"

Jim, "I'm paying it back."

Me, "So what's the problem?"

Dad, "The problem is we have a thief in the family, a liar, a cheat."

I started wondering what this dream could mean. Embezzlement? $4,000? What does that have to do with anything in my life? Nothing that I could think of came to mind. Dreams are just so damn weird.

But not so fast . . . Two weeks after the dream, my Mom called me in real life. I happened to have the stereo on while watching television, and I had to turn both off to hear her.

"I have some unpleasant news to tell you," she said.

"What's that, Mom?" I asked.

"Your brother Jim has been caught with his hand in the till."

Wait a minute . . . did she just say what I think she said? "What was that you said, Mom?"

"I said your brother Jim has been caught with his hand in the till," was her reply.

I asked her to hold on for a minute, and I searched for my journal. I flipped through all the angst-laden pages, arriving at the dream I'd recorded. The dream in the journal, I noticed, was indeed about my brother Jim, but maybe this was a coincidence. Besides, it was my Mom talking, not my Dad, who had done the talking in the dream report. But wait, the "hand in the till" was the exact phrase on the page, and who used such an expression? It was so specific and odd that, on a lark, I decided to see what would happen if I used the written-down dream as a framework for this conversation.

I read out loud into the phone from the page: "Oh. We're talking embezzlement here, aren't we?"

"Yes, exactly! He has been stealing money from the cash register where he works," she replied.

"How much money are we talking about?"

"$4,000," she replied.

I looked down at the page, and it read $4,000. I got chills.

I read my next line. "So, what's going to happen?"

She replied, "He's going to pay it back. They are going to let him off the hook as long as he pays back the money."

In the dream, it had been Jim who said this—but these were still the exact words, and I had the feeling I was in some strange, magical place.

Mom then went off script and explained that Jim would have to do some counseling. Then she paused.

I knew somehow that she was waiting for me to ask her my question, the one sitting right there on the page. I was caught in some strange déjà vu moment. I knew what was about to occur, which defied logic. I think this may have been the one time in my life when I knew exactly what someone was going to say before they said it. I absolutely knew her answer to the question I was about to ask.

My mischievous nature now grabbed hold, and I said nothing. I knew my line was "So what's the problem?" but what if I didn't say my line? Would the space-time continuum shatter? So, I paused and waited.

There was a long silence on the phone, and I could feel my mom getting uncomfortable. She finally piped up and said, "Do you have a question for me or something?"

Oh, hell, I thought, I have to ask it. "So, what is the problem?"

"The problem is we have a thief in the family, a liar, a cheat!" she announced—the exact wording on the page in front of me. She was quite upset and hung up on me.

I was dumbfounded. How the hell could this be? Frankly, I wasn't much interested in brother Jim and his misadventure, but how do I explain this almost religious vision to the Walter who had escaped the cult and now firmly believed in science and logic only

My cynical opinion of the world and how it functioned cracked open a bit in that moment. It allowed something inexplicable in, and I was not sure how I felt about that.

So many questions: Was there some unseen being out there controlling things and laughing at me at this moment? Was I destined to be dragged back into the cult of Mormonism? Oh, hell no, none of that—but what if there is something mysterious about life that has no explanation and I have to learn to live with that?

Holy Jessica Rabbit, there was something to dreams, there just had to be. I just couldn't explain to my logic-laden ego how this totally mystical occurrence fit into any slot of reason or sensibility. It was time to open a new book of understanding. Somewhere in that liminal space inhabited by things I did not know was a place of wonder and awe that I needed to find and experience. I absolutely and adamantly had to pursue this adventure into the world of dreams.

HUNTING THE SACRED BUFFALO AT ESALEN

Needless to say, I reported this strange precognitive occurrence with wide eyes and enthusiasm to my therapist, who replied, "So, what are your feelings surrounding this event?"

Not to demean therapists, but doesn't every therapist have 16 different ways to say, "How does that make you feel?"

I explained to her that I was mystified and intrigued by this strange, illogical event.

My subtle therapist went over to her desk, pulled out a catalogue, and handed it to me, telling me they conducted seminars about dreams at this place called Esalen in Big Sur, California and I should look into it. (She added that she also taught salsa dancing there.)

I looked through the catalogue, and I realized I was perusing classes of an ilk I had little or no affinity for. Filling the pages were classes with titles like "Scream Therapy, Journey into the Sacred Unknown," "Is It Love, or Is It Addiction? Finding True Love," "The Enneagram and Higher Awareness." And on and on. Yikes.

I finally found a weeklong workshop titled "Dreaming: The Magic Mirror Never Lies," taught by some guy named Jeremy Taylor. Never heard of him—plus he had the title D.Min. (Doctor of Ministry) after his name, setting off my anti-religion radar. But my therapist thought this was a cool place, so I called and signed up, resigned to hanging out with crazies in the trees and eating rabbit food for a week—but what the hell, it would make a good story.

I arrived at Esalen a bit early, so I hiked around the grounds. It was beautiful. As I stood on a bridge over a stream, watching the swirling waters beneath, I got the feeling I liked this place. Then I looked up, and there, high in a nearby tree, a burly guy in a flannel shirt with his arms around a giant limb yelled, "I love you tree! I love you tree!" I kid you not.

Then I was off to the natural hot springs baths. As I descended the path, I saw what appeared to be a bunch of naked people. Say what? All the people in the baths were nude. I mean no bathing suits, no robes, nothing—they were unabashedly naked and relaxed about it. Well, I was down with that! Off came my clothes and my attitude. I hopped into a tub full of very hot water that smelled like sulfur, where the topic was as hot as the water: yoga and Freud. I had no idea how those two subjects related and didn't really care, being totally distracted by all the eye-catching naked bodies.

I was fascinated by the little tattoo that so many of the women had at the small of their back. But that was nothing compared to the guy with the man-bun. When he suddenly stood up in the tub I found myself facing a huge three-dimensional flying dragon. Seriously, this guy's tattoos were epic. His prodigious member was the long neck of a dragon, with green scales tattooed on the top side and red and white stripes on the underside like the belly of a dragon, and a pair of eyes at the end created by a piercing. Gulp, that must have hurt. His balls were the dragon's body, also tattooed with green scales. And to complete this scintillating artful vision, radiating out across his pelvis were a pair of beautiful dragon wings. Not that I was staring at this or anything.

Welcome to the mystical world of Esalen.

And then to class. There were about 20 of us, mostly women, sitting in a circle on the floor. Jeremy Taylor launched into this mesmerizing talk about dreams speaking a universal symbolic language. He said that all dreams come for our health and wholeness. I was a little dubious about all that, but the feeling was genuine and inviting. All of us were spellbound as he wove his tapestry of stories and philosophy centered on dreams and their powerful effect on our lives.

And that night I dreamt. It was a doozy, at least for a guy who had dreams about things like embezzlement.

HUNTING THE SACRED BUFFALO

We are hunting the Sacred Buffalo in the frozen North. Where we hunt is at the top of the world. Everything is frozen solid. The ground is covered in snow in all directions. The sky is a dull gray and there is no life and no sound except the howl of the wind. I have a guide with me. He is small, wizened, wise, and the absolute master of this part of the world. He has wavy dark hair, a moustache, and a smile that twinkles. His eyes are dark and intense, and he sees everything. I am not happy about killing the sacred buffalo, but the wisdom of the guide is not to be questioned. I stand under a cliff (like a frozen wave) and when the buffalo leaps into the air, I stab him from underneath with a gold-tipped spear. He is killed instantly and falls to the ground in a heap.

The guide makes me put the carcass of the buffalo into a sacred circle that is defined by a red ring that appears when I brush back the snow. I then smash and grind the remains into a liquid. The head and shinbone float in the liquid. There is no blood. After I finish this difficult and sacred task, I drink some of the liquid and store the rest in a medicine bag that I hang around my neck. The guide tells me that I will need all this as fuel and food for my winter. I am a little distressed by this killing I have done, but I know there is extreme import to this very deep religious event. I have a new guide, and that is good, very good.

I brought this dream to the group the next morning, and I was fortunate to have it worked on. Jeremy launched into the idea that this was about frozen emotions (the ice) and self-confidence. Well, the frozen emotions I could see, but the self-confidence? He explained that my wise old guide was a part of myself that I had denied. I was projecting my self-confidence on the strange little man, and the dream invited me to own that part of myself that is totally self-confident.

Something swept over me as the work continued. This felt right to me, as a new way of seeing my own life. It was as though I was standing outside myself just a bit and seeing my strengths and weaknesses as people projected their ideas onto my dream.

This life-changing experience dropped me into a place of awe. Here I was, surrounded by people sincerely trying to help me understand something that had come without control or forethought into my being. I was forced, in a way, to own that spear, and to accept that in my nature was a powerful man, a spiritual man, perhaps with frozen emotions, but possessing the "juice" to heal not only himself, but many others. Ever since childhood, I had known I had something special, some secret thing inside the center of my body that I silently called the "ball of energy," and that ball got activated at this moment. I was genuinely moved for the first time in a long, long time. I was feeling that same immense energy that had surged through me while carrying Judy Garland.

Not everyone in the group was on the mark. One old geezer went on and on about how awful it was that I wanted to go around killing buffalos in Alaska—but most of the comments hit home. I came away with a profound sense that I was not alone in the world. I realized that this world held certain individuals who could see deeply enough, way beneath the surface, to reach right into my soul—something I had been longing for all my life. I suddenly had a sense of something sacred about my own soul. It was time to move some furniture and a few friends into the empty room that was my life.

After having my dream worked and projected all over in a loving way, my cynicism about a bunch of things melted. My ears and heart opened a bit, and I started to feel part of a community.

In that workshop, Jeremy had us work dreams with other members of the group in the off hours. I picked a woman from the group at random, who told me about a gloomy dream that took place at 12:15 and involved lots of angry male relatives. We talked about the dream for three hours. I kept noting that she seemed quite upset the entire time we were talking, which didn't seem to fit such a mundane dream. Finally, she blurted out what the dream had made her realize: she had been molested as a young teenager—by her father.

Phew. I was out of my depth there, but I had witnessed her process, and she seemed relieved from the work. That was the first dream I ever worked. I felt like something inside me had just had a good cry. Weird, but good.

The next day the woman presented that same dream to the group. After she recounted the dream, before we discussed what it meant, Jeremy put his hand to his face, darted his eyes about a bit, and then said, "You know, if this were my dream, and forgive me for being so blunt, I would wonder, since you mention the time as being 12:15, if I had been molested by my father or a relative when I was between the ages of 12 and 15."

And of course, then she blurted out everything it had taken me three hours to get to.

With each succeeding dream that we worked, I found myself walking around inside the dream and walking around inside of myself. Over the seven days of that workshop, I changed. I still had doubts and difficulties to face, but I had found something that could be probed daily to unearth meaning and purpose from my own deep interior. Life began to mean something.

By the end of that glorious week, I was part of something, something real and beautiful. I was alive in a way that I had always wanted to be. I was home in some way. I wanted to continue the work, because when I was in the thick of working dreams, I felt alive, vital, tuned, and in touch with my own emotions.

I struck up a close friendship with Mara, Jeremy's assistant, during that week. Over the next two years, she and I talked on the phone, visited in person, and worked dreams on a regular basis. She was a mentor who challenged my ideas, loaned me books, and helped me build self-confidence. With her I became that buffalo hunter with the golden-tipped spear. I also continued working with Jeremy Taylor and eventually became certified as a dreamworker through his program, but it was Mara who held the candle high over my life as I trudged through the maze in search of meaning. Without her help, I don't think I would have solidified my dream practice.

Every time I sit and listen deeply to someone's dream now—and I have listened to a lot of dreams—I connect immediately to that moment in Jeremy Taylor's workshop when people filled my soul with rich caring as they projected onto my sacred buffalo dream. And I have a bit of that magic potion left in my medicine bag to drink and to share.

CHAPTER 2

THE SCRIBE IN THE LAND OF AWES

Recalling and Recording a Dream

THE WAY IT IS

There's a thread you follow. It goes among
things that change. But it doesn't change.
People wonder about what you are pursuing.
You have to explain about the thread.
But it is hard for others to see.
While you hold it you can't get lost.
Tragedies happen; people get hurt
or die; and you suffer and get old.
Nothing you do can stop time's unfolding.
You don't ever let go of the thread.

William Stafford
The Way It Is, New and Selected Poems (1998)

DREAM RECALL

In order to work on our dreams, we need to remember and record them. All of us have different sleep patterns and experiences, which affect dreaming and dream recall. Dream recall is highly individualistic. Dreams and dream recall are affected by what is going on in our complex chemistry.

How long and how many times do we dream in a night, you might ask? It varies, but we dream from four to six times a night, and the length usually increases as the night progresses. It can start out with a five-minute dream early on, and by the end of an eight-hour cycle of sleep a single dream can be 30 to 40 minutes long. That is what the research says, but I have had lengthy dreams at the beginning of the night and have recorded up to 10 dreams in a night. Some research says the combined length of our nightly dreams exceeds two hours. Suffice it to say that we dream a lot every night.

People I know who are regular marijuana users tell me they rarely remember dreams when they are riding Puff the Magic Dragon. Studies have shown that THC, the main ingredient that takes you "one toke over the line, sweet Jesus," reduces the frequency and length of REM sleep—that time when many vivid dreams appear. Heavy drinking, taking Ambien, and other drug use that affects sleep patterns can also diminish dream recall. The dreams are still there, just not as frequent, and for most people, recalling them under such influences is difficult.

In the arena of extreme dream indulgence, I know several adventurous souls who have taken part in the consumption of ayahuasca, the hallucinogenic brew from the Amazon. They report that after a giant bout of puking their guts out, the magic potion kicked in and they found themselves on a mystic journey filled with vivid and powerful dreams and visions of snakes, gods, and other bizarre creatures. I am reticent to try this journey, since they tell me it almost always produces nausea, vomiting, and diarrhea—but perhaps someday.

Some other drugs can enhance dream memory and content. Studies have shown that galantamine, a supplement used for boosting memory and helping Alzheimer's patients, can increase by 5.8 times the likelihood of recalling a lucid dream (those dreams where you consciously know that you are dreaming). I have used galantamine, and it seems to influence the dreams' vividness as well as promoting greater lucidity. Studies have also shown that B vitamins and magnesium supplements help dream recall.

And then there are prescription drugs whose side effects include affecting our dreams and dream recall. Their effects are all over the map. Anti-Parkinson drugs can produce vivid sexual dreams. Antidepressants can bring on nightmares. In rare cases statins can produce nightmares. Withdrawing from the use of barbiturates can also cause nightmares. Propofol, the drug that killed Michael Jackson, increases the incidence of pleasant dreams, which makes me wonder if that was part of why he used this drug. Opioid users often report very vivid dreams, especially at the beginning of their use.

Putting aside all discussions of chemistry, let's talk about how to improve dream recall. Foremost, it helps to have a desire to remember your dreams. I maintain a commitment to be "in relationship" with my dreams. They don't control me or my actions, but just like a good friend or partner, they listen to me and I listen to them. They are part of me and are in contact with the deep soul that longs to share its poetry and wisdom with the Walter that gets lost in the daily routine of life. To listen to your dreams, even if you don't understand their meaning, is to be in contact with the poet, artist, dancer, musician, and philosopher resting at the base of your soul crying out to be heard.

To recall your dreams, it helps to be aware of your sleep patterns. Some people sleep through the night fairly uninterrupted, and most of their dream recall happens just upon waking in the morning. If you are that type of person, you can make a commitment to be still for a moment upon waking in the morning, to see if a dream is lingering there in that space between mystery and consciousness.

I am not so solid a sleeper as that. I have a biphasic cycle where I sleep for three to four hours and then am awake for an hour, then sleep another three to four hours. Besides that, I make a point of drinking large amounts of water before I sleep. As you can imagine, my body wakes me up a number of times to visit the toilet. This activity often flushes a dream to the surface, you might say.

There is research that shows that before the industrial revolution and the invention of electricity, people slept in that biphasic cycle, especially during the winter months (in places that have winters). People would sleep for four hours, then be up for an hour or two, sometimes having a meal, visiting with neighbors, reading, sharing dreams, or having sex, and then sleep for another four hours. Sounds great, except for the visiting the neighbors part. My dream recall happens at all times of the night, and because I have a commitment to myself to record my dreams no matter how disturbing or dopey they seem, I have volumes and volumes of dream reports.

And no, you are not the exception—a person who does not dream. Everyone dreams. They have taken people who are adamant they have never had a dream, put them in a sleep laboratory, awakened them in several REM (rapid eye movement) periods, and found a dream.

OVALTINE TO THE RESCUE

I'd better explain REM sleep. It is called REM—short for "rapid eye movement"—because during various segments of sleeping, the eyes dart back and forth rapidly under the eyelids. Rapid eye movement was identified and linked to dreams by Nathaniel Kleitman and his student Eugene Aserinsky in 1953. They weren't very interested in dreams; they were interested in the study of sleep. Sleep was an understudied area at the time—most scientists thought that only a fool would study something where nothing happened.

Interestingly, the makers of Ovaltine sponsored the sleep studies, hoping to show that their drink helped insomnia. Someone had to pay for the half-mile of paper each subject required for a single night's study, and Ovaltine stepped up to the plate.

Eugene Aserinsky first noticed that, while he had sleeping subjects hooked up to the electroencephalography (or EEG) machine, several times in sleep the subject's eyes would twitch back and forth rapidly. They later discovered that if they woke up the subjects in the middle of these twitching events, they were usually in the middle of a dream. It was a phenomenal discovery, and it became the foundation of dream studies, because researchers could wake people during or after a dream and get a reliable dream report, one not tainted by the dreamers' editing and forgetfulness. We also dream in non-REM sleep—that part where your eyes aren't twitching and convulsing. But it seems the more vivid dreams—the ones with the armies of wolves dressed in black nightgowns attacking the makeup department at Target and making themselves up as they devour giant legs of mutton while cackling witches skate around the walls painting them red—are more often encountered in REM sleep.

So, for around two hours or more in total per night, you are dreaming. Just knowing that should give you permission to remember more dreams. Tonight, before you descend into the Land of Nod, think about that—for about two of those hours of your sleep time you are dreaming. Your unconscious is furiously unloading scads of information, emotions, and experiences. Surely you can record just one small piece of a dream? Any good habit, like brushing your teeth for a full two minutes, takes a while to develop into an effective routine, but if you can cultivate the desire to recall your dreams and then stick with it for a month, you will find dream recall easier and easier.

And in case you are wondering whether Ovaltine got their money's worth, well of course they did. They didn't give a rat's ass about the REM sleep thing, but by sponsoring sleep studies, they could claim a link between their drink and the science of sleep. In fact, it is now known that magnesium promotes sleep, and there's plenty of magnesium in Ovaltine. So there you have it!

RECORDING YOUR DREAMS

So, how should you go about recording your dreams? A dream report is whatever record you produce to represent the dream—writing, drawing, and/or audio. Dreams can be so ephemeral it is important to develop some way you can record them before they disappear into the ether.

When I am trying to write words in that hypnopompic state (that semiconscious state just before wakefulness), I sometimes lose the quickly evaporating images, so I use the voice recorder on my phone and transcribe it on the computer later. That doesn't work for everyone, though. For many, the kinetic connection to writing on paper opens the flow of the dream. There is also something ritualistic and wonderful about having transcribed messages from the unconscious right there written in your own hand.

If you decide to write down your dreams, pick something to write on that is comfortable for you. You can use a sheet of paper and a pen, maybe with the aid of a clipboard. Most people use a blank-page journal you can get at a bookstore—it becomes a dream journal. That works fine, as long as you don't make it too "precious." (I bought this beautiful, hand-tooled leather journal that cost 50 bucks, and never used it because recording a dream can be a messy affair in the middle of the night, and I didn't want my precious journal defiled by scribbles.) Whatever you use, keep it next to your bed so that the instant you awaken from a dream, whether in the middle of the night or first thing in the morning, you can get down some words or drawings to represent the dream. When you look at it later, it will bring back the dream, and often more details will appear. Don't worry about logic or be reticent to write silly or painful things—just write!

Sketches and doodles are welcome additions. Make some marks that will represent the essence of the dream. Don't be concerned with getting it all down, just start.

And forget the order of events in the dream. Sometimes an earlier piece of the dream will pop up as you record. Just record it; you can put things in order and make your judgments later. Just get down as much as you can of the images, feelings, dialogue, and anything else you can remember.

Once you have it down, read it through right then. Sometimes more details will appear, so write down those things too. After I have finished recording the dream on my phone, I go back over it in my mind two or three times before I drift back to sleep. It's a way of reentering the dream and experiencing it again. Most often, what I have reviewed by walking around inside the dream after recording it will leap to memory when I write it up later.

In the strange-and-seemingly-dopey department, Charles Lutwidge Dodgson (better known by his pen name, Lewis Carroll, author of *Through the Looking Glass)* invented an alphabet and a device he called the Nyctogragh, which he used to record thoughts and dreams in the middle of the night using a complex series of holes, dots, and lines. Suffice it to say, it would be easier to write down a dream in Morse code than to use his method. It may have been genius, but it was also pretty incomprehensible.

Find your own way of recording dreams. If you try out a few different methods, you will find the one that feels right and gets the best transfer of story and images from the ephemeral connection between your unconscious and your conscious mind. Keeping in mind the importance of all this will drive you to record more dreams.

Equally important to successfully recording dreams is intention. Just before you go to sleep each night, set an intention to remember a dream. Look over at that dream journal and pen and say to yourself, "I would like to remember a dream tonight." If you are vitally interested in some particular issue that is bothering you, or you have an abiding interest in something, you can actually incubate a dream.

Dream incubation is when you ask your dreams to give you some insight into whatever it is you want to know about. You can ask something like: "Tonight when I dream, I would like to remember a dream that talks about why I am so anxious about the new baby being born." Or, "I would like to remember a dream tonight that would help me decide about my path forward in this relationship." Or, "Tonight I would like to dream about my father who passed two years ago." If you ask something of your dreams just before sleeping, your unconscious will hear that and possibly give you some insight. It's worth a try. The dreams you get may not directly answer your question, but they will often give new insight.

The longest and sometimes the most vivid dreams usually come just before waking in the morning, so when you awaken, pause for a moment and try to recall a dream. Sometimes it helps to place your body back in the position you were in as you awoke. There is a powerful, somatic connection between our dreams and our bodies. I remember dreams as I wake up better if I put my body back into the waking position, then turn my body to the opposite direction—the dream comes rolling out.

The reason we often forget our dreams is that when we awaken in the night, the long-term memory centers in the frontal cortex of the brain are still asleep, and so the responsibility goes to the short-term memory center in the hippocampus at the base of the brain. The long-term memory centers are a grumpy lot. It takes about 10 minutes for them to wake up, a lot like my dad when we used to camp. I knew better than to wake him up in the middle of the night unless I was bleeding profusely or there was a bear inside the tent.

The problem is that using the short-term memory center is like scooping up water with both hands; if you don't pour it into a container (the long-term memory centers), it will seep out through your fingers and disappear. We cannot distinguish which memory center is at work, so we think we will not possibly forget that dream, but the primitive brain, where the short-term memory resides, will often let it fade away.

Because these dreams just fade away, we miss recording them. And yet in this ephemeral world of disappearing dreams, something remains lurking. We've all had the experience of letting a dream drift off, and then in the middle of the day, something sparks a memory.

One day I returned home at 4:00 AM (don't ask) and entered the code to turn off the alarm, but it didn't work. I kept punching the code in with no results. I panicked, knowing the siren would soon go off. As I was pounding away at the keys and cursing, the recollection of a dream came flooding in.

In the dream I was on a spaceship, trying to change the course of the ship by entering the code 1923 over and over into the navigation system to no avail, and we crashed into a giant blimp, which exploded. Interestingly, my dad was born in 1923, and as a teenager he watched the Hindenburg disaster as the giant German blimp went up in flames. What could we do with that dream? Is it about not following the course my father took, going my own way instead of echoing his steps and crashing to the earth? Or is it about being too "spacey" and I need a little comeuppance and a good crash to become grounded again? Or both? Or something else?

By the way, the security siren did go off, ugh.

RECALLING NIGHTMARES

What about nightmares? When a nightmare appears, it will often wake us up long enough for the memory to get implanted in those lazy, sleepy, long-term memory centers. Nightmares come sometimes because we repeatedly ignore the dreams that really need to be heard. Since we are just sloughing them off, and the dream gods know we really, really need to hear the message they keep giving us, they change the dream into a nightmare to make sure we get the damn message.

An example: For five nights in a row, the dream gods have been trying to tell me I need to open my ears and listen to what my partner is saying instead of ignoring it. They try all sorts of dreams: the dream with the gnats flying around my ears, the dream about the alien with no ears, the dream of the dog that ignores me completely no matter how loud I yell, the one where the ship is sinking and no one pays attention to my warnings, the one where I am trapped in a plummeting elevator where no one hears me calling for help. I ignore all of them, letting them slowly purge from the hippocampus. So, the dream gods get a bit pissed off and finally send me a nightmare where an elephant rips off both my ears and hands them bloody and pulsing into my hands, hoping I will finally figure out what "the elephant in the room" is. I wake up with a start, and the adrenalin starts pumping, causing me to be awake for at least ten minutes, and I definitely will not forget this dream. And, yes, I finally figure out that I have not been listening to what my partner is saying to me.

REVERING THE ILLOGICAL

We have a part of the brain that tells us in waking life not to step off the roof, because in all reality, we cannot fly. That logical part of the brain, the dorsolateral pre-frontal cortex, is mostly offline while we sleep. With the logical part of the brain turned off, we can let loose the wild creative forces that our dour self denies us in waking life. We can fly by just bending our body, and it feels normal. We can breathe underwater and touch stars in outer space with no thought as to where the air to breathe is, interpreting the effect of touching a star not as incineration, but as gaining knowledge. We can time-travel, get killed, become animals, talk with rhinos, play chess with death, float on a leaf, mind-read, resurrect people, visit dead people, perform in a major motion picture, dance with Fred Astaire, put our forehead against a tree and hear the ocean, and watch as our body disintegrates to dust and bones (all actual dreams, by the way).

All this is so illogical and so wonderful, and yet there is a tricky part to this freewheeling world of creation. When you are writing up your dream, it is essential to keep Mr. Logic and Ms. Ego as quiet as possible. Mr. Logic will want to invent some scene wedged between the scene where I fly from the roof with ease and the scene where I harpoon the innocent whale at the bottom of the ocean to explain the transition. Mr. Logic will now and then invent something to make it more comfortable, like I must have leapt off a ship, not a roof. Ms. Ego will also want to change the innocent whale into a threatening monster that deserves to die. I mean, how would it look if I told someone I killed a beautiful whale? And sometimes ego and logic get their way, and the dream's message and the feel of the dream get perverted in the retelling.

That said, sometimes things we hadn't thought of appear as we write down the dream. Suddenly I will remember a school of dolphins swimming just above me as I killed that whale, or that the whale was resting on an old ship with the name Ahab on it. Just keep in mind that happy couple, Mr. and Ms. Logic/Ego, and make sure it is not coming from them. Try not to interpret the dream as you write it . . . Just write it . . . And then if you want to make notes or alterations, do it in a separate paragraph.

Be sure to let things in as you go over the dream. Like the feeling you get in your gut when you see a particular word, or the color of the sky as you fly—let all that in. And fire your inner editor. Even if the dream is really boring, like "I am walking down the street and I sit down on the lawn," write it down anyway. The dream gods will notice that you are attempting to recall your dreams. "Hey, Claude! This guy actually wrote down that dream about walking and sitting on the lawn that we sent him! Let's give him a corker tomorrow . . . Maybe a whale dream." Writing down dreams, even if they are fragments, will develop a habit that will help you recall more and more dreams.

In other words, make a commitment to remember your dreams, and you will remember more of them. The more you can balance on that threshold between the conscious world and the massive unconscious world you carry around all the time, the better. The greater the number of dreams you record, the more essential truths about your own life and what you need to do will be revealed. If you record dreams for a long enough period, patterns and themes will often appear and give you further insight into your life. It's like a graduate course in self-understanding, where you become the world expert on yourself.

PART 2

THE DREAM DRAWINGS

A Technique that Allows the Dream to Enter the Room and Speak

CHAPTER 3

DRAWING DOWN INTO THE DREAM

Incorporating Drawing into Dreamwork

It is only with the heart that one can see rightly.
What is essential is invisible to the eye.

Antoine de Saint-Exupery
The Little Prince

The *New Oxford American Dictionary* defines a dream as: "a series of thoughts, images, and sensations occurring in a person's mind during sleep." Well, that's a start. Sigmund Freud famously called dreams "the royal road to the unconscious," and that is where many of us who work with dreams attempt to tread. Dreams are uncontrolled phenomena, wherein the unconscious mind spews out thoughts, images, and sensations, and we have little control over what goes on, except for in lucid dreaming and Tibetan dream yoga. There is wide speculation about the meaning and purpose of dreams, a wide variety of approaches to working with dreams. Since all of us mammals dream every night, you can imagine there are as many modus operandi for dealing with dreams as there are religions in the world, and god only knows how many religions there are.

I belong to the IASD, The International Association for the Study of Dreams, an organization that promotes the understanding of dreams. It is the world's premiere organization for approaching dreams. Researchers, brain scientists, shamans, poets, therapists, writers, artists, and many more are active members exploring the world of dreams. The annual conferences are a place to learn and experience everything you could ever imagine about dreams.

Here is a list of just some of the presentations and talks from a recent IASD Dream Conference:

- Understanding, Exploring, and Resolving Nightmares: Clinical, Cultural, and Ethical Perspectives—Alan Siegel
- Terrorism, Jung and Dreams: A Jungian approach to the nature of terrorism—David Jenkins
- The Transcendent Function in Dreams at Various Stages of Therapy—Carol D. Warner
- Out-of-Body Experiences and Lucid Dreams: A Phenomenological Approach—E.W. Kellogg III
- Similarities Between the Reports of Dreams and Near-Death Experiences (NDE's)—Jacquie E. Lewis, PhD

My approach to dreams is primarily from the Jeremy Taylor/Montague Ullman modalities, which use groups to facilitate dreamwork. The central focus is the careful projection of feelings and ideas on the dream. It is known colloquially as the "If this were my dream" method; everyone speaks in the first person point of view as they talk about someone else's dream. This forces us to stay cognizant that what we are saying is a projection of our own version of the dream. It avoids any accusatory way of talking at the dreamer or telling her what she should do.

But these methods have been just a beginning foundation for what goes on in my dreamwork. I incorporate aspects of other modalities. One such approach is Gestalt dreamwork—wherein all the elements of the dream are seen as fragments of our personality, so we can become the various aspects to help open it up. I also often use Dream Theater, where dreams are acted out, as

- NREM sleep spindle frequency is associated with trait nightmare recall and pre-sleep state anxiety—DMichelle Carr
- Dreaming Autoimmunity: Exploring dreams in patients suffering autoimmune diseases—Fulvio D'Acquisto
- College Students' Erotic Dreams: Analysis of Content and Emotional Tone—Michael Schredl
- Dreaming in Auschwitz: How the concentration camp prisoners experienced and understood their dreams—Wojciech Owczarski
- Listening to End of Life Dreams: A gift for caregivers and families—Monique Segui
- Joyful Dreams: A mindful approach to the yoga of sleep, dreams, and waking up to your best life—Tzivia Gover, MFA, CDT

As you can see, dreams can be approached in so many ways.

well as Robert Bosnak's Embodied Imagination, where you locate the feelings and sensations in your body as you work the dream. And I often employ David Jenkins' method of Dream Replay, where the narrative of the dream holds sway, and we do such things as make up a movie from the dream, casting famous actors in the roles. Robert Moss does shamanic work in dream reentry, and Stephen Aizenstat does Dream Tending, where everything is alive inside the dream. These are all caring, thoughtful people whose methods have the same basic goal—to help us heal and understand ourselves and others through our dreams.

However, I branch off into my own dominion in the use of the visual in working with dreams. Which requires another story.

THE INDECIPHERABLE DREAM THAT LAUNCHED DRAWING THE DREAM

I had been facilitating dreams for a few years, mostly in the "If this were my dream" style, and was finding joy and success in doing so, when one day a client presented this dream:

BEARS, PORCUPINES, AND A MAGIC WAND

Well, my Aunt Georgie was in the basement, and it was flooded and her husband Billy told her she hadn't done the laundry right and then she comes upstairs and there are 6 bears, all blue, except one that was yellow, and then Billy takes her back down into the basement and shows her that there is a family of porcupines in the dryer, but he was painting the walls red at the time and then their son Billy Jr. starts packing his luggage upstairs and yells down that there is no toilet paper and that the bears are asking for change for the parking meter and then the sheriff shows up and shoots the yellow bear, but leaves the blue bears alone, only now the bears are all black and Billy Jr. is upset that the fireplace doesn't work unless you wave a magic wand which a small fairy supplies as she flies by and turns the black bears into porcupines that talk and the porcupines tell Billy Sr. that he is doomed.

"Oh my," I said. "Could you tell me the dream again? I was having a hard time putting all the pieces together."

So, she did, and I took notes this time, but I was still lost. I asked her to tell it a third time, a little more slowly. I took more notes; now I had notes about sheriffs, and porcupines, and bears, and fireplaces, but I couldn't remember if the bears or the porcupines changed colors, and the disparate elements got jumbled in my head, plus it seemed the story changed with every telling. There were no parking meters mentioned in version two, and in version three it was the fairy that told Billy Sr. that he was doomed and there were dozens of bunnies on the roof. I was about to abandon getting a picture of this dream in my head and just go to the feelings, relying on the dreamer to keep me afloat in this free-for-all world.

But then I had an idea. Out of the blue, I flashed back to my college days, when I performed in a production of *The Little Prince* by Antoine de Saint-Exupéry. In the story, the little prince asks the downed pilot, "Please . . . Draw me a sheep." And he does, making several sketches, but the little prince likes none of them—until the pilot draws a picture of a box with holes in it and explains that the sheep is inside. That pleases the little prince, and things unfold from there.

So I asked, "Could you draw a little sketch of the dream for me? I am a visually oriented person, and it might help me see at least some elements of the dream."

She protested that she couldn't draw, and I asked her to just use crude stick figures and lines and to write words on it to identify things.

Luckily, she complied. We grabbed a used piece of paper and she drew a house with a basement, a main floor, and an attic; six circles for bears, with B written on five of them for blue and Y for yellow on one; six balls with spikes inside a box that were the porcupines; a stick figure with a big hat that was the sheriff; and a tiny figure in the attic with a suitcase. And then, we saw Billy Sr., and was he a sight. He was coming up the stairs with his stick-figure hands raised high, and he had fangs for teeth. Aunt Georgie is nowhere to be found, and there in the middle of it all was a stick-figure fairy pointing a wand at Billy Sr.

Well, then I got it. I had a visual clue to the dream, and I ran with that. I pored over the images and was transported inside the dream. This was just a jumble when I first heard it, but now my eyes darted back and forth over the page, and I saw how it all fit together. It still may not have made sense, but I could focus on various images and ask about them. I suddenly realized that two tracks of thought were going on at the same time: I used the words to form concepts and ideas and create a narrative, and I used the visual information she put down to bring the dream to life by painting a picture of the narrative, which also gave me a picture of the emotions.

I noticed that Billy Sr. was fierce and scary. We talked about who Billy Sr. was in waking life, and it turns out he was the mean alcoholic uncle who was a "prick" (porcupine?) and beat his three kids. And we discussed the flooding in the basement. In my version, deep emotions related to this story were flooding my soul. I also mentioned that she didn't include Aunt Georgie in the drawing. The dreamer got one of those "aha" moments when I said those things, and she filled in the gaps.

Suddenly this was about her own immediate family: her silent, missing mother and the dominating father from whom she escaped, going off to college and feeling sort of "yellow" that she abandoned her four siblings. And in the imperfect world of dreams, five siblings (bears) were left when the "yellow" bear (which she identified as herself) got shot, not four. That led to another deep place, for she talked about her own child, whom she feared she was not raising right. In her version of her "new" dream, the number of bears was right, and off she went with many associations and "aha" moments. How she free-associated with all the images and thoughts matched her personality, in that she always talked about over-thinking things and struggled with taming her "monkey mind."

We were on a roll, and it was not so important that we match everything up in the dream to what was going on in her life. We didn't worry about the discrepancies, for we had opened a portal to her soul, and she was running with it. I saved talking about the fairy with the magic wand for last, because intuitively I felt it might be the key to opening up a deep connection to waking life. When we talked about this fairy, her face relaxed, and both our voices dropped into a softer tone. I asked her about the fairy and how she felt about her. She corrected me and told me it was a male fairy, and she loved how he was sure of himself and ephemeral at the same time. I talked about how in my dream this is magic, pure magic, and I am the fairy; I have a magic wand in my arsenal to help me change things in my waking life. I can change aggressive bears into defensive porcupines.

"Ask yourself, 'What would I change with a magic wand in my life if I had one?'" I said to her.

"Lots of things," she replied. And then she went silent for a moment, and we sat in that place of unspoken magic and introspection.

There was more to talk about in this complex world that arose out of her unconscious, and so we carried on, staring at that piece of paper between us as we did the work. When it seemed we were sitting gently inside the dream, I encouraged her to write what had come up, including the things she would change with her magic wand, and to work with it. What had started as a complete dilemma in working her dream turned into a productive, wonderful experience for both of us, and much of our success came from her having drawn the dream.

Oh, and what about the "aha" moments I've mentioned? The Merriam-Webster dictionary is good on this one. "Aha: Used to express satisfaction, triumph, or surprise. It is a moment of insight, a eureka moment, a time when things that were stuck or incomprehensible fall into place and suddenly make sense."

When someone has one of these moments, it can be a flash of realization, a connection to something deep, a connection between something in the heart and the mind, an intellectual connection between the words and the images and the narrative, a sudden burst of tears, an abrupt silence filled with emotion, a moment of laughter, and more. Something shifts in an "aha" moment, which makes it one of the touchstones of dreamwork. It is a point in time when the soul meets itself and rejoices in the connection. "Aha" moments are markers that the work is effective.

After this fascinating demonstration of how a little sketch of a dream could produce several "aha" moments, I introduced drawing the dream to a dream group.

I was hesitant at first. I wondered if we would taint the depth of the dream if we drew it. I thought about how when you read a book, and your furtive imagination creates all the characters and the places that appear only as words, and then someone makes a movie of the book and it is not at all your version, it can be a huge let-down.

For instance, in 2003 I worked on the lighting crew for the live-action movie adaptation of Dr. Seuss's *The Cat in the Hat.* I love Dr. Seuss. I directed a one-act play of Dr. Seuss stories in college, and it was a big hit. However, I thought this film version of *The Cat in the Hat* was a terrible idea. As I watched the production unfold day after day, it seemed to lack any magic. And when it opened in wide release, sure enough, it was a piece of dreck that contained none of the magic in the book.

What if drawing our dreams did this—got us stuck in a single way of looking at the experience, thus losing the magic necessary to do the work?

This fear turned out to be unfounded. It took some time to perfect the technique of using drawings in dreamwork. But once I landed on a suitable method, I found that drawing the dream did not impede anybody's imagination. What's on the paper is a launching point, not an end product; it leaves the door wide open for creativity and deep exploration. Using a rough sketch of the dream is like sitting in a brainstorming session as you bounce ideas off each other, designing the next iPhone or self-driving car.

In fact, stunning and magical things happened as I incorporated drawings into the work. It was as though the dream had been invited into the room and inhabited the scribbles and streaks that people made.

You will see many of these drawings as we travel along on this journey together. Just know that it is not about the artistic ability of the dreamer. These are stick figures and crudely drawn houses, mountains, animals and such, not "art." We can think of these images as inspired revelations of emotions, thoughts, and metaphors from the raw unconscious of the dreamer. As primitive as they may seem, I and others delight in their beauty.

CHAPTER 4

DREAM MAPS

A Detailed Look into the Method of Drawing and Working the Dream

The soul should always stand ajar.

EMILY DICKINSON

Here, I will lay out my own method of group dreamwork, developed over the last decade or so. I have honed its elements over the years. This system is always in flux, which is completely necessary to allow the dream to enter the space on its own terms. In actual practice, I work intuitively. There isn't a set formula, because the beauty of dreamwork is that you do not know what is going to happen.

I had a dream appear in a group that was so powerfully presented we did absolutely nothing but listen to it. Working on it would have been a mistake. In this particular case, it was like watching a masterful poem being created in front of our eyes. We were stunned into silence and that is where we left it, sitting deep in all of our souls as a poem from the center of the collective unconscious.

Other dreams call out for anything from a bit of nudging to a full arsenal of tools to help manifest what they need to say. Many particular techniques are optional for any particular dream, but here is the core structure that I bring with me whenever I am working with a dream.

1. The Groundwork

2. The Dreamer Takes the Stage

1. **The Groundwork**
   - Assemble the tools, prepare the space for the experience of working dreams, draw the dreams.

2. **The Dreamer Takes the Stage**
   - The dreams are told, a dream is chosen to work, the drawing is placed so that it becomes the central focus.
   - The dreamer reveals the emotions that occurred inside the dream as they experienced it.
   - A somatic element is added as we connect the dream to the physical body.
   - Questions are asked of the dreamer about the dream and the drawing in order to create a fuller picture.
   - Others tell the dream, giving us multiple perspectives.

3. The Group Takes the Stage

4. Bringing it All Together

3. The Group Takes the Stage

- The dreamer takes a back seat to observe.
- We carefully and respectfully project our own thoughts and emotions on the dream.
- Other tools are applied, including Gestalt, dream theater, and continuing the dream.

4. Bringing it All Together

- The dreamer returns to center stage and reacts to all that has gone on.
- Five important questions are asked.
- The Second Client, a rather bizarre way of dialoguing with the characters in the dream world, is used.

Nearly everything I will go into here applies to working one-on-one with someone or working on your own dreams, but it is geared toward group work. Every time I use this method, I get wrapped up in the experience—and most times, I stand solidly in that space of awe that I crave so much. Nothing is more thrilling to me than living inside someone's dream as this technique unfolds.

I fall easily into other people's dreams; they become my own experiences as they are being told. I remember floating along in a river as a molecule, flying into space, weeping uncontrollably in the basement of someone's childhood home, and singing along with a Black choir conducted by Mother Earth. I have also had delightful sex with a ghost, experienced a harsh reprimand by a dead parent, and have been shot at but found myself able to slow down the bullets to avoid them. Oh, then there was the discovery that I was the eye of a buffalo pounding along the plains of the ancient West. In another fantastic tale, I was dropped by a helicopter into the center of a medieval village. And then there was the time I showed up at God's house, which turned out to be a giant rug store, and hanging there was the half-completed rug that told the story of my life.

On and on these experiences go. The process of working with these myriad dreams has added to my understanding of who I am and who we are together. Empathy and understanding are a big part of what dreamwork—and life—is about.

THE GROUNDWORK

The space used for conducting this work is important and needs to be prepared in some way. In my home, where I conduct my weekly dream group, the room is filled with art conducive to presenting dreams. I have reproductions of scenes of bulls, horses, ancient bison, and a shaman from prehistoric cave paintings around the top of the room, then a lot of my own artworks based on my own dreams, and an altar with sacred objects. I find that these surroundings amplify the experience and contain the spirit of the work.

This is not always possible, of course, especially if you are conducting a workshop in a hotel, sitting in a restaurant, or online. But do whatever you can to make the space conducive to dreams, even if it's just arranging chairs in a circle, attentively laying out the materials, or including something to focus attention like a drum or a bell. I arrange the seats in my home in a semi-circle, with the open side of the circle reserved for the dream drawing.

My group sessions generally last two to three hours. Most groups do not meet for this long, but I find that when people do these simple sketches, the dream wakes up and wants to be seen, so I try to work as many as I can without shortchanging any of the dreamers.

When I first started using this method, I used standard 8½" x 11" paper and colored pencils, then we moved to pastels, and even paint. I now use large-format paper—18" x 24"—and colored felt-tip markers. I have found that colored pencils are too subtle for what we are doing; much can be missed in looking at a pencil drawing from ten feet away. Pastels and paint are messy and involve too much of the thinking process I am trying to avoid, so markers, which make bold, quick, decisive marks, are my tools of choice.

The size of the paper also matters. Using a larger format, the dreamer has an expansive field to work with. They can draw the entire dream map down in one corner, or make it into quadrants telling the dream in sections, or fill the whole field with figures and lines and waves underneath and a sun above. How they use this space often lends insight to understanding the dream.

The unconscious needs to be comfortable enough to give up some of its secrets—and that involves all these factors: the paper, the markers, and the timing. With a large blank piece of paper in front of you, markers that make bold marks with no way to erase them, and a bit of urgency in the timing, the left-brain function of trying to be correct gets repressed enough that sometimes unexpected things arise from the unconscious. Instead of trying to perfect the rendering of the dream's content, the pressure of having only 10-15 minutes to delineate something allows people to forgive themselves for its not being perfect. Even if the drawing doesn't offer any evident clues from the unconscious, we are all aware that this is not a polished piece of art, just a simple map of the dream, with stick figures and arrows, words and scribbles that are (hopefully) an honest attempt by the dreamer to conjure up the essence of the dream's content.

Some bring drawings with them to the group, but I encourage people to draw the dream in the sacred space of the dream group. Because of the quick and sometimes messy way the dream is drawn, it falls to those viewing it to fill in the gaps in their imagined version of the dream, giving each person a chance to create their own vision of this tale from the unconscious. A stick figure with a splash of red across it and blue hair becomes in our imagination that beautiful dancer in a red dress that the dreamer talks about. As she tells the story, we quietly animate this stick figure, and she whirls and dips in our minds, the blue sky spinning before our eyes, reminding us of a time we danced with abandon.

One of the reasons some people do not attend my workshops is because they dread drawing—especially people with control issues. They know that they cannot produce anything like what they see in the dream and are so afraid of being embarrassed by their lack of skill that they avoid exposing themselves to perceived ridicule. I tell them they can just be their six-year-old selves and scribble away; but for some, the self-criticism is just too deep for them to break free and draw a couple of stick figures standing on a curved line.

When people do screw their courage to the sticking place, as Shakespeare put it, and join in the proceedings, I encourage them to leave their judgments about drawing at the door and just lay down anything on the page; lines, stick figures, areas of color, doodles, words with arrows pointing at something, random marks that come while thinking on the dream—it doesn't matter. What we are after is a simple representation of the essence of the dream. It has little to do with art or beauty and everything to do with communication and sharing. Whatever appears on this large piece of paper is usually evocative, and it's fun for everyone to observe individual dreamers' various styles. Whatever materializes says something about the dream and the dreamer.

If someone does not want to draw their dream and still wants to work it, that simply means we will work the dream in a more conventional way, and the magic will appear in a different form. This is important work, and we can't let hard-and-fast rules get in the way.

THE DREAMER TAKES THE STAGE

Now that we have drawn our dreams, we are ready to start working on them. At this point, I encourage people to put the drawings aside so that others do not see them yet. That way, we can first tell the dreams without referencing the drawings, so the group hears each raw dream report unfettered from the visual aid as it is told.

It's important for everyone to be totally focused and open to this experience. No comments or questions are allowed while the dream is being told, and total focus goes to the dreamer and the dream as it pours out into the room. Dreamers can take the time they need to tell the dream. However, I encourage people to stay within the confines of what the dream actually presented and not make commentary or analysis as they present their dream. That comes later. This is a moment when we gather like a tribe, ready to hear mythic tales from wise elders.

I always find this exciting—an immediate entrance into the underworld. What often happens is called "narrative transportation," a psychological term that refers to what occurs when people lose themselves in a story. We often are transported by the narrative to a place the dream intended. We become empathetic to the characters or ideas and get swept up in the tale. We take on the attitudes and intentions of the dream figures as we immerse ourselves in this experience. In this empathic state, we take on the dream story as *our* story.

For instance, someone tells a dream about a dinosaur in a tuxedo that meets a tiny person, and the tiny person gets injected into the dinosaur's blood stream. For a few minutes, I am a dinosaur in a tuxedo roaming through an ancient woodland feeling lost and uncared for, uncomfortable in my restrictive clothing. A moment later, in the same dream, I am a tiny person who is injected into the bloodstream of the dinosaur, and it becomes my job to reassure the dinosaur that she is not alone, which is difficult as I pulse and spin in the chaotic bloodstream of this giant creature. As I take on each of these magical mantels of madness during the first telling of the dream, I may be just an observer, but I feel something and learn something. I think about how in my own life, sometimes I feel like a gigantic out-of-place, lonely being, roaming through life uncomfortable in my own skin and wondering if there is a tiny person inside of me that I can turn to for help.

After each dream is told, we pause in silence for a minute to absorb what we have experienced. We tell our dreams one at a time, with no comments or questions. It is not necessary to try and remember all the details of the dreams, since they will be told again, and we will eventually have a visual aid to remind us of each dream's content. At this stage, we can just let the dreams wash over us, noting to ourselves what strikes us or how we feel during the telling.

After everyone in the room who has wanted to share their dream, including me, has shared, sans drawings, you can feel the room fill with all those emotions, ideas, and fantastic and mundane things that have been launched into the space. We then focus on each dream one by one and see what happens.

In the dream group, I choose which dream we are going to work on first. Nightmares or distressful dreams usually take precedence; they deposit such strong emotions into the room that they cry out to be dealt with first.

Now the drawings have the opportunity to lead us into each dream's world. All the participants are in a semi-circle. The chosen dreamer takes the drawing of their dream and tapes it up on the wall or board then sits back down. The dream map completes the circle.

AN EVENING OF THREE DREAMS

Three dreams from a dream group I conducted recently illustrate the next stages of the Drawn into the Dream method.

The first is a beautiful, highly emotional visitation dream wherein the dreamer's father appears, takes her hand, and gently leads her past all the gates and fences that kept others out, onto a ship where those who have passed to the other side are waiting—including her mother, who passed recently. A feeling of magic and love arises as she tells this dream. We all feel moved by the tender moment when the dreamer approaches her mother and embraces her. Here is the drawing, which was done in about 10 minutes.

The two people in the lower left are the dreamer and her father holding hands and beginning their journey to the ship of death. They appear again next to the stop sign as the father begins to weave their way around the obstacles and barriers. On the boat, the two figures all the way to the right are the dreamer and the mother about to embrace. The boat is filled with happy people dancing. Off to the center left we see the dreamer and the father leaving the ship of death, having accomplished their mission there.

The second dream is more matter-of-fact. The dreamer is traveling in the subways of New York, where she grew up. She comes up out of this dark underground passage and has a disagreement with her friend about the location of the Museum of Modern Art. Her friend insists it's on 59th and Madison, and she insists it's on W. 63rd St.

In the picture, we see the dreamer in the lower right dominating the scene with her large presence, huge smile, confidence, and stylish, thick hair. The contrast between her and the friend is striking. The friend seems unsure, and what is with that horrible hairdo? It is just a few unkempt strands.

The third dream brought on the feeling of stepping out of reality into a magical world. A giant yellow fish has washed ashore and died and has started to smell. Someone has slit it open, and there inside is a woman and her reading light. She seems fine in there, and we don't know if or when she will come out.

The drawing adds to the mystery. Inside the dead fish, which has no eye drawn in, is the happy woman reading something under a reading light. In the dream report, it is the dreamer and her boyfriend who come upon this strange sight, but what is drawn are two women looking at one another. The dreamer was not clear at all why she drew the boyfriend as a redheaded woman or why she gave herself elfish ears, or why they are staring at each other instead of the fish. I had the feeling that on some level, the dreamer wanted to let this dream stay a mystery.

After the chosen dreamer's drawing has been taped up, the dreamer tells the dream again. When I first started this practice, I had the dreamer stand next to the drawing and point out things on the paper as they retold the dream—and then also as we projected our ideas about the dream—but that did not give the dream a chance to be as present in the room, because the focus was on the dreamer instead of the dream. So, now the dreamer sits down and uses a laser-pointer to tell the dream again while pointing out salient points and reweaving the tale.

Many people bring their dream journals with them and read the dream from the page. This is fine for the first telling, but in the second telling, I encourage people to just tell the dream from memory. When they do tell it from memory, they will sometimes leave things out, add things, or change things, which may be of help in our exploration. It is all part of the process.

As the dreamer retells the dream, pointing at the drawing with the laser, our eyes and minds follow the images; the stick figures and crude lines, the words and colors and shapes—all these suggest the narrative of the dream. This retelling of the dream usually becomes much more detailed, including facts, images, and feelings that the original report did not contain. This is storytelling, not just a report. Blending with our memory of the previous telling, the visual clues and new information bring the dream to life right before our eyes.

THE GROUP TAKES THE STAGE

Sometimes I have other people tell the dream as best they can remember it, adding another dimension to the telling and giving the dreamer a chance to step back and reflect. As someone else told the "Get on the Boat" dream, they added a dancing scene where everyone is gyrating with abandon on the deck of the ship. It added to the joy of dream, and although completely "wrong," the dreamer loved this. It drew us deeper into the drawing as we thought of this as the dance of death.

I sometimes use another technique at this point in the dreamwork, something fellow dreamworker David Jenkins does in his work, and mythologist Michael Meade uses when he tells a myth or tale. I ask each person in the group, "What stands out for you in the dream?" This gives a sense of where in the story each person in the room focuses, and it gives feedback to the dreamer about new angles on the dream. As we each share our experience of entering the dream in our own way, it creates a more communal feeling in the room.

In the case of the "Woman in the Fish" dream, one person was intrigued by how yellow the fish was. Her curiosity about yellow stemmed from her own aversion to bright colors. Because she thought that people who wore bright colors were "showoffs," the entry point for her into the dream was in that bright yellow that spoke to her loudly. Another was struck by how similar the two women at the bottom were. This person has two siblings that are identical twins and so her entrance into the dream was thinking about the concept of one person being two at the same time. To me, the women seemed to be staring at each other across a distance, which brought a feeling of mystery and intrigue. And my thoughts went here because I am a people watcher and I secretly make up all sorts of stories about relationships as I see people make eye contact.

In the case of the "Museum of Modern Art" dream, what stood out for all of us was that terrible hairdo of the friend. When we asked about that, the dreamer replied, "I think of hair as symbolic of thoughts coming out of the head, and I think I am mad at my friend for not recognizing that my studio on 63rd Avenue is a place where really good art is made. If I look at it that way, my thoughts, like my hair, are full and clear, and my friend's thoughts are scrambled and thin."

It is wonderful and so powerful that each person in the group enters the dream from a different door or window, bringing with them a unique angle of light that exposes the dream in so many different ways. It takes a village, as they say.

Once the dream has been told at least twice, I ask, "What are the emotions inside the dream? What did you feel as the dream was in progress?" It is very important to be clear that this does not refer to the emotions the dreamer felt after waking—those can be expressed later as we work—we want the dreamer to climb back inside the dream and recall what was felt in the dream, while it was being experienced. We look at the drawing and explore each emotion that came up throughout the story. In the "Get on the Boat" dream, the dreamer talked about each emotion she experienced, starting with the trepidation she felt while walking towards the cruise ship hand-in-hand with her father, then the overwhelming sadness that turned to joy as she saw her mother approach.

Once we have the basic emotions from inside the dream, it is sometimes appropriate to include emotions or facts that may be outside of the dream but that have been triggered by this investigation. The "Get on the Boat" dream brought up powerful feelings for the dreamer about the recent loss of her mother and also about the loving but rocky relationship she had with her father.

As we expose the emotions arising from the dream, it is good to connect them to our bodies. Without that somatic connection, we can easily retreat into our minds—where our wily egos want to repress emotions. So, I have us all take a pause, and ask the dreamer where in the body they are feeling the dream. This invites the dreamer to feel on two levels—emotional and somatic. This grounds the emotion in the body and gives us a clear and concise location to resonate with all that will come up as we open the dream. In a sense, we are asking the dreamer to open their heart to the process. If they can feel the dream in the body and allow that feeling to stay grounded there, everything we do from there on out will enter the body first instead of the intellect. In this way, the work becomes soul-connected, and more genuine. In the case of the dream about the location of the Museum of Modern Art, the dreamer at first thought the dream felt like it was in her gut, but then changed that to her head during our questions about the two hairdos. That information gave us a better sense of where to explore in the dream.

Once we have explored the emotions from inside the dream, allowing whatever comes up as we do this, and then grounded the dream in the body, it's time to ask clarifying questions of the dreamer. When we ask questions and later when we project on the dream, we do so speaking in the first person point of view. This is a method to make perfectly clear that we are owning the question and the projection as our own. We develop empathy by standing in the shoes of the dreamer as we pose questions and make comments.

For the "Get on the Boat" dream, we asked, "Do I recognize anyone else on the ship? How old am I in the dream? How old is my dad? Do I get a sense that the ship is about to depart? How did my dad and I slip past the guards? Is the sea calm or choppy?"

For the "Museum of Modern Art" dream, we asked, "Who is this friend? What is our relationship? Who are the people in the curved train? What is wrong with my friend's hair?"

In the case of the "Woman in the Fish" dream, we asked "How big is the giant fish that washed ashore? How old is the woman inside the fish? Does she remind me of anybody I know? Is it day or night? Do I get any sense of what the woman inside the fish is thinking or feeling?"

As we ask these questions, the dreamer often recalls a new detail they left out of the dream, or a memory comes up of an event seemingly unrelated to the dream but that was most likely triggered from the unconscious, where powerful emotions are stored. Discussing the giant fish dream, the dreamer mentioned that her father used to go to the movies with her, and they would sneak into a second film after the first one finished. It may seem totally unrelated, but perhaps the unconscious is suggesting she should cheat her way out of the dead fish without anyone realizing it.

By this point, we have talked about the emotions inside the dream and we have fleshed out the narrative and visual by asking questions about the dream. The dream thus becomes a three-dimensional, compelling story full of mystery and emotion. It is starting to come alive.

It's now time to project on the dream.

PROJECTION

What is projection, and why are we using it in dreamwork? Carl Jung nailed this with astonishing (and embarrassing) accuracy and profundity, in *General Aspects of Dream Psychology*:

> Just as we tend to assume that the world is as we see it, we naïvely suppose that people are as we imagine them to be . . . . All the contents of our unconscious are constantly being projected into our surroundings, and it is only by recognizing certain properties of the objects as projections or imagos that we are able to distinguish them from the real properties of the objects . . . *Cum grano salis,* [taken with a grain of salt] we always see our own unavowed mistakes in our opponent. Excellent examples of this are to be found in all personal quarrels. Unless we are possessed of an unusual degree of self-awareness we shall never see through our projections but must always succumb to them, because the mind in its natural state presupposes the existence of such projections. It is the natural and given thing for unconscious contents to be projected.
>
> *The Collected Works of C.G. Jung, Vol. 8*

Projection is a psychological defense mechanism in which a person attributes some undesirable or denied characteristic they have to someone else. It is as though we turn on a movie projector with all the characteristics we don't like about ourselves loaded up as images and project them onto people that most resemble the parts of ourselves that we deny. We all drag around a heavy black bag that Jung calls the shadow, and we are not getting rid of it anytime soon, I fear. We reach into that black bag and project those denied parts of ourselves onto others to great effect.

I project the loud, overbearing Walter onto the loud-mouthed guy at work, while denying that I am a loudmouth. I also project my own insecurities that I deny I have onto the silent, sheepish young woman in the dream group. I get a bit peeved as she just sits there and doesn't comment on things, but what I am really doing is seeing the quiet and introspective part of me that I deny projected onto her so that I don't have to struggle with my own doubts and insecurities.

Moreover, often the projection is correct. I may deny my own anger by pointing out how angry and unhappy a woman I was in a relationship with years ago is, but she really is angry and unhappy. She makes an easy mark for me to project my anger onto. She is not angry all the time; she can be smiling and laughing, but I assume this is just a smoke screen for her real feelings, and that way I can continue not facing my own angry self.

Projection can also consist of positive emotions and thoughts. My girlfriend is a brilliant, Harvard-trained anthropologist who speaks multiple languages and is an expert on Southeast Asia, among other things. One thing I admire about her (here comes my projection) is how she can take complex issues and fit them together into a unified, clear through-line of understanding in a nanosecond. She really does that, so the projection is true, but it feels larger than life because I am denying my own ability to do that very same thing. I have been able to own and withdraw that projection quite a bit by realizing that by writing this book I am taking complex issues surrounding dreams and awe and building them into a unified clear through-line of understanding. When I withdraw that projection and see it in my own abilities, she is still as brilliant as ever, but I am able to see my own self in the image I cast upon her, and both of us are better off.

When you withdraw a projection and own it, suddenly the person you were projecting your unwanted feelings onto becomes someone with myriad feelings, ideas, and complexities worth investigating. At the same time, you feel all those things about yourself you had been denying, not feeling or seeing as your own. Both individuals appear to change for the better.

Similarly, when I turn off the projector with the endless loop casting images of an evil witch onto that woman I was involved with, I can see the light that emanates from her soul, with all its scars from the traumas she has suffered, and maybe even a gentle smile that appears when no one is looking. It is useless to paint her as evil. Instead, I have to look at myself in the mirror and honestly see that scowl that comes from my anger at myself for my indecisiveness, which haunts me and has led to bad decisions. If I can see that and feel that, I can do something about it. Life is about learning and changing, isn't it?

Okay, we will leave all those film projectors running in the background and return to the world of dreamwork. When someone tells a dream, the information, emotions, and visual clues pour out into the room, but we can only imagine what the dream is saying from our own (projected) understanding. And that is a good thing. As I hear about the woman inside the fish with the light, the confined sense of this strikes a chord in me, and I start thinking about moments in my life when I have bound myself up and failed to climb out of a situation. I project my ideas out into the room, talking about how this woman just has to get out of this stinking dead fish, just like I have needed to get out of a series of noxious situations in my professional relationships. My projection is: "In my imagined version of this dream, I feel an urgency to get out of this damn dead fish. It reminds me of this pressing situation I am going through at work, and in my dream, I need to climb out now and jump in the ocean and cleanse myself of this horrid stench."

I have taken the dream and populated it with my own feelings and ideas, creating a movie of my own making that I load into my movie projector and project onto the dream in the room.

The dreamer and the others listen to this, gleaning from it what they will, and then offer up their own projections. The dreamer, who is more introverted than I am, is affected by my feeling of urgency to get out of the fish. She glimpses the dream in a new way, but still her own projection comes from introspection and caution. In her version of the dream, she needs to stay and read something very important, and only when everyone is gone will she quietly switch off the light and attempt to remove herself from the belly of the fish.

And with that comes an "aha" from her, as she sees a clear connection to research she's doing in her profession, and how long to stay inside that research before leaving it. I also end up with an "aha" at this moment, suddenly seeing the wisdom in her approach, of pausing before acting. I can use that insight in dealing with my work situations.

The idea that someone would project on their own dream may sound strange, but this is exactly what happens when the dreamer gives birth to the dream by delineating its form on a piece of paper. The dream has taken on a life of its own, and everyone in the room, including the dreamer, gets to dance with it by projecting on it.

Our focus during this stage is on the drawing, not the dreamer, and we keep connecting more deeply to the dream itself.

As I stare at that yellow fish, I start making up a story that it conjures. I imagine the journey the woman with the light inside the fish took to get here. I remember the story of Jonah and the whale, which is why I feel trapped and want out. And then I imagine the death of the fish. Did I kill it by being inside? Then I remember the dreamer said that the woman in the fish doesn't want to come out, so I go back over the picture again and look for new approaches. Those curly waves over the top of the fish seem fun and inviting. How does that fit? And then I think about my own life and the isolation I feel at times. In some ways I am exactly like this woman in the fish.

Meanwhile, the dreamer and others are also staring at the drawing and creating their own projections. And they express them, with care. Often someone's projection will spark a new one from someone else, and the work becomes a symphony of ideas and feelings. In this wild hot wind of projections, the dream now has many faces and multiple meanings. It is a time to think outside the box, to go in all sorts of directions in opening up the dream. Many projections fall away, while others elicit a response or a surprise, and some find emotional resonance. We can go hog-wild without getting lost in the woods of the intellect, because we have the dream drawing continually pulling us back into the dream. It is our rock, a foundation to work from.

Because people project their own shadow (insecurities, meanings, etc.) onto dreams, it is important to speak in "first person" when doing dreamwork. Each question or comment is couched in the idea that we are talking about MY projected dream here. Jeremy Taylor insisted on this, as do many dreamworkers. He would always have us say, "If this were my dream . . ." or, as he later preferred, "In my imagined version of the dream . . ."

Sometimes what comes up for someone listening and creating their own version of the dream will be a difficulty in their own life, which is wonderful, and can lend insight. The only exception to this free-for-all, anything-goes projection fest is when someone crosses a line where the passion that takes over their response is so strong that the work goes astray.

It depends on the context, but at times people lose the sense of the dream and are instead in pursuit of validation for their point of view about something. When this happens, they often ask leading questions like: "In my version of the dream I truly hate my mother, and she would never be on the same ship as my wonderful dad. Don't you just hate this woman?" If this occurs, we are captive to someone's ego, which forces the work beyond projective dreamwork and off into a personal detour, and it is my job to bring things back onto the main road.

So, at this point I politely interrupt and throw the question back at the projector: "Our emotions about our own mothers are really important, although we may have moved beyond the confines of this particular dream here. This feels to me to be a question that the dreamer need not answer. Perhaps it will be helpful for you to answer your own questions about your feelings toward your mother. We can talk about that later if you like."

It is essential to maintain respect for the dream presented, and it is my job to preserve the flow of spirit and ideas as we wade through this swamp of projection and passion. Meanwhile, the drawing holds the center, anchoring us all.

At times, another layer to the work appears at this point: the magic of the world just beyond that thin piece of paper. Through the paper, an energy connects us to the land of the dream itself, as though we have opened the door between our conscious selves and the realm that was just a few moments ago unconscious to us. The drawing comes alive and pours out an energy from some place beyond reason. If we do this right, we are experiencing something beyond ourselves and are connected to that poetic place that holds the essence of soul. We are down in an ancient cave, watching the light flicker over dream images and allowing ourselves to be carried away in the awe captured before us. The dream drawings connect us directly to the Land of Awes. It may sound strange, but as we work a dream with a drawing in front of us, those simple lines come to life and offer up a clear path into the world of mythos. Something magical goes on here.

Although projection is generally seen as masked and disguised, a mostly negative experience of denial and disconnect where we go around unconsciously projecting our own unacceptable feelings onto someone else, it works differently if we use it as a tool in a conscious way. In dreamwork, projection shifts from being a blaming tool to an act of joining and empathy. We know that we are projecting our own ideas and feelings onto our imagined version of the dream. Nothing is hidden. Our sincere wish is to present to the dreamer our own projected and honest way we see the dream. Because we are using projection with clear and conscious intent, the effect is useful and sincere. Used in this way, projection can help us grow and change and understand not only ourselves, but those around us and the world as a whole. By the time we finish working on a dream, not only have a dozen different movies been projected onto the dream, but some of the movies have merged and created new projected stories. This is similar to when people brainstorm in creating new things, but instead of creating a flying car that talks, we have created a new dream and new roads to walk down on our intrepid journey to the center of self.

If our projections go reasonably well, empathy arises. Empathy is the ability to feel and understand what someone else is experiencing. It is the invaluable experience of truly understanding someone else's feelings, thoughts, and even their way of being—not from our own viewpoint, but from theirs. It is hard to achieve real empathy, but when you do, you are dropped into that place of awe so essential to life.

So, we have projected heartily on the dream, experienced an "aha" or two in the process, and walked a mile in someone's shoes to step into the dimension of empathy and awe.

I do need to underline here that the dreamer is the final authority on their own dream. They decide what to accept, reject, and ponder in this work.

GESTALT

We can also use some aspects of Gestalt therapy to see the dream from another angle. Gestalt is vitally interested in the present, not the future or the past. A way to bring a dream into the present is to present the dream from various perspectives and see what occurs.

In the "Get on the Boat" dream, we ask the dreamer to tell the dream from the perspective of the mother. She then tells the dream as though the mother had the dream. When she does this, her body and voice change, and deep emotions of caring and worry arise. Then we have her tell the dream from the perspective of the boat. Sounds odd, but it works. Here, a deep and reassuring voice appears. The ship talks about caring for all these souls that he is in charge of as they wend their way across the ocean to the other side of life.

DREAM THEATER

We do a lot of talking during this process of opening up a dream; one way of bringing the dream back into the body is by getting up and acting it out. In the "Museum of Modern Art" dream, the dreamer casts two women from the group to play the arguing friends as they walk the streets of New York. Then she picks a man and a woman to be the two street signs: one is the sign for

59th and the other for 63rd. The dreamer directs the action as the two women walk and argue. The two signs call out to them, both insisting that their way is the way to the museum. The ensuing clamor brings to life the conflict the dreamer is feeling about her own art and her relationship to her friend.

CONTINUING THE DREAM

A powerful tool to use at this point is "Continuing the Dream." Sometimes dreams cry out to either move on from where they are or to find a completely different path. It can be revealing, healing, or resolving to make something up that continues the dream story itself into new territory. Once we have done extensive work on a dream, I ask the dreamer (and sometimes other group members), "What happens next in the dream? We will not hold you to what you say, and we can throw it out, but, what happens next beyond where the dream ended?" Dreams often stop at some arbitrary place, especially nightmares where we are awakened mid-dream. So here we can put our imagination skills to good use.

The danger here is that our precious egos, which have been standing off to the side watching all this nonsensical blathering (in their opinion) about emotions and meanings may feel invited in to aggrandize things for the sake of our "dignity." But if we have plunged deep enough into the dream's presence during this process, the ego is still held at bay while we continue the dream. Usually, the things we make up add to the depth of the work. So much work has been done by this point that what appears in "Continuing the Dream" fits nicely into a pattern of understanding and feeling.

And how do we tell when we have gone astray? How do we know when we are just making stuff up that is only amusing or that panders to the ego?

I think the best guide is the "aha" moment. If the dreamer has one of those glimmers of "aha"—usually experienced as a true body hit, often very specifically located in the body—if she does have a hit as she creates a new ending—say, where the fish comes alive again and she plunges back into the deep ocean inside it—then we are on a completely new track, and possibly headed for a new "aha" or two. So, we try on that new ending to the "Woman in the Fish" dream and see how it feels. The new ending brings up more questions about the dream: Is it a way of avoiding something, or is there new life in this magical dream fish that will take us into new self-discovery? Although it turns out this is the wrong path, this attempt at a new ending sparked other ideas about the dream for the dreamer.

Often all this rigmarole we conduct in a dream session thins the veil between worlds. And when it does, we feel things. We feel connected to the inner self, and even to the ephemeral collective unconscious where we are all connected. And that is what life is about. Really.

So, if you want to continue the dream, make stuff up, says I. Listen to the dream and speak to it. The dream will guide your path. You won't regret it. You will find home and self in the course of it. If you continue the dream, you will be able to stand on the pier and watch tearfully as your parents, safe and secure, cruise off into the afterlife. You will be able to go to your studio in your own Museum of Art with full confidence to create. And when no one is watching, and everyone has left, you will be able to gently climb out of that wonderful fish that has served you well and say goodbye.

BRINGING IT ALL TOGETHER

Nearing the end of our process, at this point I check in with the dreamer and see what they're feeling and thinking. We have opened avenues and emotions and projections, and the dreamer now voices thoughts and feelings about what has gone on. This is the dreamer's dream, and they are the authority on what has happened here. We are all ears to whatever they think or feel. With all the diverse ideas and feelings projected into the room, it would seem that we have "gotten somewhere" with the dream, but to me that is not the most important part. This is about the *experience*. The process is where the magic is found.

Our souls are fed when our dreamer on the boat destined for the afterlife stands in teary silence with both her mother and father, and we join her in that silent joy and despair of a moment with someone who has passed on. And we all experience such joy when we join the artist in that moment of realization that the "Museum of Modern Art" is, in truth, in her house. As that realization creeps across her face, our souls bend in an arc of magic and understanding, and we are better people for that experience.

When we continue the "Woman in the Fish" dream, and finally get her out, it doesn't resonate with the dreamer. And so, that woman in the fish is still in there with her light, reading away. The dreamer's insistence that she stay in there brings us all into an unfinished place of introspection, a quiet, contemplative place within us that needs expression. The tension between desperately wanting to get out of the dead fish and yet needing to stay inside opens an emotional rift that leaves us all in disquiet, standing in the liminal place between worlds where there are many questions, but no answers. This simple dream of a dead fish and a woman stands us all in this place of awe, where the great mystery of all life resides, in the presence of that giant, unanswerable question about what life is about.

And this is just one evening. Do you see why I do dreamwork?

THE QUESTIONS

I find that a single dream can elicit hours of work, but in the group process fairness comes into play—so when we feel we have at least opened up the dream and it is responding to us, it's time to find a way to end the group process and allow the dreamer to work on what has happened on their own.

At this point, I ask the dreamer five questions. This helps them to consolidate their thinking and feelings into a mosaic of their choosing and hands the dream from the group back into the dreamer's care and keeping. These questions have their genesis in the work of writer and dreamworker Kathleen Sullivan. Often when I ask them, completely new ideas, emotions, and realizations arise from unexpected sources. In dreamwork, we are doing nothing less than unearthing the meaning and verve of each of our lives in some small way. Through the magic of the moment, as we careen around inside the soul of the dream, something will be triggered in the dreamer; they will be able to weave together the threads of life exposed in this sacred process into a tapestry of soulful wholeness.

Let's use the "Woman in the Fish" dream as an example of how this works and ask the dreamer the five questions.

Question 1: Why did you have this dream, and why did you have this dream now?

This question is intentionally loaded.

The first part asks the dreamer to conjecture what their own unconscious is trying to tell them about their waking life. The second half of the question places things in context. If I come home from a huge fight with my sister and that same night I dream I'm on a ladder wrapping the beak of a noisy bird sitting on a power line with duct tape, that fight will be part of the reason I had the dream; because the fight just happened, that answers the "why now" question.

For the dead fish dream, the dreamer could respond to the first question with this: "I had this dream because the space inside the fish is private and sheltering. I think it is a place of memory; we go deep inside ourselves, our own bodies, to find that place where our memories are stored."

Say what? Most of the time we have spent on that dream was in debating whether the woman should come out of the fish or not. During the entire deep and intense working of this dream, nothing like this has been mentioned. This powerful, honest, soulful answer roars up from the deep interior with a voice that speaks up when given the chance.

The dreamer continues: "Why this dream now? It is two years since Mom died, and it could be a reflection on her death, both the less savory aspects of it and the sweetness expressed in the woman reading. My mom taught literature, and so while she is now gone, something of her lives on in me. In some ways, this woman is my mom reading to me and also enjoying quiet time with her own books."

Wow. This woman is truly taking ownership of this dream. This creates a beautiful and tender image for us all. Magic is afoot here. This clear and unexpected statement pouring out of the dreamer surprises even the most cynical of us.

Question 2: I really appreciate this dream because . . . ?

This is an opportunity to step back from all we have talked about and see the bigger picture. It invites the dreamer to reach back across the process and encapsulate what they have felt and learned through the dynamic discovery process. It is also a way to appreciate the dream itself and our own unconscious, where it came from. Like the first one, this is also a loaded question. It really asks about the emotional state of the dreamer and their gut feeling about what this dream has become in the process of opening it.

The dreamer's response: "So, it's not awful but comforting for the woman inside the golden giant fish. I appreciate this dream because it reinforces the beauty of contemplation in a private space."

Question 3: Have I learned something new here that I didn't know before we started?

This gives the dreamer a chance to integrate the work. Out of all the varying projections, the dreamer gets to express a thing or two that struck them and that they have incorporated into new understanding.

Our dreamer responds: "What did I learn from the process? Well, I learned that Walter is less tempted by the idea of reading and contemplating inside a fish." Ouch. But she is right. She continues: "Others tended to see this as a form of torture, not a refuge. It is of course reminiscent of stories of Jonah and the whale, and the way that is reworked in the story of Pinocchio. In the Pinocchio tale he is reunited with his father in the belly of the whale, so there is a story precedent to the idea that the inside of a fish can be a cozy parental space."

Once again, our dreamer uses what has gone on to find her own meaning and path.

Question 4: What can I do in my waking life to honor this dream?

This question allows the dreamer to take all the deep work we have done and connect it to their life, keeping the dream alive. It is an invitation for one small step forward in our healing process, and it also invites the unconscious to give us further guidance in the form of more dreams.

Our dreamer responds: "Honor the dream? Read and remember my mom. It's that simple."

Question 5: What is the title of this dream?

This gives the dreamer a chance to close the dream for the time being and file this experience in the soul with an easy handle.

She writes the title on the drawing: *The Woman in the Fish.* When the dreamer announces this title vocally, she firmly emphasizes the word "IN," which makes it clear that this is so not about coming out of that fish.

This is often how we end working on a dream. However, if it feels appropriate, I do one more thing that reaches a step beyond the dream.

THE SECOND CLIENT

We have asked the five questions and essentially buttoned up the dream. But let's peer through one more window on the dream and see what is there. Just as our ever-present egos relax, thinking they have finished battling all these outlandish ideas, it's time to throw them one more unexpected curve ball, to shake up the process and open one more path into the unconscious. This intuitive tool can be used anywhere in the process, but I find it is most effective as an added lightning bolt at the end of the work.

This step is called "The Second Client," and I have David Jenkins to thank for this idea. David is vitally interested in what goes on in the dream world itself and with the characters there. Normally in a therapeutic setting, you have the therapist and the client. But in dreamwork, we have a second client to deal with, because there are two "I"s we are looking at. The first "I" is the waking self—the human, the dreamer, the one who buys the cappuccinos at the movies, writes poetry that no one will see, and knows everything there is to know about the French Revolution. Then there is the second "I," the dream self, the character who takes over at night while we are sleeping, who flies like Superman, walks through walls, and gives Buddha a pedicure while he sits under the Bodhi Tree pontificating about life. Some dreamworkers call this the "dream ego." The waking "I" and the dreaming "I" are partners in the same business of pushing forward our life's journey, so it is only natural that they should consult one another once in a while. We set up a powwow between these two very important figures, and something surprising often pops out.

In working with the "Woman in the Fish" dream, using the Second Client technique is just not appropriate. The quiet, introspective dream feels completed when we finish the questions.

The "Get on the Boat" dream is another matter. In this visitation dream, where the father brought the dreamer past barriers and got her onboard the ship to see her mother, it seems as though something else under the surface here might be accessed using the Second Client.

I tell the dreamer, Catrina, "We are going be a little creative and do some role-playing. If this were a movie and someone was playing you, who would you choose?"

She hesitates, then replies, "I would pick Nicole Kidman. I like her boldness and assuredness."

"Okay, so, like any great actor, Nicole Kidman has researched your life and knows a lot about you. She has played you in this movie based on your dream, and now she gets to tell you her impressions of what happened within the dream. She might see you from an angle you never saw, so let's ask her about her experience. I know she's making a movie in Australia right now, so *you* will have to be the stand-in for her and speak as though you were her.

Catrina now speaks as though she were Nicole Kidman, as we do a bit of dream theatre. "Well, what grabbed me as I played this role is the warmth and affection between my father and myself. I know from my research that you, Catrina, never felt the extreme warmth, support, validation, and faith from your father that clearly arises in the dream. In the dream, this guy is key to getting past all these barriers that stop me from getting on the boat of life, embracing the celebration going on there and also embracing myself, represented in the dream by the mother. Are you following my logic here? Perhaps one thing I can share with you from my perspective of having been in your shoes is: love is all around you, and the extreme traumas you have suffered have made you blind to that, if I can be blunt. Open your eyes to the love around you. Allow that love into your life! Embrace life and get on the boat!"

Well, that was a revelation we never saw when we were working the dream.

"Now, let's turn the tables and have Catrina speak to Nicole," I say.

Catrina is into this now and is unusually animated as she revels in this moment of theatre. She readily agrees to give some advice to the dream figure. "You know what, Nicole? You don't need your dad to get past all those barriers on the way to the boat. You have everything you need to get past all these traumas brought on by your divorce and all the other shit life has thrown at you. You may have suffered, but stand at every one of those barriers and ground yourself, breathe that life force up into yourself, then move on. Get on the boat! Get your ass on the boat, woman! Embrace life! Shake off the traumas and embrace life like you embraced your mother. You have lived as an invisible being for long enough. You do matter, you are seen, you are loved. Get on the damn boat now!"

Wow, that adds a new wrinkle we also didn't see in the work we did earlier. This particular dreamer is a very quiet, contemplative, introverted being, and the force of her inner strength had a chance to be given voice here in the theatre of the Second Client. As we did this work, the dreamer was surprised at her own boldness and clarity. She not only found a way to sidestep her ego and her instinct to hide, she also connected to her own unconscious for a few moments of self-created awe.

When things like this occur, who cannot love dreamwork?

This is just one way that using the Second Client can work. Each dream and dreamer presents different questions and different answers. The main goal is to step outside the ego in an imaginative way and allow the unconscious to express itself in some form. We also gain from having a second "I" onboard for all this powerful work in that we are not alone in our journey. Someone else is vitally interested in the well-being of this intrepid poet, and together we can heal and grow and find magic. We may have friends and family and a group of dreamers projecting on our dreams to aid us, but having a second "I" to sit with in solitude can be where much of the magic happens.

It must be said: so much of the work of dreamwork goes on after the dreamer goes home and thinks about what happened and what they felt. So many people have called me up a week or two after some dreamwork and expressed that the dream was still working on them, and new insights and new dreams had appeared to clarify even more things they had realized through the process. Dreamwork truly is a gift that keeps on giving.

EMPATHY AS AN OPENING TO UNDERSTANDING

This entire process is a guideline for how to open the dream. I'm not looking for answers so much as opening all the windows I can find. I can climb on my ladder, lantern in hand, and look in each of those open windows, seeing the dream from different angles and in different lights. I can look in on this tale-from-the-deep and see the living, breathing, and personal myth from a variety of perspectives. I hope to open enough windows that the magic inside wakes up and engulfs us.

The most important concept in all of this is to listen with empathy. Listen with your ears, your body, your mind, your heart, and your soul. Get your ego out of the way and listen to the dreamer, listen to others in the room, listen to that unspoken quiet inside of you, listen to the dream itself. Look for emotion—and allow it in. Hold still, and hold the moment. When Catrina talks about embracing her father and mother who have passed over on the cruise ship, we need to slow things down for that tender moment and allow it to linger. In that moment of lingering, empathy arises.

Empathy is the key to understanding others, and, reflectively, to understanding ourselves. When we attempt to stand in the space of someone else and feel and see what they do, it serves them, and it serves our own soul. We can connect to the artist/musician/dancer/philosopher/poet in each of us through dreamwork, whereby we are deposited in the Land of Awes. Dreamwork puts us in loving contact with our own soul, and with kindred souls, in a connection that we all crave and deserve. This communal experience would change the entire world if people practiced it more.

PART 3

DREAMS AND THE MIND

The Delicate Dance of Dreamer and Dream

CHAPTER 5

DIVING BELOW THE SURFACE

Exploring Consciousness, the Subconscious, and the Unconscious

Everything of which I know, but of which I am not at the moment thinking; everything of which I was once conscious but have now forgotten; everything perceived by my senses, but not noted by my conscious mind; everything which, involuntarily and without paying attention to it, I feel, think, remember, want, and do; all the future things which are taking shape in me and will sometimes come to consciousness; all this is the content of the unconscious.

CARL JUNG
The Collected Works, Vol. 8

Dreams are a direct connection to the unconscious, so they can be a source of unimaginable power, understanding, and healing. Everyone dreams on average between two and four hours a night—a ton of experiences if you think about it. It's like going to the movies every night and watching a symbolized documentary about your own life for two hours. Little of this plethora of dreams is remembered, however, and the bits we do remember are often strange, illogical, confusing, and/or upsetting. But they can be of great use if we can recognize what is bubbling up from the unconscious.

Understanding the unconscious is like that old analogy of the iceberg falsely attributed to Sigmund Freud: "The mind is like an iceberg; it floats with one-seventh of its bulk above water." He never said that, but the concept is valuable nonetheless.

Our conscious selves are working with a boatload of knowledge, thoughts, emotions, memories, and desires that exist above the water line in our conscious world. But all that consciousness is dwarfed by the myriad machinations going on below the surface in the unconscious. The bulk of who we are lies in our unconscious selves.

Since a plethora of terms can be used to talk about consciousness and unconsciousness, I will elucidate these concepts insofar as they bear upon our dreamwork: consciousness, the subconscious, and the unconscious.

CONSCIOUSNESS

The study of consciousness and its meaning encompasses everything from Descartes' dictum "I think, therefore I am" to quantum physics and artificial intelligence—but that is a rabbit hole we will not plunge into here. We will focus instead on our experience of consciousness rather than the philosophical ideas surrounding it.

Merriam-Webster defines consciousness as "the quality or state of being aware especially of something within oneself." Consciousness is individual awareness. It is my awareness of my own unique thoughts, sensations, memories, feelings, and environment. Our conscious experience is continually shifting and changing. It is a fluid state wherein we are constantly letting go of thoughts, memories, and visuals and replacing them with other thoughts, memories, and visuals.

The conscious mind's working memory, also known as short-term memory, can only store three- to four-items at the same time (one of the reasons phone numbers are broken up into three and four number sequences). For example: I am aware that it is chilly here on the dock, and I am aware of the ripples on the water, and I am aware that I am hungry and that it is around 5:00 PM. Then I become aware that a fish just jumped out of the water, and that someone just yelled my name. Those two last things, however, push the awareness of my chilliness and my hunger out of consciousness for a moment. And the jumping fish reminds me of my dad, who was a fisherman, and I become aware of my feelings about him and how I disappointed him in my inability to fish properly, and that makes me lose the sense of what time it is. I let the awareness of the fish jumping fade from my conscious thoughts as I turn to see who has called my name and become aware of a group of rowdy guys across the way, as I remember my dad yelling at me when we were fishing together. Then my body reminds me that I am hungry and cold, and my consciousness turns back to that.

Consciousness is slippery and complex. It shifts and flows like a river current, evaluating, learning, comparing, and connecting all that it comprises. Since consciousness is connected to memory, the whole business is a huge challenge to navigate, and yet our conscious selves seem to manage pretty well as long as we are not overwhelmed.

THE SUBCONSCIOUS

The next layer—the subconscious—is tricky, because the definitions of subconscious and unconscious are almost exactly the same in many references, and people use them interchangeably, which is incorrect. We will separate them here.

The prefix "sub" literally refers to something beneath; something subterranean is underground. The subconscious is the part of the mind functioning just under the surface, containing thoughts and emotions not currently in focal awareness. It is connected to consciousness and may be easily accessible or accessible with effort. The Freudians call it the preconscious. I find subconscious more expressive and accurate.

How cool is it that the body/mind does this? If we had all the information and chatter living in the subconscious going on at the same time in our conscious minds, we would fail to function. Talk about monkey mind! We're lucky the mind/body limits the number of things we can hold in our consciousness at the same time. If too many were released into consciousness, the circuits in the brain would likely overload, like someone on a bad acid trip when too many things fill their awareness at the same time. (Not that that has ever happened to me.)

Yet much of what's subconscious is easily accessed. Sometimes all we need to do for the subconscious to supply the information we're looking for—like where the car keys are—is to look up to the right and scratch our head for a second. However, other things in the subconscious may take more thought and concentration to recall. This is where we store our childhood home address, our best friend's phone number, the fact that dry ice is CO^2, and a multitude of things that hover just under our consciousness but are available if we try. Somewhere stored in my subconscious is the name of the restaurant in Santa Monica where I met that gorgeous woman in the indigo dress, what the case was about when I served jury duty two years ago, the feeling of dread when I was about to take my driver's test at age 16, the answer to "How much wood could a woodchuck chuck, if a woodchuck could chuck wood?". Indeed, we access the subconscious all the time as we grind through our days slaying dragons and ordering lattes. We can also access the subconscious without even knowing it—for, as we know, we often work on autopilot.

THE NIGHT I ALMOST KILLED GREGG ALLMAN

You won't be surprised that this brings up a story for me.

During the 1990s, I was working at Paramount Studios in Hollywood, doing lighting on various television enterprises such as the *Star Trek: Voyager* series, *Cheers, Taxi,* and *The Arsenio Hall Show.* I was hired as the director of photography for a broadcast originating from Stage 29 at Paramount, to be carried live via satellite to the prime-time audience in Japan: a live performance by Gregg Allman of Allman Brothers fame. They scheduled the broadcast for 8:00 PM in Japan, which was 4:00 AM in Los Angeles. Not an ideal time, but we be show folks, so we geared up for the event. The two producers visiting from Japan for this were polite and enthusiastic as, on the day before the event, we came up with a "look" for the broadcast.

In the center of the stage, we had a perfectly tuned grand piano sitting on a shiny black floor. Gregg Allman would sit at the piano and play and sing one song solo, and that would be the entire deal. I had five cameras to cover the action: one to show his hands, one for a close-up of his face, one for the wide shot taking in the entire stage, one hand-held to roam and shoot interesting angles, and a fifth to use as a tracking shot, moving back and forth. We set up the shots and rehearsed with one of the Japanese producers sitting in as Gregg Allman.

I created the lighting look, starting simply with a follow-spot just off center into the face from a fairly low angle, but not so low the cameras would create shadows, adjusting it and the piano so the mic shadow fell where it pleased me and the nose shadow looked right. Then I added a light on the hands, a hard amber backlight to make the hair pop, and various other lights. In the deep background, we had a series of swag curtains that I lit with streaks of deep blue.

We asked the producers what they thought. They both hesitated, then said they liked it very much and this would do fine. Hmm . . . something told me their politeness was masking the fact they weren't over the moon with this. I was determined to knock their socks off.

I added a sweeping series of colored lights to the look, timed with the playback track of the song we used to rehearse with. I got a similar response. I then removed the curtains and replaced them with 60 feet of Mylar mirrors that would reflect the images of Gregg Allman and the piano and added smoke to the room so you could see the moving shafts of colored light. They mentioned that they liked the mirrors a lot, but we were still in muted-response land.

Well, being me, I was hell-bent on getting a visceral response from these two, so I went to the music for inspiration. The song was Allman's hit "I'm No Angel." That gave me a crazy idea.

I ordered up a series of powerful fog machines that used dry ice to create a thick, rolling ground fog. We had used them on the Warren Beatty movie *Heaven Can Wait* for the scene with the SST airplane that sat on top of a cloud, so I knew these suckers put out enough fog to do anything we wanted. We snaked the feed tubes around so they wouldn't be seen on camera and strategically placed fans to create the cloud-like look I was going for. I rolled the fog in, and I turned all the sweeping lights blood red and added a series of blood-red lights on the floor, creating an otherworldly series of rippling red clouds that Satan himself would have smiled at.

I got one of my producer's assistants to sit down and pretend to be Gregg Allman this time, so both producers could watch on monitor. I lit it up like before, but on cue, I let loose the massive waves of ground fog and cued in the blood red lighting effect while the cameras went through their motions. The reflections in the mirrors and the dynamic visual elements at the piano were stunning.

This time the demure and courteous Japanese producers lit up like roman candles, saying all manner of things in Japanese and pointing at me and saying in English, "That was good! No one in Japan has ever done that! You are good!"

At last, I had cracked that reserved exterior.

We now had a look and a plan, and we just had to wait for Mr. Allman to show up. He was to arrive at 1:00 AM, we would rehearse twice, and then he would go to hair and makeup before the 4:00 AM broadcast.

1:00 AM came and went. 2:00 AM came and went, then 3:00 AM, and my two producers were pacing and muttering loudly in Japanese. They made phone calls and kept looking outside for the limo, but to no avail. At 3:50, still no Gregg Allman. The producers called Japan, and they moved things around so that the live hookup would begin at 4:15 AM.

At 4:10 AM, the two producers ran out the door, and a minute later they reappeared with each of their heads under an armpit of a totally drugged-out Gregg Allman. Oh, dear.

As soon as I saw them, I cued in the ground fog and put up the lighting look. They staggered to the piano and deposited him on the piano bench. But this was a disaster in the making. Gregg Allman was slumped over, his head unceremoniously resting on the just-polished piano top. What would happen if they cut to us, and all we had was a comatose rock star and a bunch of red fog?

The two producers yelled at me, "What do we do? What do we do?!!"

We only had three minutes before we were on air. I suggested we play the prerecorded version of the song we had used in rehearsal. I would have the cameras widen out to long shots and turn off the front lights that hit his face, and hopefully no one would figure out that there was an unconscious rock star hiding behind the smoke and mirrors. We also had a huge mirror ball hanging overhead; I suggested we turn that on and hit it with the follow spots, and it would hide a lot. These were terrible ideas, but they were all I could come up with.

As I was saying this, the two producers let out huge groans, pointing wildly at the piano. I turned around, and there was the piano lit up, the red fog rolling beautifully across the floor, but no Gregg Allman. Holy hell. Apparently, Gregg had stood up and moved the piano bench a few inches, and not being in the most stable condition, had fallen to the floor and was lying somewhere in the midst of the dense fog.

I went into a full panic. As I dug up from my subconscious at the time, dry ice is CO^2, and CO^2 displaces oxygen when you release it. I had a famous celebrity lying on the floor sucking in CO^2 instead of air.

Holy shit, I just killed Gregg Allman! I rushed to the piano and kicked everywhere, trying to find the body, screaming at my guys to kill the fog machines—which they did—but the fog lingered. Finally, I kicked a body squarely in the ribs, took a deep breath, and pulled a limp Gregg Allman up out of the CO^2.

I started to drag him off the stage, thinking Japan would be compelled to figure something else out.

But at that instant, he came alive, pushed me back, and said, "I'm fine man, I'm fine. Let's do this."

And this is where his subconscious kicked in. He sat down at the piano, played a few chords, and gave us a thumbs-up. The producer, wide-eyed and pouring sweat, counted down from 30 seconds, and Gregg Allman started the tune as though nothing had happened. He performed magnificently as the fog rolled, the cameras moved, and everything looked just like we had planned. After he finished the short performance, he stood up, staggered out the door to the limo, and off he went to who knows where. Evidently the people in Japan were very pleased with it all, and the two producers have a story they probably tell to this day.

That moment where something in Gregg Allman's subconscious just took over when it needed to was a testament to the power of these stupefying minds of ours. I suspect he hardly remembered being at the piano that night, but in his subconscious was everything he needed to construct a memorable performance, including the emotions and the kinetic ability to play and sing—and it is like that with all of us.

Under the surface of our consciousness are these magnificent minds that can call up the emotions, thoughts, and memories to guide our lives, or at least get us through the day. Gregg Allman had performed this song so many times, he could do it on autopilot.

Some things in the subconscious come readily up to consciousness, while other things may require concentration or help or prompts. When I am hanging out with my brothers and they are telling stories from our youth, those stories suddenly unlock memories from my subconscious I could not access until something prompted them.

Oh, and I am sure you want to know how much wood a woodchuck could chuck if a woodchuck could chuck wood. I checked with my subconscious, and the answer is: As much wood as a woodchuck could, if a woodchuck could chuck wood.

THE UNCONSCIOUS

Unlike the subconscious, the unconscious cannot be accessed directly. "Un" as a prefix means "not," and this differs from the subconscious, where things are just "under" the surface. The subconscious is like a vast library where we can move up and down the aisles and retrieve many things, but the unconscious is the library's special collection that can only be opened with a key. All this immense unconscious is not sealed off from us, it's just not accessible directly from our conscious minds. Nevertheless, it affects our behavior and emotions. It sits there silently influencing us, but we are not completely aware of it.

Perhaps when you were an infant, your mother grabbed your head and pulled it inches from her angry, threatening face as she reprimanded you loudly. Now, years later, when someone gets close and looks you directly in the eye, you recoil and move away instinctively, even though you have no conscious memory of your mother taking out any self-loathing on you.

Or perhaps your mother used to get her face close up to yours and smile broadly, holding your gaze for a long time, and now in your conscious life you love it when people get close and look you directly in the eye, even though you have no conscious memory of that loving gesture on your mother's part. Even with Herculean effort, that memory from babyhood cannot be accessed.

Our intuition and our gut feelings are tied up with the unconscious and its unseen influence on our lives, all part of this quiet, wonderful, enormous underbelly of who we are. The unconscious leads us into relationships and embraces certain ideas and systems that seem to fit with the essence of our souls. A lot of life hums along with the silent connection between the conscious self and the unconscious self, and it all works just fine.

But what about the messed-up parts? Sometimes these emotions and memories interfere with our forward movement. What happens when we desire a change? Perhaps it's time to deal with an aversion to looking people in the eye that was acquired from that nasty mother. How do we do that? How do we access the vast expanse of the personal unconscious?

Therapy can be extremely valuable in accessing the unconscious, particularly to address things that are preventing us from moving forward. Often in the process of talk therapy, things from the unconscious are revealed. If we are aware of abuse suffered in childhood, we can talk about it and express our feelings. By doing that there is a road to recovery that will allow us to right the ship and eventually, for example, experience the intimacy we so desire in our relationships. When someone has an aversion to looking people in the eye, the therapist might guide and probe her way into a memory of the mother's scolding, allowing the client to see that her fear of intimacy stems from this and helping her develop new habits and feelings. Often the actual memory will not be found, but if the therapist has a bit of Sherlock Holmes in her, the clues will appear that show various aspects of this fear of intimacy, and together the therapist and client can form a path to recovery.

Some therapies are designed to work directly with the unconscious. Carl Jung used Active Imagination to work with a dream, image, or memory from waking life, letting the unconscious express itself by playing with the images so they could take on a life of their own. Fritz Perls developed Gestalt therapy, which uses role-play to engage the conscious mind while the unconscious expresses itself within the role.

Hypnotherapy has also proven useful in accessing the unconscious. When a hypnotist guides people down into a trance, the unconscious is sometimes accessed. In this state the patient can access repressed memories and emotions, both positive and negative, which could be key to some form of recovery or progress. This requires a skilled, caring hypnotist, especially since memory is tricky to deal with. Hypnotism can be abused. Memories can be implanted or remembered incorrectly in this state, so you don't want to be hypnotized by your cousin Betty, who used to work in the circus as the crystal ball swami.[1]

And finally, we can access the unconscious through our dreams.

---

1. A fabulous book on the correct use of hypnosis is *The Pregnant Man and Other Cases From a Hypnotherapist's Couch* by Deirdre Barrett, Ph.D., who is on the faculty at Harvard Medical School. The book explores seven cases in her own practice when hypnotism was used to explore the deep unconscious. Used correctly, as Dr. Barrett does, hypnotism becomes an opening into the unconscious mind and can be a path of healing

THE SUBMARINE

In *The Red Book,* that long-squirreled-away secret tome wherein Carl Jung passed through his own madness, he wrote something to the effect of, "I drew something today, but something else appeared." His unconscious had another idea of what that day's artwork should be, and so that is what he drew.

When we draw our dreams, we allow our unconscious to express itself not only through the dream itself and the words we choose to tell it, but also through the act of drawing.

In this example, the unconscious created an entire drawing completely unexpected by the dreamer.

JOURNEY HOME

I am on a journey. I have to get home. I am frustrated by this trip. First, I get in a submarine and navigate through a marshland. Now I am in a giant valley between two giant mountain peaks. It is hot, and it is a desert with cactus. I walk and walk for a long way under the hot sun. Then I see my set of compounds in the distance mounted on two side-by-side hills. That is my home. There is barbed wire all around both underground compounds, but I can see the black metal roofs of the compound entrances. Then I realize that people have been going in and out of my compounds and it pisses me off. Someone, maybe my mother, has given every damn person in the town the combination to getting into these completely sealed and protected places. Oh, hell, I will change that!

For context, our dreamer lives in an apartment in a city and has never owned, lived in, or been in any compound described in the dream report.

Let's look at the drawing on the next page.

Well. I mean, well. What do you see here?

When the dreamer put up the picture, all of us attempted to not laugh out loud. What was here on the page was totally evident to everyone in the room except the dreamer. The dreamer did not understand she had drawn

a body—perhaps a hermaphrodite body at that, or perhaps a pair of bodies engaged in that most delightful of physical activities.

We all stayed stoically silent as she took us through the dream, starting at that submarine passing through the marshlands, up through the dry desert and then to the compounds. As she circled the compounds with the laser pointer, showing us the circle of barbed wire, it suddenly dawned on her that something else was going on here.

With wide eyes, she exclaimed, "Oh, my god! Those are my mother's breasts. Somehow, I have drawn my mother's breasts! Oh, wait! Those are my breasts! They must be my breasts, and those are my nipples. Oh, hell, the whole thing looks like a body. And I have a penis. Why would I have a penis? Or is that someone else's penis? Yikes!"

The unconscious artist had really done a number on her here. In doing so, it opened a giant revelation to the dreamer about how her mother had not nourished her and how she was not nurturing others around her—especially men, whom she had locked out of her life. Her discoveries thrilled her, and this drawing became a touchstone for a great deal of positive corrective work she did on herself.

The unconscious can be a spectacular artist, leading us into a deeper understanding of our complex lives. When you draw your dreams, try to not impede that silent, unseen voice that wants you to make a sloppy drawing of a submarine that turns out looking like a penis. Hand the marker over to the unconscious now and then and see what happens, says the Wizard of Awes.

CHAPTER 6

LUCID DREAMING

Bringing Consciousness Inside the Dream

Humankind is being led
along an evolving course,
through this migration
of intelligences
and though we seem
to be sleeping
there is an inner wakefulness,
that directs the dream
and that will eventually
startle us back
to the truth of
who we are

RUMI
from *Inner Wakefulness*

Lucid dreaming is the rare occasion when consciousness is applied inside the dream. In this one area, the unconscious and the conscious mind are in the same place at the same time, which makes for some interesting and powerful experiences. To be lucid in a dream means that you are aware that you are dreaming while you dream. In a sense, you wake up inside the dream. How cool is that? Can you imagine the possibilities that this makes viable? It becomes a chance to consciously connect with aspects of the unconscious that can be explored and learned from.

THE HISTORY OF LUCIDITY

Dutch psychiatrist Frederik van Eeden coined the term "lucid dream" in his 1913 article "A Study of Dreams" to describe a dream in which the dreamer is consciously aware that they are dreaming. The phenomenon of being aware in a dream reaches far back into history. The ancient Indian practice of Yoga Nidra and the Tibetan practice of Dream Yoga both encourage dreamers to cultivate the ability to be aware that they are dreaming during a dream. Aristotle also was aware of it and wrote about the practice.

The first scientific proof of lucid dreaming came from British parapsychologist Keith Hearne in 1975. He hooked up a man who reportedly had lots of lucid dreams to a multi-channel chart recorder and told him to make seven or eight left-right eye movements when he was aware that he was dreaming. The eye muscles are one of the few muscle groups not affected by temporary sleep paralysis in REM sleep, so it was a nifty idea to use them to signal to the researcher that he was in a lucid dream. Keith hung out all night, watching the readout showing the REM periods and such. Around eight in the morning, the lucid dreamer was about half an hour into a REM state, and sure enough, he moved his eyes back and forth seven times, just as planned. Keith couldn't believe his eyes. He was so jazzed he had a hard time not immediately shaking the guy awake. When the dreamer woke up, he confirmed that he had been lucid and had sent the signal. And that was the start of the research into lucidity that continues madly apace now.

Most likely no one has hooked you up to a machine to find out, but chances are you have had more than one lucid dream in your life. As Melissa Dahl states in her article "People Who Can Control Their Dreams are also

Better at Real Life" *(New York Magazine,* September 11, 2014), "Most people have experienced a lucid dream at some point during their lives, and frequent lucid dreamers—those who have a lucid dream more than once a month—are fairly common, too, somewhere between 19 and 37 percent of the population."

PRACTICING LUCIDITY

For some folks, lucidity comes naturally, and for others it is a learned skill that requires a great deal of practice and tricks. I fall into this latter group. Most of us common dreaming people are not hell-bent on becoming lucid. We don't think of the word "lucid" when we have a dream where our father appears and we realize inside the dream that he passed two years ago and know we are dreaming at that moment. We become spontaneously lucid, but it doesn't occur to us to take conscious control of the situation. I think that is just fine. The lucidity serves as a beautiful reminder of the relationship with the dreamer's father, and the intrepid soul has a moment of awe realizing what an important part he still plays in their life. In this spontaneous passive lucidity, we do not exert any influence on the dream, but the dream can take on greater importance due to the lucidity.

But what if we make a conscious effort to become lucid and take some control of the dream? And what would be the purpose of doing so?

If I am dreaming and become lucid, realizing that this is a dream, I can discover things not readily accessible in a non-lucid dream. I can ask figures in the dream questions and look around corners I would not have noticed. I can fly to my childhood home and hover over it, then see through the walls. I can have wild sex with dream figures, which is one of the reasons, methinks, that a large following of enthusiastic young men are vitally interested in lucid dreaming. Flying and sex seem to be the two most common activities that lucid dreamers attempt when they become advanced enough to control things in a dream.

But many possibilities open in lucidity. I can ask the railroad engineer where we are going and why she is in my dream. I can connect with those who have passed to the other side. I can fly into outer space and visit stars and planets. The options are endless.

There are levels of lucidity, of course. Those steeped in the practice have developed the skill to bring their consciousness fully into the dream and still maintain the dream. It is a delicate balance to stay lucid. If excitement and emotions rise too much, the lucidity can vanish, and we wake up. That balance is a bit like really great sex, if you catch my drift.

If you do start a lucidity practice, be patient with yourself. At first you may gain control of just one small thing. It may be something as simple as this example:

PARADISE FOUND

I walk into a bar and look at my watch and it is 2:00 AM. *I look away and then look back at the watch and it reads 4:30* PM. *This makes me realize that I am in a dream since time does not change like that in waking life. I am dreaming and I know I am dreaming! So, if that is true, I can do something else instead of walking into the bar! So I do not enter. Instead, I step back and look up at the red neon sign over the entrance, which reads Paradise Lost and Found. Wow! I then walk into the bar and immediately forget that I am dreaming. The dream continues with a country western band playing in the background while I toss back beer after beer.*

That small stint of lucidity, that single moment when the dreamer looked up at that sign, has delivered a clue about what the dream might be trying to say. In this example, the dreamer in his waking life had broken up with his girlfriend who had moved to New York, but he was in the process of reconnecting and making it into a long distance relationship. The concept of paradise lost and then found encouraged him to continue this important love connection.

One of the earmarks of being in a dream is unreliable technology. Another is that things like locations and objects shift. Since the logic centers are pretty much asleep during dreaming, naturally all sorts of crazy things can go off the beam in a dream, like flying, being naked in public, and talking to animals (or, rather, animals talking to us). One trick that lucid-seekers use is known as the reality check, which you might try if you want to become lucid. During the day, look at a clock—then look away and back and ask if you are in a dream. Do the same thing with text in a book, or on a sign. Do this over and over while awake, as a way of rehearsing for becoming lucid. In waking life, nothing will change, but often in dreams, the text or time will change radically.

If clocks or text appear when you are dreaming, your consciousness might be awake enough to remember what you rehearsed and have you look away and look back to confirm that you are dreaming. If that happens, your consciousness and unconsciousness are hanging out together in a dream. From there you can explore the dream, if you can maintain that very delicate balance of logic and magic.

Other proven ways to become lucid include constantly checking the validity of the reality around you during the day. Take a moment to take in what is before you, and ask if it is real. "I see the tree, I see the car, but are they real? Let me look closely at them." Or you can attempt to push your index finger through the palm of your other hand during the day. That can coax the dream ego to try the same experiment in a dream and succeed at impaling your hand, signaling that you are in a dream. (I would be careful who is around when you do this, however. Someone might want to lock you up!) Also, try setting an intention just before sleeping, such as a question you want to ask in the dream. Or, you can say to yourself, *When I dream tonight, I will know that I am dreaming,* or something along those lines.

Lucidity is a skill that can be learned, and just like art or tennis or making love, it gets better with practice.

One of the most beautiful uses of lucid dreaming is to help people with PTSD (post-traumatic distress disorder) and/or people with distressing nightmares. Since lucid dreaming is a skill that can be learned, when those suffering from PTSD nightmares learn to be conscious in the nightmare, they may be able to change something inside the dream, which can lead to relief and healing. Such work is to be lauded and cherished. If you do suffer from PTSD or other serious emotional or mental difficulties, do not just jump into a lucidity practice. Consult your therapist or other medical professional before attempting to look into it.

I have to admit, my greatest hesitancy about lucid dreaming has been the control factor. I have always thought of dreams as something sacred that you just don't want to mess with. These messages from the unconscious rise in response to our needs and health. Exerting control in a dream seems to invite the ego to bend the dream to serve egotistical purposes. We can ignore the old lady in the corner and instead fly off somewhere exotic to have sex with multiple characters. In doing so, we may miss the significance of that old lady, and therefore the themes and feelings that the dream intended. Lucidity seems to muddle the pure experience of the dream.

But you know what? Many find that too narrow a view. I asked Robert Waggoner, an expert in the area of lucidity, about this, and he replied:

> The sailor does not control the sea; neither does the lucid dreamer control the dream. A sailor learns they must relate to the winds, the waves, the current, and many things in order to arrive at their destination (and that is not guaranteed). Similarly, the lucid dreamer learns to relate to a dynamic confluence of conscious and unconscious beliefs, expectations, focus, and energies within the lucid dream. Lucid dreaming does not mean "control"; rather lucid dreaming means more aware relating.

Well, that is a great point. Also, when you develop the skill of lucidity, it doesn't mean all or even most of your dreams are lucid. Even avid lucid onieronauts (a fancy, somewhat pretentious term for dreamers) only experience a very small percentage of their dreams as lucid. Robert tells me less than ten percent of the dreams he recalls are lucid.

And even if I miss talking to the old lady in the lucid dream, she will likely return in some form in another dream to give me another chance at understanding something about my path. The dream gods are ultimately patient and will keep sending dream after dream, trying to help us fulfill our destiny and live in our genius. With that in mind, you can see how thoughtful consideration of trying a bit of lucid dreaming is not such an off-the-wall idea.

HANDS IN THE FACE AND MUMMIES WITH ZIPPERS

I have had many lucid dreams, but most often I have failed to exert my consciousness with any will into the lucid dream. In an attempt to get lucid in my dreams, I had been using a technique first used by Carlos Castaneda that Robert Waggoner showed me. You stop many times in the day and look at your hands, while repeatedly saying to yourself, "Tonight, when I see my hands, I will know I am dreaming." For many people, this trigger makes them realize they are dreaming and elicits lucidity.

So, there I was, walking around for days looking at my hands, feeling a bit foolish, but I persisted. Then one night, just before I went to sleep, I set an intention to see my hands in a dream and become lucid. And this dream appeared:

HAND IT TO ROBERT

I am at a dream conference and I realize that I am totally naked walking around with everyone else dressed. I head to my car to get some clothes. I rummage through my luggage in the trunk of a station wagon, but all of my clothes are dresses and bras and corsets and high heels. As I am doing this, Robert Waggoner walks up. I am a little embarrassed that I am standing there naked with a bra and high heels in my hands, but he doesn't seem to care. He raises his right hand directly in front of his face and says, "Hi." I drop my clothing and raise my hand in front of my face in return and also say, "Hi." This is odd. He does the same thing again and I also do it, but why would anyone hold their hand in front of their face while saying hi? Maybe there is something important about looking at my hands? No, they are just my hands. We keep doing this until I finally ask, "Why are we doing this, Robert?" He replies by putting his hand in front of my face and says, "I don't know, Walter, why are we doing this?" I have no answer, so I grab a dress and some heels from the station wagon and head off into the woods to Germany.

What a funny dream. I mean, could someone be more clueless than this? All the triggers were there, even the king of lucidity himself, but it never occurred to me until I woke up that the hands were a signal to become lucid.

I doubled down and kept seeking lucidity night after night, and finally this dream came, with a screaming possibility of me being a fantastic lucid oneironaut.

ZIPPING THE MUMMY

I am in the back room of an ancient museum. I am privileged to be present as they are zipping up a mummy: an ancient Egyptian mummy in his original zippered plastic case. The room is brightly lit and there are a multitude of mummies here. I look at my right hand for some reason. Why am I looking at my hand? My hand is just in the way of seeing the mummies, and yet I keep holding up my hand in front of my face. Why am I looking at my hand? I think there is a reason, but I don't know what it is. Then I see the hand of the guy zipping up the mummy.

I zoom in on the zipper. Wow. I watch it in slow motion and extremely close up as the teeth pass through from one side to the other. That is an advanced, complex machine really, this zipper thing. It doesn't fit with being so ancient. I know—I must be dreaming!

They didn't have zippers in ancient Egypt. They couldn't have had them! Could they? I really am dreaming, that must be it! I announce to the room that I am having a dream. The guy who is doing the zipping looks at me askance and tells me clearly, "No, you are not having a dream, these are ancient zippers that the Egyptians invented."

I am crestfallen. "Oh . . . are you sure? Zippers were invented in the 19th century or later, I am so sure of it . . . . I must be dreaming, this has to be a dream."

The dour bald-headed tall pale-skinned zipper guy in a long white robe gives me an exasperated look and says, "I assure you, you are not dreaming. All the mummies here have these ancient zippers. Who would know better than me?" I am resigned to the fact that I must not be dreaming and the zippers are ancient. He must be right.

But then one more thought strikes me and I say to the zipper guy, "Wait a minute. What about the plastic? How did they have plastic in ancient Egypt? I really must be dreaming!"

He doesn't even reply. He just gives me one of those withering looks my ex-wife used to give me, which makes me think, "Oh, stop Walter. Stop doubting everything around you. Just go back to sleep." And I do.

I suppose this is my just desserts for being a trickster-storyteller. The Walter trickster got tricked by the zipper-trickster.

I have since had success in becoming lucid, and even changing things in a dream, but it is not something that sits naturally in my wheelhouse. But with huge effort, it is achievable.

In some circles, lucidity is the extreme sport of dreamers. People who have practiced lucidity for a good length of time become comfortable asking questions of the dream figures and roaming around in the dream landscape at will, including flying to exotic locations. In these explorations, they can gain greater understanding of themselves and others. A sense of awe is readily available in this unique place where consciousness and unconsciousness walk around hand in hand. Many times, when I have become lucid in a dream, something wells up in me as I feel the sense of wonder and awe vibrate through my body. The problem is that this is so exciting to me, I often immediately lose lucidity and am jolted awake.

Besides talking to the dream figures and asking them questions, in a lucid dream you can ask a question of something Robert Waggoner calls "the unseen awareness." The unseen awareness or "wisdom behind the dream" is a bit like the man behind the curtain in *The Wizard of Oz.* It is the something that is possibly pulling the levers and the source and inspiration for the dream. I talk about "The Dream Gods," as though there is a group of beings that make up and send us dreams at night. This is probably the same as the unseen awareness—or the "lucid light," as Clare Johnson, another lucidity expert, likes to call it.

ALL YOU NEED IS LUCID LOVE

Here is an example of how someone asked that "wisdom behind the awareness" a question when he was in a state of lucidity and received some wisdom he needed. Bob is a regular, skilled practitioner of lucidity. His marriage to a wonderfully bright woman has been long-term, and very strong. In recent years, his wife has been slipping into dementia. Because of that, Bob has been going through a difficult passage on both a practical and an emotional level.

ALL YOU NEED IS LOVE

That day I had been stressing about what it is I need to get through an evolving situation with someone I am caring for that has dementia. I have no idea where this is going and what I will need to do to get through it. That night I was dreaming that I was in a marina boat yard filled with old rotting and rusting boats (an aside: boats in my dreams always relate to my creative journey through life—which is now impacted by the caretaking concern). Suddenly I realized I was dreaming. Knowing that there is a "wisdom" behind the dream (Jung called it the Collective Unconscious, some consider it the higher self), I called out "show me what I need to get through this situation." At that moment I was lifted up into the cosmos and found myself in a universe of crystal light which I felt totally at ONE with, yet still a separate personality.

There was celestial music consuming everything. I held up my arms and could see through them realizing I too was made up of crystal light. I felt an intense BLISS greater than anything I have ever experienced before or could even imagine experiencing. I dwelled on the pure ecstasy of being absorbed by this sensation, almost forgetting who I was or how I had gotten there. But then I remembered—I had not gotten an answer to my question. So, I stated, "This is really wonderful . . . but what do I need to get through this situation?" At that moment tiny three-dimensional red hearts began to appear in the crystal matrix, floating around in a clockwise circular manner. They formed the outline of a giant red heart in front of me. I could now hear a tune or singing among the celestial music in the background—so I listened carefully. It gradually increased in amplitude . . . it was the Beatles tune "All You Need Is Love." I smiled in amazement—I had my answer . . . which I immediately knew to be true . . . I knew that is really all I can depend on in this situation.

LUCIDITY RESOURCES

I have two friends who are experts in the field of lucidity, and if you are interested in this area, I would recommend reading their work.

Dr. Clare Johnson can be found at *deepluciddreaming.com*, and her book *Llewellyn's Complete Book of Lucid Dreaming* is a masterful guide to techniques and use of lucid dreaming—and a good read, also. Here is a quote:

> Waking up in a dream usually means finding ourselves in an environment that is as super-real as that of our waking life, where thoughts can change reality, gravity can be weak or strong and time

is not linear. This means we can imaginatively create whatever we like by thinking about it with intent and expecting it to happen.

Robert Waggoner can be found at *lucidadvice.com,* and his book, *Lucid Dreaming: Gateway to the Inner Self* is a clear and concise look at lucid dreaming, showing what a powerful tool it can be as he weaves story after story into the mix.

These dreamers are onto something powerfully healing and significant.

CHAPTER 7

MAKING THINGS UP

The Endless Pursuit of Ego-defense Penetration

To confront a person with his shadow is to show him his own light. Once one has experienced a few times what it is like to stand judgingly between the opposites, one begins to understand what is meant by the self. Anyone who perceives his shadow and his light simultaneously sees himself from two sides and thus gets in the middle.

CARL JUNG

Good and Evil in Analytical Psychology (1959)

From the moment a dream appears and we record it, to the last insight we find in the work, the ego often battles us. I think the reason that most people ignore their dreams, and that the general public does not have a deep abiding interest in dreams, is that most remembered dreams, in my experience, are basically "negative," which can trigger the ego-defense system and allow us to disregard or sublimate them. One of the largest obstacles for accomplishing meaningful progress in understanding our dreams is getting past this ever-aware, dictatorial, self-serving, narcissistic, constantly changing barrier to the real self.

What is the ego? The Oxford Reference Dictionary defines it as: "A person's sense of self-esteem or self-importance" and then includes a psychoanalytical definition: "The part of the mind that mediates between the conscious and the unconscious and is responsible for reality testing and a sense of personal identity."

The ego is a necessary part of our existence. When there is a balance between the ego and the self, we can find harmony and are able to be steady and stable, and still keep forward motion. In that place, we neither beat ourselves up for our shortcomings nor do we suddenly think we are the greatest thing since sliced bread.

Problems occur when we are out of balance and the ego becomes inflated or defensive. When the ego becomes inflated, the journey to self-realization can be thwarted or stopped, at least for a time. It can also be dangerous. Having spent decades in the film and television industry, I have watched many souls who have come into fame, often for good reason, fall prey to believing that they are the sole creator of the magic that is all around them. They are surrounded by writers who toil over the words they will say, producers who compliment and coddle them with innumerable perks and tons of money, agents who are cheerleaders protecting them from uncomfortable truths, and audiences who believe that those words and emotions roaring out of their carefully made-up faces are their own. Many fall into the gaping maw of this self-deception. With that disconnect in place, they turn into raving jackasses as they revel in their inflated egos. Donald Trump is a prime example of someone whose inflated ego can cause huge damage to the self and to others.

On the other hand, Tom Hanks is a famous person who hasn't let his ego take over. He fully knows his own strengths and shortcomings. He immediately realizes when someone is blowing smoke up their butt. He keeps things simple and is always interested in what other people have to say. I once sat with him at lunch and he wanted to know what I did and how the magic of lighting happened, and actually listened to what I had to say. It was a deep and very real conversation.

Most of us have a balance in our souls that keeps the ego from dictating every move. But let's face it—we all make stuff up. We rewrite our history and the history of others. We lie to ourselves and to others, hide things, bend the truth, are mute when asked a direct question, and ignore things that just don't fit with the tailored truth locus we have built for ourselves. We are a deceptive bunch, we humans. We listen selectively to almost everything. But you know, that's okay, as long as we recognize that we are doing it. However, the more we weave those small perversions of the truth into our life story, the easier it becomes to believe our own varnished "truth." Just like some famous people, we can believe the smoke we are blowing up our own butt if we are not careful, selecting the "truths" that fit our ego's desire.

Dreams symbolically and metaphorically show us things that are stuck or have hurt us, or things we should embrace that make us uncomfortable, and who in their right mind wants to wake up with something like that in their head? They will have a dream about being naked in public, or not being prepared for a test, or strangling their mother, or getting caught stealing, or being shot at, or crashing a car because the brakes fail, or having their teeth fall out, or masturbating, or killing someone, or a thousand other things. When the waking mind gets presented with these uninvited experiences, it wants to deep-six them to Never Never Land. The conscious mind does not realize that these images and feelings are important keys that can unlock insight and lead to a clearer and better self. In fact, so consistently do we shy away from self-critical images and emotions that I often encounter dreamers who conveniently, in telling the dream, leave out the ego-bashing parts, thus whitewashing the experience.

It may be slightly cynical, but when I hear or see what appears to be a life-affirming, positive dream, my radar goes up and I become a little suspicious, and I will probe to see if the ego is hiding something lurking in the shadows. When everything seems rosy and wonderful, I look for the undertow of the dream that is there, hinting, begging to be discovered. Often the ego has hidden nothing, but now and then a very important fact or emotion is stepped over by the dreamer. Omission can be a powerful tool for the ego to protect itself. I cannot tell you how many times someone has suddenly remembered something in a dream that they kind of, sort of, forgot to tell.

"Oh," confided one dreamer after we had spent a long time working on his dream, "remember when I told you that I looked in the mirror and I saw myself and I was naked? I forgot to mention that what I saw was a woman. I was a beautiful naked woman. Oh, and I think I was aroused by seeing myself as a woman. I think I forgot that part." Oh, that shady, sneaky ego was at work. He hadn't forgotten this at all; his ego just couldn't handle what he saw and felt.

> The dream is a little hidden door in the innermost and most secret recesses of the soul, opening into that cosmic night which was psyche long before there was any ego-consciousness, and which will remain psyche no matter how far our ego-consciousness extends.
>
> Carl Jung, *The Meaning of Psychology for Modern Man* (1933)

THE SINS OF OMISSION

Precisely during the time when I was writing about how our egos often coax us into omitting things from the dream report, I had the following dream:

MOUNTAIN MIRACLE

There are a bunch of us climbing across the face of a mountain that is steep and sheer. Far below are the pounding waves, which even at this height are spraying us with salty water that we can taste. I am with a woman and we inch along this narrow path as we talk excitedly about the meaning of life and empathy. There is a problem, though. A huge 'L' shaped silver pipe that is like an air conditioning duct has fallen in the path, partially blocking it. There are a series of these pipes on the sheer face of the mountain and this is the only place there is a break in them. Something must have happened for this to break open like this. This is obviously a closed, tight system of air weaving up the mountainside and I imagine this has stopped the flow of air.

I take the woman's hand and we climb over it, but when we do, we fall. We plunge forward and we pass that point of balance where you cannot recover. I know we are headed for sudden death. With all my might, I throw the woman over my left shoulder, at least I will just possibly save her. She lands back on the path and miraculously I also land back on the path. Oh, my god that was close. Some magic must be afoot here, because I know I could not have recovered from this fall.

I yell down to the many people down below among the rocks that I need a couple of guys to move the pipe from the path. Two guys get in a boat and manage to remove the errant pipe. Meanwhile, I am reliving the staggering feat I performed, telling it to a guy with us and I keep repeating specifically about that point of no return we reached.

The instant I finished recording this dream, I remembered that I was working on the ego and dream conflict. I was fairly confident that I had recorded the dream accurately, and normally I would have passed back into the Land of Nod, with my slurry, groggy voice-recording ready for later when I would write it up. But since I had been writing about the ego that very night, I slipped quietly back across the dream to see if my pesky ego had raised its hackles while I was recording.

One thing that seemed ego-driven was a very strong desire not to remember the dream. The instant I awoke and focused on the dream, I realized a whole impressive scene had occurred before we were on the cliff, but while I focused on the pipe and cliff part, the whole other scene had faded away. That made my ego angry. *I am the dream guy, I should be able to recall dreams better. But if I can't remember the whole thing, what's the point? And I want to sleep, and if I record this half-ass dream, I will not get back to sleep. Grumble, grumble.* The only reason I continued was because of my long-term commitment to recording my dreams.

I turned the recorder back on and carefully and quietly went back over the dream in the most detail I could. I made a conscious effort to remember all the images, ideas, and narrative in their purest form—without judgment or editing. When I did that, the dream changed.

Evidently my ego had not been entirely asleep during my recording process.

So, the initial recording is fairly accurate . . . that is, until I get to the fall. But in going back over the dream, I realized that when I throw the woman over my shoulder and she lands back on the path, she actually pulls me back with her. In other words, the woman saves me, after I save her, but this does not get mentioned in the initial report. Looking back, I realized that I initially left that out because in my waking, conscious (although groggy) state, my ego quietly liked me being the hero. It takes away from my heroic image if the woman has saved me. It is not a conscious thought that says I want to be the hero; it is subtler—some ego-force just steps in and takes over for a second, giving me a chance to like this dream instead of dismissing it. It took two or three passes at the dream to realize this subtle shift, but I found it.

Going over it again, I realized I had left something else out of the dream report as well. When I get to the point where I call down for a couple of guys to remove the pipe, I pause in the recording, and what flits across my mind—that I don't say into the mic—is that a clear-eyed woman, robust and quick, climbs up towards us and volunteers to help remove the pipe. Reawakening that part of the dream, I can see her face and body clearly. She is in a tight black climbing outfit that looks like a bodysuit. She is obviously strong, and she is very attractive. Her hair is very, very odd, though. It is jet black and resembles a series of ocean waves. In this newly remembered part of the dream itself, I dismiss her. "No, not you, I need men to do this," I say with disdain.

I sat with that realization for a time as I carefully thought about what was going on when I made the original recording. Why would I leave out something so seminal? I was finally able to retrieve a subtle conversation that my precious ego had inserted into the process. That short three-second gap in the recording contained not only the story of the woman with the sea-wave hair, but also Walter's ego saying: "Now how would that look, me turning down the help of a woman, and doing it with disdain? That's not me, not at all. I love and respect women." So, my ego talked me into not including that in the report. How would it look to people if I told them I was a complete jerk to a woman? That damn tricky ego.

And finally, Master Ego and I left out another part of the dream. At the end of the dream, as I am telling my tale of bravery, another guy shows me an electrical circuit, some wires with a bulb on it all, and tells me he will install it above the highest part of the path because we have no double circuits on the high path. Well, Master Ego thought that just made too little sense and adding that to the end of the dream simply confused things. I was already thinking about the meaning of the dream, even in the groggy state, and all that electrical stuff was just too much to consider and add in. It was such a bother to think about, I just left it out. No one would know.

All these changes and omissions I made to the dream while recording it came from a very subtle place, so subtle that I had to sit ever so quietly to find them. In ways like these, our egos can really shift the foundation of dreamwork if we are not careful. If I had worked this dream without the additional honesty I added after, I might not have seen that the dream was trying to talk about my relationship to the feminine, because I had overlooked the importance of the two women who were trying to help me.

But fret not, fellow dreamer, all is not lost, even if our dream report is tainted with ego thrusts. Often the missing or perverted pieces will appear later under the loving scrutiny of dreamwork. I suspect if I had presented the dream to a dream group, I would have suddenly recalled the face of the woman with the distinct hairdo of a sea goddess—as the group passed over and over the narrative and stared for a while at my drawing of the dream.

What I made of the dream before the additions was that it was an affirmation of the path I am on, and about my strong, loving relationship to the feminine. With the additional information, however, this dream speaks of my lack of recognition of my own feminine and the feminine in general. The flow of my progress represented by the air conditioning duct has been stopped (by me, I bet), and in order to restore the flow of my life, I need the help of the feminine. The sea goddess, or the archetype of the unconscious feminine, rose up from the unconscious—the sea—to help, but I denied her. I also failed to recognize that it is my own feminine that pulls me back onto the path of life. And if that is not enough, a light bulb goes on supplied by the electrician who was installing a "double circuit on the high path"—which I take to mean both the feminine and the masculine must work together in a "double circuit" to give light on the high path of life. "Aha," says I. I am learning multiple things from my dreams.

This illustrates how important it is to get as much of the dream down that you can, warts and weirdness included. What you do with that information is subject to discretion, of course. Often it is just fine not to share some part of a dream, because when we work a dream with someone, especially

a group, we need not only to trust, but also to respect privacy. A woman once shared a graphic sexual dream with me before the group gathered, and then when the group met there were four men present, and she totally skipped the sexually laden portion when telling the dream. That was just fine, since that was the level of comfort she felt in the situation. She and I worked on the dream privately later to great effect.

This is a delicate world we are plodding around in. And it is not black and white. Sometimes as we are recording the dream, things shift and appear, and other parts of the dream come flooding in. Being honest with ourselves and including the entire scope of the dream—without omissions our egos would like—will help us see what the dream is trying to convey.

One of the biggest dreams of my life, in which I meet the Dalai Lama and discover that death is just another place, almost got forgotten because of my ego. You can read about that dream in *Chicken Soup for the Soul—Dreams and Premonitions* by Amy Newmark and Kelly Sullivan Walden.

The bottom line here is: be open to things in your dreams, let little bits like the dirty dish on the table, the bad teeth on the tiger, the brown shoes in the closet, and the subtle anger you have for the guy that keeps interrupting you be included in the dream report. Try not to edit yourself. Editing and sublimation are a function of the ego that wants you to look good and avoid conflict. Let it all in, and tell yourself you can throw stuff out later.

When I record a dream, my rule is that I allow myself to say anything, feel anything, and do my best to keep myself out of my way. I can fix this later, I tell my ego, which seems to always be present, even in this shadowy hazy place. No one ever needs to hear this recording or written record. If I am both dead and alive at the same time, or a duck is pulling a baby carriage down into the sewer, or I am having sex with a man, I just step out of the way of the dream and record it.

That pen or recorder is the link to your own unconscious and the bridge to the Land of Awes. Use it, and you will find your soul woven through those words or images.

PART 4

DREAMS, AWE, AND ART

Dreaming Is the Magical Poetic Wellspring of the Soul's Vitality

CHAPTER 8

POEMS FROM THE SOUL

Why Dreams Speak a Symbolic Language

And the smith his iron measures hammered to the anvil's chime;
Thanking God, whose boundless wisdom makes
the flowers of poesy bloom
In the forge's dust and cinders, in the tissues of the loom.

HENRY WADSWORTH LONGFELLOW
from *Nuremberg*

Life is chock-full of symbolism. Art, literature, poetry, and music all rely on the audience to see, feel, or hear the symbolic messages. Movies, clothing, buildings, plants, sounds—almost anything can be a symbol of something. Our minds shape the incoming signals from all five senses and paint a "reality" related to what we have already experienced and stored in our memory. Moreover, how we interpret symbols has some common ground with other beings roaming the planet. Somehow, we all know that when we see a red traffic signal, it symbolizes stop. (Well, except for my son Philip.)

We learn a vast symbol dictionary throughout our lives, and often can relate to what others see and feel and experience because of common established ground. However, our lives and the ways we live them vary widely. We carry around so many experiences and hurts and joys and facts and emotional triggers that almost everything gets twisted when we experience it. The way we finally see things is unique to each individual. Sometimes a cigar is just a cigar, but often it is not.

GETTING CROSS WITH THE CROSS

For instance, take the Christian cross. What comes up for you when you think of or see a cross hanging around someone's neck?

Most people think of it as the symbol of Jesus and Christianity. It is the device used by the Romans to kill Jesus. To Christians, it represents the sacrifice Jesus made for our sins, and when they see it, there can be a connection to a deep sense of devotion and respect. If I feel a similar devotion, the person wearing it and I have a silent connection. For some, it means nothing at all; it is just a piece of sparkly bling. For ardent non-believers, it can symbolize a silly, naïve belief. They look at a cross-wearing person and see them as foolishly immersed in a false narrative. For others, it is a symbol that represents the needless death of millions in various religious wars. All in all, the cross is a symbol loaded with meaning that shifts radically with each person.

My relationship to the cross shows how complex this can be. I fall into the non-believer group, as you can imagine, so I see it hanging around a neck and I think, "Poor deluded fool." But that harsh judgment is not all that comes up for me. I also respect faith, so it becomes, "Poor deluded fool, but good for her as she reaches into the unknown and tries to connect to something deeper than herself." But my history enters in as well. In my time in Mormonism, there were no crosses anywhere. You will never see a cross in a Mormon church; they eschew them as symbols of death. And because the Mormon Church hates crosses, and I still hold a (possibly undeserved) grudge against Mormonism, I now embrace the cross as a symbol of the willing sacrifice archetype, and display a few in my house as art objects, because I find meaning in this ancient symbol. If I dig a little deeper, I suspect I will find just a taste of spite lingering as well.

So, when I see the woman fiddling with the cross around her neck as she talks, I think to myself, "Poor deluded fool. No, wait. She is trying to connect to something deeper than herself, and the cross is more like an archetypal symbol. She's attempting to listen to her own unconscious. We are all in this life together, and if I look at it right, that cross is like a door to the inner self. Maybe I should wear a cross—just to piss off the Mormons! Hmm. No damn way."

And indeed, everything is this complex and conflicted. We all bring tons of baggage and experience to the dance, and it affects how we see and experience things.

So, when we work with symbols in dreams, it's important to think about what those symbols mean not only in general, but to the dreamer in particular.

WHY DO DREAMS SPEAK A SYMBOLIC LANGUAGE?

To unlock the messages of the following dream, it was necessary to think about the symbols the dreamer's unconscious had sent—both in a universal and an individual context.

REFLECTING ON THE GHOST

I look in a mirror and I can't believe my eyes. This can't be me, but it is. The woman in the mirror has short hair, but I don't have short hair! And whoever colored the hair didn't finish the job. The roots are full of grey gunk and whatever color this hair of mine is, I am not sure because it is still wet. They will have to fix this. I go in search of who did this to me. I am not happy.

There is no clear, direct message here, so as with most dreams, we have to prowl around and feel into the metaphoric and emotional content. The dream does come to say something, but what is it, and why so hidden?

This is one of my favorite dream drawings. I am not entirely sure why, but it jumps out at me. The direct simplicity is disarming. The reflected self stares directly at us—one arm to the hair and the other to the heart area. The mirror frame is a perfect square within a square. There is no attempt to depict the dreamer looking at herself, so we are the stand-in for the dreamer, making this very personal as we look at our own reflection. All the lines are deliberate and clear and purposeful. Nothing unnecessary is portrayed. The hair is the only thing with any disorder, which draws our focus to it. The perfectly round face sits inside a perfectly square pair of squares. That leads me to the phrase "square the circle," which means to solve an impossible problem. Could the dream be talking about solving an apparently impossible difficulty? I think so. And if I reach further into the symbolism bag, we have a circle, a symbol of the feminine, inside two squares, which are symbols of the masculine. Is this about a woman and two men on some symbolic level?

After discussions of feelings and the obvious reference to this being a "reflection" of the self, I ask the dreamer about the short hair. Hair grows out of the head, that place of thoughts, so that is another symbolic track we can follow as we try to understand the poetry of this visitor from the unconscious.

"When was the last time you had short hair?" I ask.

She replies that it was in 2016, a time when she made a deliberate change in her life. She was a highly successful professional model and made the decision to cut off her hair (something that she was known for in her career) and change professions. We are onto something, then. The dream is recalling a time of giant upheaval and laying that experience against her current life for some reason.

That was also a time when her father passed, and in that same time period she discovered in a massive, shocking moment that her husband had emptied their bank account, using it for drugs and prostitutes. She had spent large tracts of time modeling in Japan, Europe, and elsewhere—building a nice nest egg for their future—only to come home to an empty bank account and a cheating husband with a huge drug habit. Yikes. In a sense, this was the moment when the male role models in her life disappeared. Those facts came rolling up in an emotional and profound way as she found herself in a place of awe, processing this "aha" that had arisen spontaneously. She reflected on the contrast of having a loving father and a (seemingly) loving husband at one moment, and then in the next losing the father and being betrayed by the husband. The short hair is a symbol of this loss, not only in that it happened at that moment in her life, but also because shearing off her beautiful locks represents the cutting-off of the loving males from her life. When the unconscious drew that perfect circle framed by two squares, perhaps it was poetically talking about the relationship between the dreamer and these two men who "framed" this passage in her life.

Have I mentioned how much I love doing dream work? To sit with someone and watch and participate in such personal revelation and clarity fills me with awe.

But why does this dream come now? What is it trying to say?

When she had the dream, it was after finally getting the asshole husband "out of her hair" by divorcing him. The dream is using that time when she had cut her hair to think or "reflect" about the new self. Although there is still some gunk at the root of this new self reflected in the mirror, it is time to restore her faith in her animus and allow loving relationships to appear. That was the "aha" that the dreamer got. At the end of the dream, she goes off to a new life by seeking to have the gunk at the root of the problem removed so she can discover a restored, beautiful, happy woman. It is a hopeful and positive dream. What color will her life take when this newly dyed hair dries?

So, why did it take all this Sherlocking to get to this place? Why couldn't she have had a dream where a man appears and simply says, "You remember that time you had short hair and you liked men and trusted them? Well, you have been through a ton of crap, and it is time to return to that same feeling, put all this distrust of men behind you, and gain new relationships with men."

But dreams rarely do that. One reason that dreams probably do this symbolic dance is because of heredity, our history as a species. Dreams most likely preceded language, so millions of years ago, when we didn't have words to express things, the dreams did that speaking. Likely the brain is hard-wired to produce dreams in symbolic form, and/or that form was left still functioning within, even as we developed language. But that is all conjecture.

I put the question of why dreams speak a symbolic language to Bob Hoss, the executive officer of the International Association for the Study of Dreams, a dream scientist, and the author of *Dream Language: Self-Understanding through Imagery and Color,* a thoroughly engaging book that not only gets deep into the science of dreaming but also offers a way to work with color in dreams. In response he sent me some of his ideas from his book:

> The "language" of the dream is primarily that of metaphor or picture-metaphor—a symbolic representation of the unconscious association between emotions, memories, concepts and processes taking place as the dream attempts to express and resolve a problem. Dream imagery is formed in the "associative cortex" of the brain—an area that unconsciously forms associations or "meaning" between what we see (an image) and our personal store of experiences, emotions, and beliefs. In the dream that brain center continues to create imagery associations—but in this case creates images that relate to the issues we are dreaming about. It is also a center that speaks in metaphor, thus what is created is a picture which is metaphorically related to the unconscious meaning it has for us—a picture analogy of a memory or feeling or concept. This is what Sigmund Freud and Carl Jung called a symbol or as Carl Jung put it, "the unconscious aspect of any event is revealed to us in dreams where it appears not as a rational thought but as a symbolic image . . . an emotionally charged pictorial language."

So, the associative cortex in our brains creates a language of metaphors. The science of it clearly answers the question, but surely there is more to explore here. There is such a lyrical feel to dreams that seems deeply connected to this mysterious, symbolic language, so I went looking deeper.

I put the same question about why dreams speak a symbolic language to Kelly Bulkeley, Ph.D., an author of many books about dreams and a psychologist of religion specializing in dream research. He has created something called the Sleep and Dream Database, which is an open-access online archive and search engine designed to promote the scientific study of dreams, so the guy is way serious about dreams. Kelly became interested in dreams partially because of a series of recurring monster-chasing-me nightmares he had with (amongst others) Darth Vader from *Star Wars* pursuing him, and I feel a kinship to anyone with that sort of imaginative spirit engaged in the study of dreams. Beyond the brain science, I feel like something poetic happens as dreams pour out from the unconscious in this highly symbolic form, so I asked Kelly about dreams as poetry. He wrote me back:

> Dreams speak in this language because this is the best way to communicate new and complex truths about ourselves and the world. Symbols and metaphors use imagery we know to convey meanings we don't yet know. . . . This is in fact an expression of the genius of the human spirit, that we can continually leverage our current knowledge to help us mentally journey into entirely unknown realms and realities. Dreaming is the bubbling alchemical caldron in which that process is kept at a steady, healthy boil. Or, as you put it, dreaming is the magical poetic wellspring of the soul's vitality.

Kelly reminded me of a phrase I had coined—Dreaming is the magical wellspring of the soul's vitality. Wow. Wonderful.

As I turned this phrase over and over in my mind, it sent me down a rabbit hole to my soul's deep interior and brought together thoughts and feelings that had been brewing for a long, long time. This produced a huge "aha" for me and dropped me once more into that glorious abyss, the Land of Awes.

DREAMS ARE THE POETRY OF THE SOUL

Dreams and poetry are multidimensional. Both poetry and dreams can use a single symbol to mean a variety of things at the same time. A washed-out bridge in a poem or in a dream speaks of a path interrupted, but so much more. It is also a place from which to look back along the path we were on and a place to look down into the swirling waters of our emotions. Poetry is so damn beautiful because it washes over us in a symbolic form and lifts us beyond the mundane world of logos into the magical world of mythos. It takes us to the edge of that washed-out bridge and allows us to question our existence, to reach into the world of metaphor and symbolism as we pause and center ourselves in this revelry of magic. I think we are poetic beings at heart. When we allow it, the natural poet in all of us lifts us out of our mundane selves and allows enough mystery in for us to stand in the place of awe and feel alive and whole.

Dreams are the emissaries of poetry. The poetry of our soul bubbles and churns in our unconscious, waiting with fervent anticipation to be released and heard. Each dream is a poem from the heart seeking kinship with our conscious being. Magic happens when we connect these two kindred worlds of the deep self and the conscious self.

Dreams offer up visual poems intended to open our souls to a landscape of symbols that express the true nature of our being. We do not have to understand the poetry of our dreams to be affected by them. As our soul sings to us in our sleep, we find connection and healing, even when we do not remember the wondrous dream-songs. Every night we are sung to by our unconscious. And just like the lullaby of a mother, soothing us and connecting us to her soul, the dream songs remind us of our divinity, our unique threads of life, our gifts, our foibles, and our purpose.

When people are continually woken up due to stress and other factors and deprived of REM sleep, where many of our dreams appear, things go awry in their waking lives. If our souls cannot sing us their songs while we sleep, we risk becoming angry, mean, stupid, irrational, even vindictive. As Rubin Naiman noted in his article "Dreamless: The Silent Epidemic of REM Sleep Loss," "REM/dream loss is an unrecognized public health hazard that silently wreaks havoc with our lives, contributing to illness, depression, and an erosion of consciousness."

We need to be sung to every night, and our dreams do just that.

Not all the songs, however, are pleasant. Many dreams have moved me to tears. Deep hurt and pain roar out of these missives from our unconscious, but they are no less poetry than the others. Whether the dream comes to teach us something, affirm something, warn us, inspire us, or connect us to something or someone, it comes in the form of poetry, the language of our soul.

As I sit in reverence, listening to someone's dream, I can see the gates of eternity open and silent wisps of soul spill out, vibrating slowly, the colors and the light sweeping across my soul. Dreams are the agent of transference of the powerful, poetic forces of nature that can be best experienced in a symbolic form. Thus, in being in touch with our dreams, we are in touch with creation itself.

Michael Meade talks about how myths are lies that tell the truth, and dreams are the same. For example, it is a lie that we can breathe underwater, but if we have a dream where that happens, it represents a new way of taking in life. If we think of water as symbolic of emotion or the unconscious, poetically we are taking in those emotions or communing with the unconscious with each breath we take underwater. If we can recognize the poetry in our dreams, if we allow ourselves to surrender to this poetic process, we will stand firmly in the Land of Awes, where we can access our true nature. Where life happens.

WE ARE ALL MUSICIANS, ARTISTS, PHILOSOPHERS, DANCERS, AND POETS

There is a vitality, a life force, an energy, a quickening that is translated through you into action, and because there is only one of you in all time, this expression is unique. And if you block it, it will never exist through any other medium and will be lost.

MARTHA GRAHAM

I believe that at the core of our being, at the source and in our simplest self, we are all musicians, artists, philosophers, dancers, and poets. We are each unique, and our true voices manifest in different ways, but when the true Self talks to us, it does it in a symbolic language, just like dreams do.

What I am proposing is that if we could reach down far enough into ourselves, beyond the learning, the ego, the detritus of society, family, and the myriad attitudes we have taken on in this life, we would find this glorious beautiful soul who stands silently with full knowledge of who we are. This is the being who is ready to speak to us through music, art, philosophy, dance, and poetry.

You have probably met such beings on occasion. Like the time you started harmonizing with your sister in the bathroom to an old Cat Stevens tune and both of you found something both comical and magical about the moment and you were suddenly wrapped in an inexplicable sense of awe. Or the time you were in art class and something came over you to smear the entire self-portrait into a wild bouquet of expressive streaks of color that spoke so much louder. You got in trouble, but it was so worth it, no? Or the time when, engaged in outrageously glorious lovemaking, you suddenly knew the meaning of life. Or those splendid moments when your body moved in abandon to the splashing of a sudden summer downpour in Paris, twirling and cavorting in the delightful rain, feeling the connection between the chaotic raindrops and your spinning body. And then there are those love poems you wrote when the emotions you were experiencing were so overwhelming you were driven to use symbolic language to express it all. In that moment you were connected to your poetic self and allowed it speak clearly, careening back and forth at the command of that voice, crossing some things out, making others more lovingly obscure, putting words together that seemed totally foreign to you.

These creative beings become manifest in our dreams. Let's look at each of them.

WE ARE ALL MUSICIANS

Why does music moves us so deeply at times? It is because at our core we are all musicians. That deep Self that is a musician and speaks to us in melodies hears something rich and beautiful in the opera we attend, and suddenly we are in communion with that symbol-laden musician at the core of our being. And that inner Self cries out to be heard and when we hear it and respond, emotions pour out pell-mell. In that moment we are connected to not just the music, but ourselves and the universe.

A simple example of how at the core of our being we are musicians is the well-known story that the entire melody of *Yesterday* written by Paul McCartney came in a dream in 1963. As he tells it, "I just fell out of bed, found out what key I had dreamed it in . . . and played it." Even someone whose entire life is shaped around music found perhaps his greatest contribution coming from that deep inner musician, delivered up by a dream.

And the original title you ask? "Scrambled Eggs." The lyrics went like this: "Scrambled eggs, Oh, you've got such lovely legs, Scrambled eggs. Oh, my baby, how I love your legs." Thank god the dream only supplied the melody and left the rest up to the creative team.

The story of the "Yesterday" dream reminds me of this fun and memorable encounter with its dreamer.

I was working in Burbank, California as the director of photography for a behind-the-scenes production company. It was the week of the Grammys and we were shooting rehearsals and interviews with all sorts of musicians and bands. I was in the room with B.B. King when Madonna stopped by and the two of them were vocalizing and goofing together. It was magical. Those are two people who seem to have a clear direct connection to the musician that exists so deep inside each of us.

As I walked out into the parking lot to go to another stage, there taking a break was Paul McCartney talking to two blokes. I've been around a ton of stars and famous musicians, but this was freaking Paul McCartney! I tried to be nonchalant as I came up to the three of them. I'm sure it was obvious to Sir Paul that I was a tiny bit star-struck, but of course he's used to that. He caught my eye, smiled, and extended his hand.

"Hi. I'm Paul. Who are you?" he said.

WE ARE ALL ARTISTS

Some of the most stunning art ever created was done during the Upper Paleolithic period in Southern France and Northern Spain. Some 20,000 years ago the people who lived near modern-day Montignac in the Dordogne region descended to total darkness inside the caves of Lascaux with small stone pots of animal fats, wicks, and flints. There, they lit their pots and created magnificent paintings using pigments mixed with water, saliva, animal fat, urine, and blood. These ancient people created something so astonishing and spiritual it will take your breath away. They created it because their pure deep Self screamed out so loud that they were compelled to honor that voice from within, that essential artist that is in all of us. My take is that these are images of dreams that were seared in their souls, that demanded

Like there is a single human on the planet who wouldn't recognize Paul McCartney, I thought to myself.

"I'm Walter," I said.

"And what do you do here?" he asked.

"I'm the director of photography for all the behind-the-scenes shooting," I replied.

"Sounds like a fascinating job," he said.

"It is. And what do you do?" I asked, cheekily.

"Oh, I am a musician," he replied.

"Oh, dear," I said. "I hope that works out for you. It's a tough profession to make a living at."

"It's worked out okay so far," Paul said with a wink. "But you never know."

The two blokes looked at me as though I was crazy, but Paul and I laughed. I was elated that I held it together long enough to bring out my Trickster nature and speak with Sir Paul.

to be given shape in this deep hidden cathedral. All of us have that same artist in us attempting to express something that demands expression.

Painting of an auroch, from the Lascaux complex of caves

PAINTING IN

I am sitting alone in a restaurant in Paris at a small table overlooking the city. There is a guy next to me to my right. Oddly, he is painting a painting at his table. "Only in France," I think to myself, "would someone paint a painting at a restaurant while eating."

Strangely, the canvas is all white, with the outline of an all-white Eiffel Tower, which is barely discernable since it is white on white. The guy has a pile of white oil paint laid out on the white table and he is using a palette knife to paint more white on the white.

I now see a painting in front of me on my table, only mine is a collage. It is composed of pictures from my life that have been masterfully put together in an array that tells the story of my life. I suddenly realize this is an art piece that I created.

The pictures that are collaged here are not complete. There are heads cut off, legs cut off, scenic views cut off, and where the pictures meet there is a build-up of black encaustic paint that is very rough and almost dangerous to touch. The black encaustic paint sits up about an inch from the surface and forms a rugged barrier between these incomplete pictures.

The dapper waiter comes up and stands between us and takes a bit of the white paint off the table of the Parisian artist and smears it across the surface of my collage. How dare he! Interestingly, it brings depth to the collage and I realize that he is onto something. I have a pallet knife and I grab a bit of the guy's white paint myself and scrape it over the picture of me on a bicycle wearing a blue jacket. As I scrape it across the sleeve of the jacket, I notice that the white fills in some of the shadow and the picture starts to have depth and starts to come alive. Oh, this is fantastic! I will have to do this to the rest of the picture. I wonder what messages will be revealed about my life as these pictures come to life and start to talk?

This dream is a clear attempt by my deep Lascaux-like painter self to speak to me about my life and how I need to integrate so many disparate aspects of my existence. After this dream, I started looking at all those different parallel lives I am living. I am still making attempts to integrate these dissimilar paths I am on. I also created a number of art pieces trying to reflect this integration.

Remember all those silly drawings you drew without much thought as a child, that were just so fun to draw? Well, it's time to be that child again and allow the inner artist to speak.

WE ARE ALL PHILOSOPHERS

Philosophy literally means "love of wisdom." There is something intrinsic about wanting to understand the nature of knowledge, reality, and existence—that is the bailiwick of philosophy. Besides our conscious self, which is always wondering what happens after we die, our deep self is also vitally interested in the meaning of life and other philosophical things that will help us grow and connect us to a greater sphere of understanding. Our dream life will often wax philosophical in its effort to make us understand and apply greater understanding and empathy to ourselves and those around us on our lovely jaunt here on Earth.

THE PHILOSOPHY OF IMAGINATION

I am with a philosopher in a three-story building that is blue. This place is filled with people, and I go to a table and sit to the right of the philosopher. A woman is seated across the table from us. She asks the philosopher, "What is imagination?" He pauses for a minute, then looks at me, and I take it as an opportunity to answer the question. I respond, "Imagination is a portal that puts us in contact with the 'other'." As I intone the words "The other," the philosopher does it at the same time in a harmonic way. We both smile, and in this moment I feel like his equal, like I have finally made it to another level and it feels great. We then have a long conversation about imagination and how important it is, especially as we get older since that's when we tend to move away from it versus in childhood when we thrive on it.

I think this is a perfect example of how that magnificent philosopher inside of us can reach up through a dream and speak to us. I love how the dream plays with the philosopher and dreamer and makes them one and the same as they finish the sentence together about imagination. I feel like the inner philosopher is lecturing us on the importance of imagination, encouraging us as we age not to leave him, or the artist we all are inside, behind. The dreamer had never thought about imagination in this way. How cool is this idea the dream has given us? Imagination is a portal that puts us in contact with our deep inner self. It makes me want to go find a deep cave and use my imagination to fill it with art. How about you?

WE ARE ALL DANCERS

And how are all of us dancers at our core? You need only watch a baby that hasn't learned to walk yet to figure that out. Dancing is the somatic connection where the soul and the body meet. Watch carefully as someone tells a dream, and you will always see them dance. They raise their hands high over their head and spread their fingers every time they mention the dragon in the dream, and this is a dance. They gently touch their heart as they speak of their mother, and this is a dance. They clench their fists and tighten their body and open their eyes wide as some unknown force sucks them head first down the toilet in the Pope's bathroom, and this is a dance. They slump in their chair and wiggle their arms as they describe how they turn into liquid in the New York subway and slink away to avoid the killers who have just shot a young woman, and this is a dance. Even the dreamer who sits stoically with no movement while telling of being launched into space hanging onto the outside of the rocket is dancing in that stillness. The body is such an important connection to the unconscious and has its own language that speaks to us through sensation and dance.

I recently worked a dream where the dreamer dove through a grass-lined green portal to another dimension and discovered strange statues. She then realized that each of these statues was a representation of a deeper part of the person they depicted. And right there was a statue of her own deeper self, which had a blue boot for a heart. The statues came to life and danced with their other selves in delight. So, she also danced in delight with her own statue with a blue boot for a heart and it was thrilling.

Now, how do you make stuff like this up? I believe it is that dancer-self in the unconscious talking here, wanting her to feel the beauty and abandon when she dances with her deeper self. The dream is so interested in being clear that this is about the dance of life, it turns the heart into a blue boot as though the heart is also dancing. Why blue you ask? Blue is the color of the sky, and spirit, and the throat chakra, so perhaps this is about voicing delight in the dance of life. A dream like this just begs for projections as we do a little dance to honor it.

The next time you tell a dream, make yourself aware of how your body moves and you will feel the dancer-self participating in this glorious tale of Self.

WE ARE ALL POETS

What about the poets lurking in all of us? Dreams, like poetry, give a special intensity to the expression of feelings and ideas through the distinctive rhythm and style unique to that dreamer. In that deep soul of yours, in your unconscious, you are weaving poetic tale after poetic tale every night. A lot of what you dream may not seem poetic at all, but going deeper, we find the poetry in these symbolic missives. They rarely have the polished, carefully thought-out patterns of most poetry, but they are highly concentrated and poetic nonetheless.

This is one of my dream reports that seems poetic, which I put in poetic stanzas to make the point.

PLAYING THE DREAM TRACK

I can control the music.
Somehow, the scars on my arm control the music.
I touch and move along the lines
Of those old bitter scars
to control the vibrations and feel.
I don't create the music,
I just control it,
pressing my finger into
these old deep scars
and tracing the lines of the scars.
It is painful,
ever so painful.
Everyone is listening
and connected.
I am aware of everyone's needs
And how their own scars dance
at this moment
as I decide how the music will play.
So, play on, scars, play on.

For me, the ideas and feelings that arise in listening to this dream report do the same thing that a poem does—they take me into both deeper thought and wonder. Do we not all play the music of our lives by touching our own scars? Isn't exposing and digging into those old scars painful?

But, in exposing those scars and allowing the music of our soul to be heard by others, do we not speak to their needs? Does this not lead to all of us healing just a little?

If I think of people (and myself) in this poetic light, what a difference it makes. As someone describes the incredible catch someone made in the latest football game—which normally for me would be a big snore—I can instead see something that the person's inner poetic artist is connected to and appreciate the sparks of life that connect us all.

Dreaming really is the magical poetic wellspring of the soul. Inside each of us is a magnificent being that composes music, creates masterful works of art, organizes complex ideas into a whole, dances like an uninhibited ballerina, and spews out poetry the likes of which the world has never known. It is our destiny to recognize and dance with our uniqueness. Look to your dreams to see and feel that uniqueness and embrace it.

CHAPTER 9

FALLING BETWEEN THE CRACKS OF REALITY

Awe, Art, and the Collective Unconscious

> *Have you noticed that all your foundations are completely mired in madness? Do you not want to recognize your madness and welcome it in a friendly manner? You wanted to accept everything. So accept madness too. Let the light of your madness shine, and it will suddenly dawn on you. Madness is not to be despised and not to be feared, but instead you should give it life.*
>
> CARL JUNG
> *The Red Book*

FACETS OF AWE

As you have gathered by now, I search out experiences that take me to the Land of Awes. Working with dreams is one entrance into this marvelous world, but there are many other paths down into this sublime repository of wonder. And exploring these other paths in turn enhances the experience of working with dreams.

What is awe? Let's go to the dictionary, which does help here. *The American Heritage Dictionary* online defines *awe* as: "A feeling of respect or reverence mixed with dread and wonder, often inspired by something majestic or powerful."

Wikipedia adds some angles:

> Awe is difficult to define, and the meaning of the word has changed over time. Related concepts are wonder, admiration, elevation, and the sublime. In *Awe: The Delights and Dangers of Our Eleventh Emotion*, neuropsychologist and positive psychology guru Paul Pearsall presents a phenomenological study of awe. He defines awe as an "overwhelming and bewildering sense of connection with a startling universe that is usually far beyond the narrow band of our consciousness." Pearsall sees awe as the 11th emotion, beyond those now scientifically accepted (i.e., love, fear, sadness, embarrassment, curiosity, pride, enjoyment, despair, guilt, and anger). Most definitions allow for awe to be a positive or a negative experience, but when asked to describe events that elicit awe, most people only cite positive experiences.

In spite of their thoughtfulness, words cannot truly capture or encompass the experience of standing in the place of awe. These definitions refer to awe as an emotion, but I look at it also as an *experience*, not just the emotion alone. It is a state of being for me, a place where you can connect with something outside yourself.

The difference between the *concept* (and definitions) of awe and the *experience* of awe is akin to the difference between the concept of love and being in love. I can feel love, but being in love is an immersive experience that comes with magic. The same is true of awe. I can feel awe as an emotion, but when I am *in the experience of* awe, I have moved beyond the emotion to a state of being.

When you are in that place—and I find it to be an actual place—other things happen that are beyond explaining in words only. Experiencing true awe is always magical. In that state, the ego diminishes, and the senses become heightened, but most importantly, the magic connects you to an experience outside of yourself. You are standing in a world that is not your own and experiencing emotions that come from that place.

I am reminded of the first moment I held my granddaughter, Ashlynn. I cradled her in my arms just minutes after she was born. She looked up at me, twisted her head slightly, stared right through me, and smiled. And guess what? I fell into the Land of Awes headfirst. I was suddenly delivered up to a place where there was a flow of love between us, and I was experiencing not just my own emotions, but also hers, as she struggled to understand what this was all about. And yet, this child full of magic, knew, on some level, exactly what was transpiring. She was the one who reached out and made the connection, turning me into a participant in the dance of life, as I melted, transfixed in a state beyond myself. At that moment, we were both experiencing something beyond words. I was dancing with one foot in this reality and the other in some other place of magic. I could smell the soup of life being stirred in a giant pot just around the corner. The nurse had to come and pry this conduit of awe out of my hands.

How do you set yourself up to experience awe? The answer is elusive, but I can suggest some things and give examples that offer helpful hints. This sacred place is at all times around us and within us, but it must be said that experiences of awe do not always come from our own efforts. Sometimes they just land on us like a sudden summer shower in Paris. To experience such awe you must unlock your soul to the experience. You can stare at a gorgeous sunset for a long time, but until you allow it to affect you, it is just an incident, not a trip to that inner place. Part of what's necessary to cross over into the Land of Awes is to bypass the ever-present ego and logical mind that control so much of our conscious life.

The key to every experience of awe is to be open to it.

PINA BAUSCH WORKS HER MAGIC

In 2007, I attended a performance in Los Angeles of *Ten Chi*—a dance piece choreographed by the dancer Pina Bausch. *Tenchi* translates from Japanese as Heaven and Earth, which should have given a hint about what the performance was about—but it didn't, at least not at first.

This was a strange affair to say the least. Onstage in the center was the giant tail of a humpback whale. About 45 minutes into the performance, white snow (or cherry blossoms?) started falling and continued to fall for the rest of the performance. Women in flowing gowns leapt out and danced erratically around the whale's tail. The music was a staccato mix of strange sounds that started and stopped abruptly. A woman walked along the front row, slowly wiping audience members' hands with water and encouraging them to snore. Meanwhile, many other things were going on offstage and onstage. A man with a baritone voice was pronouncing over and over words like "sushi" and "Sony" and "Hitachi" with different intonations.

I had entered "The Twilight Zone," and I wasn't liking it. Interesting, but it just did not make sense at all. My mind tried to get a handle on this: The water on the hands related to the ocean and the whale, right? And the intonations were about Japanese culture, right? And the guy taking coat after coat off of another guy was about . . . hmm . . . layers? And the guy pushing the chair across the stage moaning was . . . ? Oh hell, this was a nightmare, and I became irritated. I could not put it together, and every time I saw a pattern or got a sense of something, something else ripped me away into more madness.

So, I gave up trying. I consciously washed my hands of the whole mess and just checked out into a meditative place, rinsing all thought from my fervent brain.

And that is when lightning struck. Once I gave up trying to figure out what the hell I was watching and let loose the reins of reason, I fell into the place of reverie that Pina Bausch in her genius had fully intended. I was suddenly on a carnival ride, and it didn't matter which way it twisted and turned and burped and groaned; I was in sync with whatever the underbelly of unreason was presenting. It was no longer about thinking; it was only about experiencing. Pina Bausch had ripped me from my narrow thoughts and ways, and thrown me into a psychic stream of unconscious magma, which I joyfully bubbled and churned in until the whole indecipherable mess came to a crashing close.

Wow. This was living in the Land of Awes. My soul connected not only to the not-yet-speech-ripe experience that Pina Bausch had laid out for us to fall into, but I also connected with the threads of my own life that moved and danced and glowed to the strange staccato rhythms this whole encompassing experience engendered.

Now, that was my experience. It was one of those moments where who I am on the deepest level and my life story and my emotional state at the moment all came together to deliver up something remarkably consequential for me. For you, it will be different.

VISUAL ARTISTS AND AWE

A core and potentially transcendent way of crossing the threshold into the Land of Awes is by experiencing art, in its many forms. Visual artists create captivating images that draw us in to experience what they experienced when they were drawing, painting, sculpting, filming. Their work is tangible, expressing what they felt compelled to create, to communicate. Some labor for hours, others can dash off a sketch in a minute. For the viewer, it can take work and sometimes study to see into the passageway of artful delight, but it is all around us all the time. Sadly, much of the time we ignore it—and then wonder why we are not joyful. At other times, we are struck as if by lightning.

Art is personal in its effect on us. A Jeff Koons piece leaves me empty and bored, but the paintings of Jackson Pollock, which many people think their kids could create, totally suck me in. We need to find what vibrates with our soul and dive in, wherever it appears.

I am reminded of the painter Lucien Freud, the grandson of Sigmund Freud. He painted a series of portraits that, for me, reveal an understanding of the people he painted far greater than anything his grandfather understood about his patients. At first glance these works are hideous, and you could just ignore them as the art of a madman. But a bit of preparation or investigation comes in handy here. Once I learned that people would sit for 130 hours or more for a single portrait, I looked closer at this strange work. Can you imagine that? Sitting four hours a day for a month while such an intense man painted and repainted and repainted you on a single canvas? It must have yielded unbelievable insight into who the subjects were and who the artist was.

When I see these portraits, I can't help but be transported to the Land of Awes. I cannot explain what exactly they are about, or even how they affect me, but in an unspoken and unknown place, they grab me by the throat and slam me to the ground in the most delightful and undelightful way. I feel like I am looking directly into someone's deeper soul, warts and all. Freud's portraits become symbols for what is beyond the surface of the paint, beyond the surface of our own lives. With a little study and knowledge about the sitters and their experience, about the artist's thoughts and ideas, we let go of reason and ego and drop deep inside something both disturbing and pleasurable. All this is brought on by colored splotches of paint put together in an inspired way.

Art is a touchstone, a catalyst that allows us entry into something greater than ourselves. In that moment when we fall under the spell of a great piece of art, we allow the artist's symbols to connect with our own deep self. When I am standing for an hour in front of a Jackson Pollock painting, I am transported into a vast space of chaos and music. My guard is down, my judgmental self melts, my ego gives up and hides, and I am left with the feeling that the threads of my life are intertwining with those of Jackson Pollock's as I spin deeper and deeper into the beautiful chaos of artistic genius.

When we can allow this, the door between the personal unconscious and the collective unconscious swings open, and we sense the vast greatness of our own soul connecting with the vast greatness of all of humanity. This is not a place of words, but a place of experience.

And yet, paradoxically, the universal door that great art opens seems to access a room of mirrors where each of us thinks we are seeing what everyone else is seeing, when we are actually seeing a version of ourselves cued up by a symphony of symbols from deep within the soul. If I were to assume that everyone looking at a Jackson Pollock painting is transported to that sublime place of release and self-understanding, I would be wrong. Instead, we bring to any potential portal to the sublime our own ideas and understanding and find our own music and joy—or distaste—in the process.

This all directly relates to dreamwork.

Every time I work with a dream, the dreamer, the others in the room, and myself are processing something that came from the unconscious of the dreamer. It is our job and our pleasure to be drawn into that place of empathy necessary to working with a dream.

For instance, someone presented a compelling dream in which an eagle with an arrow through its wing was flying in search of an elixir to heal himself. The way the dreamer told this tale felt magical, inviting all of us into that place of empathy for the eagle. The more we looked at this dream and talked about it, the more empathetic we felt, as our eagle landed in different locations, desperately searching for the elixir that would save him. Nothing compares to that feeling of being in tune with others in this way. The journey we took while working with this dream was much like the journey that comes with being in the presence of great art and allowing ourselves to pass into the artful experience.

These missives that come pouring out of the unconscious naturally connect to awe. In truth, I so relish working with people's dreams because it almost always lands me in the Land of Awes, where dreams are permanent residents that wander out at night to deposit their magic in our souls as we sleep. They are tales woven by the Dream Gods to help us heal and understand ourselves as we battle through this existence.

The Dream Gods are like a Hollywood movie production team. They are writers, producers, directors, costumers, historical researchers, counselors in psychology, visual effects artists, continuity advisors, and lighting specialists. Every night they gather and create specialized movies for each of us based on our needs, problems, and history, with one eye to the future and the other to the past. They deliver up these strange tales steeped in symbolism in the form of dreams every damn night. They are the silent artists of our soul.

STANDING IN THE PRESENCE OF THE COLLECTIVE UNCONSCIOUS

In *The Structure of the Psyche,* Carl Jung discussed two ways of studying what he called "the collective unconscious":

> The collective unconscious—so far as we can say anything about it at all—appears to consist of mythological motifs or primordial

> images, for which reason the myths of all nations are its real exponents. In fact, the whole of mythology could be taken as a sort of projection of the collective unconscious . . . We can therefore study the collective unconscious in two ways, either in mythology or in the analysis of the individual. *Collected Works, Vol. 8*

Life can be a lonely place, and even the most gregarious of us spend a huge amount of time alone, either in solitude or surrounded with others but not connected. Most of us want company in the subtle seclusion that comes with this life of ours, and so we do all manner of things not to be alone. If we have a true friend who knows us, we may talk endlessly about our feelings until this other person moves into a space where they experience their version of those feelings, thus giving us a feeling about their feelings—in a kind of reciprocity of empathy. In that moment, we are not so alone. We are connected across a series of symbols that have brought us into an experience we are fully sharing with someone else. And in that sharing, we not only learn what is going on inside the other, we also learn more clearly what is going on inside our own soul. And, dare I say, we are even likely connected to the collective unconscious, that place where we share unconscious archetypes that roam around in that underground chamber of mystery.

Jung developed the concept of the collective unconscious to talk about our psyches' patterns (archetypes), which we share with all other humans and that access the history and tendencies of all humankind. According to Jung, a mind-boggling arena of thoughts, emotions, stories, instincts, connections, pleasures, pains, memories, and complex matrixes functions just under the surface of these powerful lives of ours.

If Jung is right, we not only have our own unconscious—with all our repressed memories and feelings—but we also have access to a vast library of all humankind's stories and archetypes in a common understanding or identification beyond our conscious minds. The idea of all that floating in the unconscious is almost incomprehensible. It is also a wonderful indication that we are all in this vast endeavor together as a united group of beings struggling to understand ourselves and others.

This was a dream I had that powerfully connected me to the collective unconscious and acted as a catalyst for important changes in my life.

KILLING THE GREAT MOTHER

I stand on the deck of an ancient sailing ship with five gods looking into the distance where two powerful rivers come together that we are about to navigate. The old wooden sailing ship has a narrow prow and a single extremely large white sail.

The five gods brought me above deck to experience something that few ever have encountered. They warn me that when we arrive at the tumultuous joining of the two swift rivers, I'll need their protection or be torn to shreds instantly in the ensuing chaos. My body tingles with excitement at this prospect.

The five gods surround me, get on their knees and hold hands in a circle. They give each other knowing looks, bow their heads, and cry out in unison a magic word. This incantation, together with their unified will, creates a clear bubble of energy that ripples with light just large enough for me to stand upright in.

As we reach the junction of the two rivers, the fierce storm drops like an anvil on the ship. Powerful energy fields stream across us from the narrow prow and pass behind us and I am amazed the gods can withstand it!

This is not just weather we are enduring here; emotions and experiences tear at the bubble. As my body is lifted and thrown to the deck, I realize that what I'm experiencing is the collective unconscious pouring over us. Every emotion in my soul is triggered at the same time. I am giddy with excitement, filled with love, torn with pain, guilt, anger, and complete rage. The blood pounds in my ears and my body shakes uncontrollably, as I am thrown to the deck again and again.

I see a griffin and a bull fly by. Voices cry out, thousands of voices—the noise is deafening. Emotions tear at my skin as they pass. I feel we are passing through all of history, through every emotion, every terror, every joy, every memory that has ever been let loose. It is utterly overwhelming, and only the bubble protects me from destruction. I am despairing and frightened.

Then a few brightly lit sections of the storm sweep across us and I feel joy. I'm lifted off my feet, only to be slammed again to the splintery deck by more dark waves of emotion.

This is some form of initiation, and I barely survive it.

The center god is a powerful tall bearded man wearing a Native American white beaded loop necklace in the shape of a "V." His beard is odd, long, and sculpted like a topiary; his chest is bare. He takes his finger and slowly slides it down his chest then makes a gesture with his finger at his heart as though it were a knife plunging into his heart. This is a signal to me of what I must do, now that I am initiated. I know that he cannot speak about it, and even doing this simple gesture is highly dangerous, because below deck is the Great Mother who can read thoughts. It is she who holds us all in a spell on this long journey.

I know from what he has indicated that this means the only way to break the spell and finish my quest is to kill the Great Mother.

Now it is night and I am below deck, in the center of the ship. There is something strange about the lighting here—it moves around in waves, not in straight lines.

I am making love with my young beautiful chosen companion. She and I are naked and tied together in an erotic knot like the twisted bread from a Parisian bakery.

The Great Mother's blue-turbaned consort/sorcerer/genie quietly indicates to me that it is time to sleep with the Great Mother.

I realize I must kill him first if I am to survive this. I pull out my silver spike and plunge it into his body. His body morphs into the shape of the bottle from "I Dream of Jeannie," and around the base is a clear, red band. I plunge my spike into this band, five times, letting out the air, which is somehow his life. He is dead with no reaction from him as I end his life and no remorse from me.

Now it is time to go to the Great Mother. I look up and there she is. She is enormous, and there are waves of energy coming off her, distorting my vision. Her flesh is grey and her body hideous and distorted, but I am drawn to her. Her breasts are 20 feet from the deck, the place I know I must reach. She resembles a giant statue of Buddha, only her face is like a strange animal. She is in a meditation pose, with eyes closed.

I ascend by sliding up her enormous naked body, starting at the feet, which are folded. There also appears to be a giant tail of some sort tucked under her crossed legs. She opens one eye and telepathically indicates to me that I should move up to rest between her gargantuan breasts. I climb up to just below these breasts, but there is no way to get there until she lifts them up and out of the way allowing me to climb into the space between them. She then enfolds me into the darkness of that space at the center of her body.

Enveloped in the heart of the Great Mother is the place of madness the gods warned me about. Her energies are so overpowering that mere mortals go mad, and I feel it starting to overcome me. The Great Mother's heart is beating so loudly that I don't know exactly where it is here in the enveloping darkness. I have to trust my instincts as I raise my silver spike high over my head and plunge the spike into what I hope is the heart of the Great Mother. As the spike enters her body, a shock wave of energy emanates from her and ripples through the ship, and the light changes from wavy lines to straight lines as her body shudders and shrinks. A deafening endless mournful thunder shakes the entire ship—my aim was true. I'm thrown against the rough wood of the ceiling by a shock wave so strong,

it almost tears my body apart. I am blinded by the light emitted from this furious death, and I tumble blindly to the wet splintery floor in a heap as the thunder and lightning cease.

There is no blood, and no remorse or resistance as she dies.

The feeling changes immediately. I've broken the spell. The Great Mother disappears and the vessel itself leaps in the air as gravity disappears and I float cross-legged in mid-air, like the Buddha. I am weightless, and filled with light. This is a beautiful feeling I have never experienced before. There is light churning inside me in circles and I feel connected to some other being that I am inside.

I wake up alone with a bright light that shifts back and forth with the swaying of the ship. I must tell the gods of my success in breaking the spell, but I sense they already know and have fled to do the things gods do.

The experience of this dream was so vivid and moving that I remember every detail of it, and that is why the dream report is so long and comprehensive. You may have had a dream like this—a dream that is so full of detail and feels so real, it overwhelms your senses and wakes you with a start, and you wonder for a brief second which reality is reality. This dream deeply affected me, and it has stayed with me, seared in my memory and my emotional self. And it changed my life.

Something powerful coursed in the emotional undertow of this dream. Waking up from it, I was in a place of awe, overwhelmed by something that stopped time and landed me in wonderment. As I recorded the dream and went over it, that feeling still lingered, the feeling that I was so involved in the story that it had changed who I was. I was emotionally exhausted and tingling in some spiritual aftermath. It was as though something deep within me had opened to something it had always wanted to be with but had always been denied. I felt silently connected to something beyond my own self that I couldn't name.

It also felt as though this was an actual myth or tale that I had never read. It felt like a combination of "Sinbad The Sailor" and the "*Kama Sutra,*" and it also had the feel of an Indian or Sumerian tale. This was a "mythic dream" because of the presence of gods, mythic figures, and the outsized themes that pervade myths and legends. But I could not imagine that it referred to any actual myth. I mean, in what myth would they kill the Great Mother? So, I let it go and just assumed that I was on my own in this strange, twisted tale of death and betrayal. I was reticent to work on it. I hated that I killed two people—one of them a mother—yikes.

But then I decided to search for references to killing mothers in myths, and I discovered this in Babylonian mythology:

> Killing the mother: When generations went blood-thirsty in a bid to create the earth, sky, and humankind.
>
> Tiamat was the great mother of all gods; in her body resided all her children. All was well until the children made so much noise that the old gods demanded the destruction of the new gods. The first time this happened, Tiamat warned her children. The second time this happened, Tiamat ordered her consort to destroy the new gods. The new gods rallied around Marduk who, after a furious fight, defeated Tiamat and her consort and all the old gods who sided with them. From the body of Tiamat, Marduk created the earth below and the sky above. Tiamat's tears became the rivers Tigris and Euphrates. The blood of her consort was mixed with the red earth and from this was created humankind. As the spawn of the old gods, humanity was forced to serve the new gods forever. Failure to serve the new gods led to floods and storms. This tale is told in the *Enuma Elish.*
>
> Devdutt Pattanaik,
> from "10 best mythological tales from around the world"

From other sources we learn that Tiamat is a sea dragon or hideous beast, her consort is named Apsu, and Marduk is the storm god.

This is a creation myth, one of the oldest known.

Well, "shiver me timbers," as Popeye used to say. Strangely, this Sumerian/ Babylonian myth, which I had never encountered before, actually lines up with my dream in many ways. One could say this is just coincidence, but perhaps something else is afoot here. Perhaps, just perhaps, we are plugged into something magical. And even if that is not true, the importance of a myth lining up with a dream is in the effect it has on the dreamer, and perhaps on others.

Let's look at some of the similarities. First, two rivers came together in the dream. In the Tiamat myth, Tiamat is the primeval cauldron of salty water where everything begins. That great salty being joins together with the sweet waters of Apsu, her consort, and the blending produces many gods, who are their children. So that maelstrom produced in my dream where the two rivers came together was like the joining of these two creation forces that produced something new—in the myth, new gods; in the dream, a new way of seeing and feeling.

Even though this is the Great Mother of creation, it turns out that, in the myth, Tiamat is not only the benevolent mother of all; she is also a vengeful dragon that needs to be slain. The idea of her also being a dragon was hinted at in the dream by the dragon's tail I saw sticking out between the Great Mother's legs.

Slaying the Great Mother/dragon in the Sumerian/Babylonian tale is the job of Marduk, the great warrior. In some versions, Marduk kills Tiamat by shooting her in the heart with an arrow—not exactly a silver spike, but close. The actions I took in the dream run parallel to those of Marduk. Those tricky gods in the dream knew exactly what they were doing. They made me a part of the plot to kill the Great Mother, assigning me the role of Marduk, and I killed both the consort and Tiamat, the Mother.

Unlike in my dream, the mythical Marduk cuts the corpse of Tiamat in two, using half to make the firmament above and the other half to make the earth. Her giant udder forms the mountains, and the tears from her eyes form the Tigris and Euphrates rivers that join and flow into the Persian Gulf. In the mythic tale, the red blood of the consort is mixed with red earth, and that forms the human race. That feels similar to me, and echoes the red band of the consort's I-Dream-of-Jeannie-bottle body that I pierced with my silver spike.

Of course, I have unanswered questions about the dream, like: what was with the Native American necklace on the god? And why were animals flying by like the cows that whiz past Dorothy in *The Wizard of Oz*? But let's not dig too deeply into symbols here: let's go right for the jugular. Why did I, like Marduk, kill my own Great Mother and her consort in the dream?

I think it points to my own psychology and life path. When I had this dream, I was struggling mightily with my relationships to women. Like Tiamat's children, I was both distrustful of women and feeling devoured by them. What was required in order to move on from this stuck place of failed relationships was to take a silver spike and plunge it into the heart of my ideas of both the masculine (the consort) and the feminine (the Great Mother).

I had to break the spell of my own mother and the spell of other women I had substituted for my mother, and at the same time, I had to kill off the male part of me (the consort) that was in league with my twisted view of the feminine. It took a long time, but I managed to do just that. I am still a work in progress, but I broke the spell by modeling my behavior on this dream. As deep and searing emotions tear at me in my life as they did on the deck of that sailing ship in ancient Babylon, I take them in and experience them, allowing myself to become deeply emotional. Then I take action by expressing those emotions to others and by finding ways to change behaviors, like reaching out to those around me with similar difficulties and practicing true empathy with them. This is sticking a silver spike in the old male and female parts of my being and letting out the inflated air of my ego.

The important point about the connection to the Tiamat creation myth is that we identify with the characters in our dreams and what they are going through just like we identify with the characters in great stories and movies. Our lives can bend and change and improve as we see laid out before us these bigger-than-life experiences that echo in our beings.

A dream like this also allows us to stand in the presence of the collective unconscious and actually experience the deep forces just under the surface of life. These forces are crouching there patiently waiting for us to open the door, lift the rug, open the window, and allow the wind to caress us, the water to overwhelm us, the fire to consume us, or the darkness to envelope us. It is time for the veneer of the ordinary to crack open and allow our true souls and spirits to spill out into our lives.

PART 5

WHEN DREAMS SCREAM

The Value of Difficult Dreams

CHAPTER 10

FRUSTRATION DREAMS

There's a Tsunami Coming and Nobody Seems to Give a Damn

What good is a dream that doesn't test the mettle of the dreamer? What good is a path that doesn't carry us to the edge of our capacity and then beyond that place? A true calling involves a great exposure before it can become a genuine refuge.

Michael Meade
Fate and Destiny, the Two Agreements of the Soul

NOW IS THE WINTER OF OUR DREAM DISCONTENT

It's wonderful when our dreams provide epic stories that land us effortlessly in the Land of Awes, that sparkle with magic long after we wake up. But what about the dreams that leave us unsatisfied, stuck, and frustrated?

The Cambridge Dictionary explains frustration as: "The feeling of being annoyed or less confident because you cannot achieve what you want." Frustration dreams are those where things just don't go right, usually in a big way. They have unresolvedness and discontent hanging all over them. I wait and wait in line at the airport and they give the last seat to the guy in front of me and shut the door in my face and take off and I watch in anger as they do spectacular loop-de-loops without me. Or everyone ignores me as I implore them to run from the tsunami. Or I'm being chased by a gang of thugs, and my feet are moving like I'm in molasses. Or I am about to eat this incredible meal, and my teeth fall out. So why do the dream gods do this? Why frustrate me with all these seemingly obnoxious and useless scenarios?

The ego looks at things like this from an egocentric viewpoint, of course, and ends up bellyaching about the unfairness of losing my seat on the airplane. So many people ignore these frustration dreams because they seem to point out our faults and inabilities—and damn, we just don't like that. I mean, really, am I going to make any effort to remember, let alone bring to a dream group, a dream where I look like an ineffectual dope?

But what if we look at it from another perspective? Perhaps the guy in front of me in the airplane dream is a part of me that soars off into that creative space. And part of me is just not accepting myself as someone who can soar. The dream says I am perfectly capable of soaring, but I am holding myself back from doing so.

The frustrating airplane dream was someone's real dream, and I encouraged the dreamer to ask himself, "So, where in my waking life am I holding back from soaring? Is there an area where I am holding myself back?" He did not have an immediate answer, but the question worked on him for a few minutes. Then he blurted out that he had long had a desire to paint small paintings of different colors that would express certain emotions, but he had no training or experience, and no reason to do it. "Well, you have a reason now, so go get yourself some paints and small canvases from the art store and just play," I said. And he did that, to great satisfaction. In this case, the frustration was the impetus for creation.

A deeper understanding of why something frustrating drives itself into our dreams lies in the nature of conflict and the use of imagination. As my screenplay teacher used to say, "Without conflict there is no drama, no story, and no movement." We need not go around looking for a black eye all the time, but it is often through conflict that the opportunity to move forward opens up. Sometimes you need something to push against in order to move forward. Michael Meade says when there are two opposing forces that cannot resolve an issue, a third thing needs to rise at that moment, and that third thing is imagination.

> The point of tension and conflict in this world is to generate a third and creative thing. Whenever there is an intense polarity, what is really trying to happen is a deeper awakening that produces the third thing that no one saw until the tension became great enough.
>
> MICHAEL MEADE
> *East and West Must Meet*

This is not unlike the triad of ideas that appears in philosophy: thesis, antithesis, synthesis. The thesis states a point of view, and the antithesis contradicts that idea, which is where the frustration comes in. It is in the synthesis that resolution happens. All three of these are necessary to move forward philosophically into new ideas. Frustration dreams attempt to give us a thesis and an antithesis, but they leave the synthesis up to us.

During the crisis of the COVID-19 global pandemic, I worked dozens of frustration dreams centered around the reality of the virus. Threatening "bugs" appeared, characters in the dreams were isolated and lonely, and other aspects of frustration surfaced. Once we recognized that the dream was a reflection of the fear associated with the pandemic, we attempted to use our powers of creativity to bring a synthesis to that frustration and fear. The danger was still there, but in the creative process of bringing the emotions to light, the dreamers found a possible path forward to living more comfortably with them.

SWEPT AWAY

To illustrate the movement towards creativity in frustration dreams, let's use a pair of tsunami dreams. I have worked dozens of tsunami dreams, and while they are totally individual in nature, they also often have the common theme of the dreamer being overwhelmed. Here is one from a woman in her mid-forties.

NO ONE LISTENS

I am at the beach. It is a beach I have never seen before. It is a bright day and I squint out into the ocean and see a giant cresting dark wave so enormous that I know it will wipe all of us out. It's a tsunami! I run down the beach, screaming for people to get off the beach. No one listens to me! They look out to the ocean, but no one is the least bit concerned. People look at me funny as though I am crazy! I stop a woman and tell her a tsunami is coming. She smiles and moves on. We are all going to die and no one gets it! The wave is crashing! I wake with a start.

There are at least two ways to look at a very frustrating dream like this (which is also technically a nightmare). My feeling from the telling of this dream is that all the people on the beach are unified in the pleasant, non-threatening feeling that might be a key to approaching this dream. Maybe the dream is pointing out that the dreamer is out of step with things and emotions around her. This is a projection on my part, of course, but let us go down this path for a minute.

If we step back from the dream and look at it from the viewpoint of all the other people on the beach—as opposed to the viewpoint of the dreamer—we can see it differently. As adding a bit of imagination can be helpful, we asked the dreamer to step out of her own dream ego and take on the perspective of the others in the dream. She told a new version of the dream that she made up from the other people's view. Here is how it was told when she was thinking and talking as the other people in the dream, not herself:

> *We are a few dozen people and we are walking along the beach. Suddenly, this woman with crazy hair appears and runs down the beach, screaming that there is a tsunami coming. We look at each other and smile. We are the locals here and there are some strong sets coming in, and this may be a tsunami, but we always get through this, no sweat. We have seen this before and it falls to us to help this woman understand how things work here among us at the beach. We will find a way to calm her, we are sure.*

In telling the dream from the perspective of the other figures in it, the dreamer felt her frustration start to dissipate. She started to see how events in her life were related to the dream. She brought up the fact that her grandmother was "on her last legs" and she was sure she would die soon, and she felt frustrated that she could doing nothing to change this. She was completely consumed with anxiety about it. The dream portrays this anxiety in the form of a tsunami. The impending death is like a tsunami that literally knocks people off their feet. When we look at it from the perspective of the others on the beach, we realize the death will come and the emotions will indeed overwhelm us, but it does no good to run around screaming about how overwhelmed we are when we're thinking about it. The "aha" the dreamer got was to listen to others who might have a calmer, wiser view of this event.

One essential thing to do with a true frustration dream, in my experience, is to continue the dream. Dreams, like movies or stories or folktales, have to continue on beyond the point of frustration if they are to make their point. Where we left the tsunami dream is like the point where Little Red Riding Rood gets eaten by the wolf. She is still alive in there, and the story ends? No way. Now, what can we make up for our tsunami dream?

In working this dream, we already had a solid "aha" moment, but the dreamer wanted to go further in resolving the frustration in it. We had the players and the story, so the dreamer continued the dream from her own viewpoint, making up this new narrative:

> *I keep trying to tell these idiots that there is a tsunami coming, as the wave looms so large it blocks out the light. The people gather around me and assure me that everything will be fine. They are nuts! I guess it doesn't matter now; the wave is crashing.*
>
> *We are all swept up inside this violent wave, all together, and I find myself grabbing a woman's hand as I face certain death. Just as I am about to pass out, here in this murky underworld, the woman, who looks like a mermaid now, but also reminds me of my grandmother as a young woman, grabs me and swims to the surface with her arms around me. On the surface, there is a small white rowboat with oars. I climb aboard in relief. The woman smiles at me and telepathically tells me, "You are one of us now."*

Now this is a totally made-up ending to the dream, pulled out of thin air by the dreamer—or so it may seem. In truth, we had laid the groundwork for something like this to occur. Because we went through the process of working the dream—discovering the emotions, asking questions, projecting on it, feeling it in the body, acting it out—something was already primed to come up from the unconscious. Because of all that, something magical happened: what she made up as she continued the dream came out of an inspired creative place.

When I used to direct live theatre I would rehearse and rehearse acts one and two, but not touch act three until very late in the process. By the time we let loose on act three, the actors were so steeped in their characters, emotions, and motivations that act three would virtually block itself. With the actors intuitively knowing where to move and how to pause and find the right cadence in the lines, the entire play would fall into place. Magic always happened when we arrived at act three, because we had laid the groundwork.

The same is true here with our tsunami dream. The dreamer in this case totally surprised herself with this made-up continuation of the story. It helped her resolve the frustration she had around the impending death of her grandmother. It also opened something else for her. She connected this dream and the feelings around it directly to her feeling of being overwhelmed by others in her life and a longing to connect with people on a deeper level. She wondered what would happen if she secretly looked at things from the perspective of the people she was around, who seemed so foreign to her. It was a good new beginning, and possibly at least one more thing the dream wanted her to see.

Frustration dreams can invite creative ways to face the frustration, giving us a solution from outside the dream that often has some bearing on the frustrations we face in waking life. I'm telling you, listen to your dreams, and they will give you a path forward in this frustrating world of ours!

The other way to look at this type of frustration dream is the polar opposite. Here is a second tsunami dream, from a man in his twenties.

THE BIG WAVE

I have been surfing for a couple of hours at my usual spot. It's overcast. Suddenly I see a huge wave approaching. It's gotta be one of those tsunamis! I run down the shoreline trying to get people to run for high ground, but no one listens to me! No one will even look at me. It is going to be a disaster. The wave crests as I wake up in a panic.

In this dream, the same frustration appears, but with hints that this could be the opposite of the last dream. The dreamer is the authority here. He is familiar with the beach and even surfs it. His frustration is justified, as he tries to wake people up to the reality of the impending disaster. In my projected version of this dream, the people walking along are not wise and discerning. They are stand-ins for the complacent parts of myself that are not tuned in to what is going on. I am the one who has the knowledge and vision, and I need to wake up the sleepy parts of myself and help them see what is going on.

So, in working this dream, we explored and projected as we usually do, but this time I had the dreamer stay focused on the dream ego/surfer dude instead of moving the focus to the people on the beach. I had him continue the dream like we did in our last example, making something up of his choosing.

> *I realize that it is too late for any of us to escape this giant wave, so I herd everyone together on the beach and we huddle in a tight, very tight circle as the tsunami washes over us. We hold each other tightly, but the wave overwhelms us and washes us all out to sea. We hold together somehow and we discover that we can breathe underwater. We finally emerge and swim ashore and share stories of our experience.*

The conclusion the dreamer came to after inventing this ending to the dream was that a giant wave of emotion was approaching in his waking work life, and the dream addressed his frustration with not being able to control it. He had been thinking about starting his own business but was deathly afraid of the risk. That would be like a tsunami overwhelming him, so he had sat in the state of frustration, and the emotions piled up until they formed a threatening tsunami. The dream had offered up the frustration, but it was up to him to fix it.

In this case, I did something unusual. I had the dreamer draw the dream *after* we worked on it. This led to some further understandings.

Let's look at the drawing. Notice how everything is circular. The story winds around the central image of the group holding hands underwater.

The story starts in the upper left with the solo surfer. It continues in the upper right, where the surfer warns people of the impending tsunami. Then the story moves to the center, where the people hold hands in the circle with our hero as the tsunami overwhelms them. They are then washed out to sea from the center of the picture to the lower left, where they are still holding hands and breathing underwater. The breathing underwater was such a strong image in the dreamer's mind that he felt compelled to draw a close-up of himself at the bottom center declaring he can breathe underwater. Then we move to the final scene in the lower right, where the surfer is hanging with his new friends as they share their tales of survival.

The drawing invites our focus to move in a circular fashion forced by those curved blue lines at the center. It turns out this circular, continuous movement is exactly how our dreamer functions when he is at his best. He is in his element and greatest joy when he is helping people. When he does that, it always feels like waves, vibrations, and circular motion. The "aha" the dreamer got from discussing the drawing was that the stuck place he was in could be solved by joining up with others and helping them pass through the same emotional waves that had engulfed him recently.

This ended up as an inspiration for a lengthy journey into owning his own business. He now owns a crystal shop near the beach, and his greatest joy is helping people in their spiritual journey. He attempts to guide people into finding which stones "vibrate" the best with their needs. He also does sound healings with circular crystal singing bowls. This simple frustration dream and the drawing helped to bring one soul into his true rhythm of life.

If we look at a universal application, this particular tsunami dream is trying to get us to move forward by clearly showing that we need to deal with something that frustrates us. We wake up wallowing in this dreadful field of frustration, but by inventing a new ending, we have gathered the reluctant parts of ourselves and hunkered down as the tsunami of emotion overwhelms us. We have magically learned to breathe inside the tsunami of emotion and are now united in moving forward. Frustration dreams are an invitation to take action.

LEAVING A CLOSED DOOR CLOSED

In my experience, frustration dreams can often be difficult to work. In the frustration dream (unless we become lucid) we don't have a key to the prison door, we never locate the car, we lose our wallet and never find it, the phone doesn't work, we never find our own house, we can't stop the water as it floods our apartment, no one listens to our brilliant idea, we can't stop the menacing dark figure as he chases us wherever we go, and so on. These are all frustrating situations, bringing distress and offering no clear path in the dream. Upon waking, this frustration is locked into the dream.

The difficulty is that people just hate being frustrated and often do not see the way forward. And that is where some invention and creative thinking can come into play. Other types of dreams often have the resolution built into the dream somewhere, but frustration dreams leave it out. The frustration dream forces us to feel the frustration, identify it, and then resolve it outside the dream. The unconscious wants us to fix this pressing problem, whatever it is. So, when you get frustrated in a dream and see no clear resolution, use your imagination and creative tools, artificially remove the frustration, and see what happens.

Bang on the prison door until someone opens it. When that frustrating phone won't work, take it apart and make a sculpture out of it and see what happens. When your house fills with water, go rent a huge water pump and drain it. When you are frustrated that the brilliant idea you write down in the dream disappears off the page, write something down as you work the dream. Turn around and confront the dark figure, pull his mask off and ask him if he would like some dark chocolate. Frustrations invite creation.

But even these approaches may well fall flat. When we use creativity and address a frustration dream, the dreamer can get an "aha" or at least find a path to work through the frustration—but many times it just doesn't work. Let's look at a frustrating prison door dream.

THE DOOR

I am inside a prison. I have been here a long time. It is dark and there is no way out. It feels like I am underground. In front of me is a locked door and there is no way to open it, absolutely no way to get it open and it is the only way out, but there is no way to open it, no way. It is hopeless.

As the dreamer told this dream, you could hear in her voice the extreme agitation that she couldn't get the damn prison door open. Her tight, gesticulating body also radiated intense frustration, as she sawed the air with her arms. I asked her what emotions she felt inside the dream. She replied, "I was angry, frustrated, and sad too. I hated being in there, and I also felt helpless. There was nothing I could do."

Well, in the obvious department, the approach seemed clear. I asked the dreamer, "Could you invent a way to get the door open?"

"It is an impenetrable door with no key to open it, and it simply cannot be done," she replied.

I then asked her, "So, what would it take to get this door open?"

"There is no way to do that," she replied.

I suggested we bring someone into the dream who could succeed at getting it open, say Bruce Willis or Dwayne Johnson in one of their movie roles, and she agreed. She brought in Dwayne Johnson, whom she finds quite attractive, with a machine gun and dynamite, and had him blow the door to smithereens. Aha, thought I, we are getting somewhere.

"So, what happens next?" I asked.

"Nothing, really," she said sheepishly.

I pushed her for a response. "Really? The door that has frustrated me is now open and clear to walk through, and what happens?"

"Oh, I guess I walk through the door and go home," she said in a quiet voice.

"Is this solution okay with you?" I asked.

"Not really," she replied.

I then suggested we go back to the time when the door was still intact, before Dwayne Johnson blew it open, and rethink this. "What do we do now?" I asked.

"I don't know," she replied. "I guess I am just in the dark prison and there's nothing I can do."

She had despair in her voice when she said that, and we ended up stuck in that place. None of the other suggestions I dreamed up seemed to have any impact. Digging a tunnel, having someone unlock it from the outside, walking magically through the wall—nothing fit the dreamer's idea of what to do.

So, we left it there, unresolved, and that is fine. Logic and reason do not always hold sway in dream work. The frustration here called out to be resolved, but that was not the path we were able to take with this dream. Frustration dreams can be fertile brewing grounds for something that hasn't yet become "speech ripe," as Jeremy Taylor has said, and it is possible this dreamer had more work to do or more emotions to experience in this locked prison.

Perhaps we didn't ask the right question. Or perhaps we needed not to ask a question. Perhaps this uncomfortable place of unresolvedness was where the dreamer needed to be. Perhaps magic was hiding in this dark place, working slowly to resolve something. Perhaps magic was in the frustration itself. Being frustrated can lead us down into that liminal space between spaces where words fail us and awe has a subtler form. Sometimes you just let a dream be what it is, and don't look to unearth anything about it; you let it just wash over you.

I tried one last time to address this frustrating place we seemed to be in by asking the question "Is there a place where I feel completely trapped in my life right now?" The response was a steely look that said, "Not in seven hells . . . I am not answering that question."

That we had clearly addressed this frustration was a beginning for the dreamer, and we will see what future dreams bring that may give further insight into this frustrating prison.

In other words, frustration dreams can be, well, to put it bluntly—frustrating. And that is fine. In telling a frustration dream, we have opened ourselves up to things that are not readily resolved. The approach to them needs to be open, creative, and accepting. I was going to say more, but isn't it appropriate to leave a discussion of the nature of frustration in a place of frustration?

CHAPTER 11

NIGHTMARES

The Mad Scientist and the Boy with Stone Eyes

GO AMONG TREES AND SIT STILL

I go among trees and sit still.
All my stirring becomes quiet
around me like circles on water.
My tasks lie in their places
where I left them, asleep like cattle.
Then what is afraid of me comes
and lives a while in my sight.
What it fears in me leaves me,
and the fear of me leaves it.
It sings, and I hear its song.
Then what I am afraid of comes.
I live for a while in its sight.
What I fear in it leaves it,
and the fear of it leaves me.
It sings, and I hear its song.
After days of labor,
mute in my consternations,
I hear my song at last,
and I sing it. As we sing,
the day turns, the trees move.

WENDELL BERRY, from *Sabbaths*

Let's talk about nightmares. Why are they called nightmares? The "night" part is obvious: this part of the term was added to indicate that they happen in the night. And although you may think of a "mare" as a horse, here it refers to a demon. It comes from the Old English *maere*, which means monster, and if you dig deeper, that comes from the Proto-Germanic *maron*, which is an imp or goblin. So, a nightmare is a goblin that appears in the middle of the night.

SLEEP PARALYSIS

Have you ever woken up in the middle of the night out of a dream and not been able to move? This is referred to as sleep paralysis. It is estimated that around 40% to 50% of people have experienced it at least once. It is that condition where you have little or no control of the voluntary muscle groups. It can be extremely frightening—and is sometimes accompanied by hallucinations, which makes it even worse, but that is rare.

It turns out that our astonishing bodies have developed this trick to keep us from jumping out of bed and chasing the talking pink flamingo during those vivid dreams during REM sleep. One major scientific theory tells us that during some parts of our sleep cycle, a chemical messenger called gamma-aminobutyric acid (GABA) is secreted, and it acts as an inhibitor that stifles the activity of the brain's motor system. It is what allows us to dance *The Nutcracker* in our dream without doing actual pirouettes on the bed. This occurs most every night for us teeming millions. We are rarely aware of it because it usually happens in a deep sleep cycle (REM sleep), and we are not conscious of what is occurring.

In a normal sleep night, we pass through five levels of sleep; the first three are steps down into the deeper stage four, or Delta Sleep, which lasts for approximately 30 minutes. After that, we go back to stage three, then stage two, and then into REM sleep—a separate stage of sleep from the other four stages. It is where most (but not all) of our dreams occur. The whole

Here is some of the latest science on the matter:

"Rapid eye movement (REM) sleep is generated and maintained by the interaction of a variety of neurotransmitter systems in the brainstem, forebrain, and hypothalamus. Within these circuits lies a core region that is active during REM sleep, known as the subcoeruleus nucleus (SubC) or sublaterodorsal nucleus. It is hypothesized that glutamatergic SubC neurons regulate REM sleep and its defining features such as muscle paralysis and cortical activation. REM sleep paralysis is initiated when glutamatergic SubC cells activate neurons in the ventral medial medulla, which causes release of GABA and glycine onto skeletal motoneurons. REM sleep timing is controlled by activity of GABAergic neurons in the ventrolateral periaqueductal gray and dorsal paragigantocellular reticular nucleus as well as melanin-concentrating hormone neurons in the hypothalamus and cholinergic cells in the laterodorsal and pedunculo-pontine tegmentum in the brainstem. Determining how these circuits interact with the SubC is important because breakdown in their communication is hypothesized to underlie narcolepsy/cataplexy and REM sleep behavior disorder (RBD)."

Jimmy J. Fraigne, Zoltan A. Torontali, Matthew B. Snow, and John H. Peever,
REM Sleep at its Core: Circuits, Neurotransmitters, and Pathophysiology,
Ed. Patrick Fuller, Harvard Medical School,
Quoted in Frontiers in Neurology (May 29, 2015)

Whew. I hoped you survived that. My spell check hates about 20% of those words.

sleep cycle experience takes about 90 to 110 minutes on the first go-round, including about 10 minutes of REM sleep. We go through about four to five cycles in a night, with the REM sleep period getting longer and longer as the night progresses, sometimes lasting up to an hour.

At the outset of REM sleep is when our brilliant mammalian bodies and brains produce that temporary sleep paralysis to protect us from extinction. With our voluntary muscles paralyzed, we can get to work in our dreams—flying, having sex, dancing a ballet, and performing brain surgery—all without harming anyone, including ourselves.

Thank goodness for sleep paralysis. If not for our friend GABA, I am pretty sure my ex-wife would have strangled me in my sleep as she acted out her greatest desires in her dreams. Oops. There I go projecting again.

WHEN THINGS GO AWRY

When things are running smoothly in our sleep patterns, we pass back and forth through these five stages of sleep. Sometimes there will be a short break of being awake for a few minutes about halfway through the night—more if your sleep pattern is disturbed or if, like me, you consume lots of water. We end up with around two to four hours of dreams that most often we remember little of, but which affect us anyway. You don't always have to remember the dreams to get the benefit. A good rest with uninterrupted dream time can clear the brain of clutter and help us organize our lives better.

Sometimes, though, things go haywire with this wonderful protective system of ours. When things go awry in what is usually an unnoticed series of moments in our REM sleep cycle, two different things can happen. The first is when the temporary sleep paralysis doesn't take effect properly, and we act out things in our sleep. This is where sleepwalking fits in.

Here is some of the science around sleepwalking, from neurologist Antonio Oliviero of the National Hospital for Paraplegics in Toledo, Spain. ("Why Do Some People Sleepwalk?" *Scientific American,* February, 2008):

> During normal sleep the chemical messenger gamma-aminobutyric acid (GABA) acts as an inhibitor that stifles the activity of the brain's motor system. In children the neurons that release this neurotransmitter are still developing and have not yet fully established a network of connections to keep motor activity under control.

> As a result, many kids have insufficient amounts of GABA, leaving their motor neurons capable of commanding the body to move even during sleep. In some, this inhibitory system may remain underdeveloped—or be rendered less effective by environmental factors—and sleepwalking can persist into adulthood.

This condition can be brought on by sleep deprivation, other underlying medical conditions, and also some medications. I once had a girlfriend who was a heavy Ambien user, and she would wake me up in the middle of the night and act out all sorts of things.

One night she shook me awake and pointed to the end of the bed and yelled, "You have to catch the baby!"

"What baby?" I asked as I woke up, startled.

"The one coming through the window! Catch her! She's coming through the window! Catch her!" she yelled.

"What window?" I said, still not really awake.

"Right there! Catch her!" she said, as she frantically pointed again to the end of the bed.

So, I crawled to the end of the bed and made like I was catching a baby in the direction she had pointed. Evidently, I didn't get it right.

"You missed her! You're a fucking idiot! Why didn't you catch the baby?"

"Sorry, where is she now?" I replied.

"On the floor, right by the rabbit. What the fuck is wrong with you? Why don't you ever listen to me? You are a complete fucking idiot!" she ranted.

I reached over the edge of the bed and tried to pick up the imaginary baby. That's when she pushed me off the bed onto the floor.

"Do I have to do everything myself?" she said with indignation. She then reached down on the other side of the bed, scooped up the imaginary baby, lay back down cuddling her, and immediately fell back to sleep. Oh, my god, could that woman snore. I went out to the couch and tried to sleep there, afraid to stay in that bed.

In the morning, she had absolutely no recollection of the baby-catching incident. Needless to say, this relationship didn't last long. It is hard to sleep with someone if you're worried you might wake up being choked because they think you are an evil pterodactyl clawing at them.

Most often, these instances are not dangerous, just bizarre. And, yes, you should wake up a person who is sleepwalking or experiencing something like this.

These experiences are not considered nightmares; they are known as sleep terrors or night terrors. The distinction is that night terrors or sleep terrors are not recalled by the subject, whereas nightmares are.

Now let's examine what happens if temporary sleep paralysis, instead of ending too soon, stays too long. In this case, there are some links to nightmares. Sometimes, the GABA inhibitor that immobilizes us during a dream works too efficiently or for too long. If we wake up before it totally dissipates, we become aware of the paralysis. We are in a conscious state, and yet we can't move our arms, legs, or head. Yikes! This is often accompanied by the feeling that something is sitting on your chest and you can't breathe. When this happened in times of yore, the assumption was that it was a demon plaguing you. They believed that there was an evil spirit, an incubus (a male demon that rapes and tortures women) or a succubus (the female demon that rapes and tortures men) sitting on your chest.

This is the complete opposite of our sleepwalking and night terrors scenario. Instead of getting up and doing something like chasing a wooly mammoth, we wake up but cannot move. This is a situation where nightmares can appear.

The artist Fussli's depiction of a nightmare was an instant hit in 1782 in London, where he first exhibited this dark work, attracting morbid fascination. The horse coming through the curtains is a visual pun on the idea of night "mare." The woman is sleeping alone with her head off the bed, which, as folklore had it, was an invitation for a nightmare to occur. I must assume that she is deeply engaged in temporary sleep paralysis with a full

The Nightmare by Johann Henrich Fussli (1781)

dose of GABA coursing through her system. I mean, wouldn't you jump up if there was an imp on your chest and a ghostly-eyed horse snorting in the background?

It is possible that what is reported as a nightmare in this state of paralysis is just the anxiety and panic that comes from not being able to move. One other possibility is that the dream we are having in a REM sleep period jolts us awake too early, and we find ourselves frozen, further adding to the frustration and thus moving it into nightmare status. I once had a nightmare where an old hag chased me up a tree, then flew up and impaled my right eye with a huge needle. As the needle entered my eye, I woke up, trying to scream, but nothing came out, and in addition, I couldn't move. The paralysis lasted only seconds, but it sure added to my panic.

THE FUNCTION OF NIGHTMARES

So, nightmares may wake us up before the body is done with its temporary paralysis, adding to the fright. But why do these miserable damn things come to us, anyway? Couldn't we just get by with a quiet discussion about the meaning of life with the smelly, 12-foot monster with sharp teeth and claws, instead of being chased by him and then having his claws rip into our back as we try to flee around the corner? What good does it do to have these harrowing experiences that disturb our sleep and upset us?

I don't think there is an easy answer to this, but let's give it a shot.

One theory that is plausible but not entirely fulfilling is the idea that dreams, especially nightmares, are used for our survival through threat rehearsal. A nightmare can be a rehearsal of how to act when things go wrong in life. Imagine one of our cave-living ancestors who has a recurring nightmare of being attacked by a saber-toothed tiger. Over and over in his nightmares, this stealthy cat sneaks into the cave and attacks him. The first time he is too slow in reaching for his bone knife, and the cat digs its long teeth into his legs, and he wakes with a start. In the second nightmare he has his bone knife ready, but the cat attacks him from behind, and he is again impaled with those long teeth. In the third go-round he is ready for Mr. Sabertooth, and they fight fiercely. He plunges the bone knife into the back of the tiger, and awakes in a sweat. These nightmares are a way of rehearsing the real saber-toothed tiger threat in waking life. When the actual tiger enters the cave, our ancestor has rehearsed grabbing the knife and killing the tiger so many times in his nightmares that it becomes second nature and saves his life. We do the same as we find ourselves facing our own darkest worries in a nightmare.

However, I don't think this explains very much of why we have nightmares. Let's dig deeper.

We can perhaps envision the purpose of nightmares if we consider our natural tendency to avoid unpleasant things. Our reticence and tendency to dissociate become barriers to dreams that try to talk to us about painful things we need to work on. Sometimes a nightmare is the only way for the dream gods to get through to us—which is to say the only way to get through to ourselves.

For example, the dream gods have been involved with my becoming a writer. They watched as I took an illuminating writing class at USC and they saw how much I enjoyed it. They know that some threads of my destiny lay in writing, but they watched for six months, and I hadn't written a damn thing. I had dissociated somehow from the joy I felt in writing. And so, they sent me a dream about finding a blank journal in the street and opening it to find my name in it. I woke up and thought, *that is pretty cool,* but then I just turned over and went back to sleep, and the dream drifted away.

The dream gods sent me more dreams with libraries and bookstores and clouds with words on them and scenes from childhood where I doodled on the back of birthday cards. When I still ignored all of that and just turned over and snored, the dream gods got more aggressive, hoping against hope I would listen to my inner being, who truly wanted to tell its compelling story through writing.

This time they sent a full-on nightmare:

> *I am locked in a room with an elephant that bellows loudly and then charges me at full speed. Yikes! I race to the door and find it locked with a combination lock. Damn! But wait, I have a piece of paper in my pocket that I wrote the combination on! I pull out the paper, but holy hell, it's blank! I remember now—I forgot to write it down! I pull and pull at the lock, but to no avail. The elephant is on me and smashes me against the door. He then wraps his trunk around my body as I scream in protest. He lifts me in the air and brutally uses me as a battering ram to smash open the door. I am a bloody mess and worried that I might die. I awaken with a start.*

So there I was, in the middle of the night—adrenalin pumping, heart racing, eyes wide open, as I tried to shake off the very real feeling that I was dying. No turning over and drifting off was possible. Dreams are usually stored in the short-term memory centers because the long-term memory centers are asleep, and they quickly disappear from consciousness. But when a nightmare comes, the long-term memory centers get a wake-up call, and the dream gets recorded in a place we can remember it. Finally, the dream gods had gotten their point across to the conscious self that the "elephant in the room" was about writing. It made it imperative that I write something down in order to open the door to the next phase of my life. It was time to become a writer.

Children have more nightmares than most of us jaded older humans. One reason for this is that so many powerful changes are going on during childhood, and nightmares reflect those changes. The nightmare of the monster chasing a child that comes the night before they start school is probably the personification of some fear of that change. Childhood is a time of heightened imagination, which also contributes to having and remembering nightmares. Seventy percent of adults report remembering a vivid nightmare from childhood.

Anxiety and post-traumatic stress are also huge factors in the production of nightmares. When we suffer from trauma and anxiety, our souls cry out to find a way to express the pain and correct the perilous situation. Repetitive nightmares spawned from deep traumas, such as witnessing or experiencing sexual abuse or other types of violence, often depict some aspect of the actual abuse or trauma over and over. They are termed replicative nightmares. Because this is such a dynamic reenactment of something so overpowering and disturbing, the nightmare reignites the trauma instead of becoming a healing event.

This is where therapists and other professionals come into the picture. Image rehearsal therapy (IRT) is a field of therapy geared to working with nightmares that plague people with post-traumatic stress disorder (PTSD). In this technique, a trained therapist guides the PTSD patient in rehearsing the replicative nightmares they suffer using different endings and different scenarios within the dream. After these rehearsals, patients often find the nightmares less intense, and oftentimes they do not recur.

In this same field, if a therapist can teach the PTSD patient to become lucid while still continuing to dream, and they can alter the nightmare while inside of it, they may experience great relief. If my elephant dream were a replicative nightmare, and I could become lucid at the beginning of the dream, everything could change. I could write down the combination on the paper before the elephant charged, or ask the elephant why he was there, or use my flying abilities to escape the situation. There is no cure-all for what underlies the problems encountered in PTSD patients, but this can help.[2]

Nightmares can be a debilitating experience requiring professional help. If they plague you, talk therapy and other professional help is available.

THE NIGHTMARE AS AN UNFINISHED DREAM

A powerful way to look at a nightmare is as an unfinished dream. We almost always awaken in the middle of the story, just as the monster drives a wooden stake into our heart, or as the bomb goes off, or at the moment Big Foot throws us out of the airplane. Such moments are so horrific that they startle us awake, effectively leaving out the last part of the story, like a movie ending right in the middle of the climax. Furthermore, because a nightmare is so dramatic and full of emotion, we tend to freeze it in that moment, leaving us in an uncomfortable place. Sometimes we can discover the reason a nightmare has come if we allow it to continue. Nightmares, then, are fertile ground for applying the technique of "continuing the dream."

So, what if we ask: "What happens next?" This launches the nightmare into different directions; it also may replace the lingering horror and

2. For more information about how lucidity can help with PTSD, see the study: Brigitte Holzinger, Bernd Saletu and Gerhard Klösch, "Cognitions in Sleep: Lucid Dreaming as an Intervention for Nightmares in Patients With Posttraumatic Stress Disorder." Published in *Frontiers in Psychology,* Aug. 21, 2020.

discomfort with a way to understand why our unconscious was so insistent that we wake up and deal with whatever it sees as something we need to be aware of.

For instance, let's take a look at the nightmare that wakes us up just as the wooden stake is driven into our heart. First, we should think about the meaning and symbology associated with this. Wooden stakes through hearts are an obvious reference to vampires, as one of the few ways you can kill them. So, in our dream, that would make us a vampire who dies. To "continue the dream," we start where the dream leaves off and make something up to continue the story.

In my imagined continued version of this dream, the wooden stake plunges into my heart, and suddenly I see myself die and turn to dust. My family then surrounds this pile of dust and applauds, then blows the dust away as they cheer. I stand nearby, shocked that my own family would act in such a way. They then see me and come over and embrace me. Thus, the dream has a new meaning. Perhaps there is some way in my waking life I am being a "vampire" to my family? Or is there some way I am sucking the lifeblood out of some of my relationships? Is it time to let the vampire in me die? That is one possibility. By continuing the nightmare with a new ending, we have moved beyond that stuck place that most nightmares leave us.

WORKING WITH A NIGHTMARE

Let's look at a particularly vivid and horrid nightmare I had and see if it gives us some further insight.

THE MAD SCIENTIST AND THE BOY WITH THE STONE EYES

I stand in the middle of a dark room that is sealed, with a mad scientist/doctor in a white lab coat, dark hair, and a face without form. It is a scary place. There are piercing bright hard lights beaming down on an operating table with a young boy strapped to it.

The mad scientist is here to transform this innocent boy. I look closer and I realize the boy is encased in clear plastic. It is like a form-fitting coffin. He is naked and coated with a layer of wet mud the color of light brown shit. My heart goes out to this boy. This is awful. I can tell from his face he is horrified.

The doctor holds two brightly colored stones high in the air, then reaches up under the plastic and takes the two stones and forces them into the eyes of the boy. He uses so much force they crush his eyes and replace them. I am speechless and frozen as I watch this horrid torture.

He then takes a circular saw and cuts open the throat, destroying the voice. Oh, my god this is awful! He is making the boy blind and mute. There is liquid flying everywhere as the saw proceeds down into the body. I am sprayed with water and shit and blood. The spray is so massive that it impairs my eyesight. My god, he is making him into a Jesus figure! This is horrific and mean. As the saw moves towards the heart, I am panicked and sick. I can't take anymore. I wake in a sweat, screaming.

The first thing that arose as I awoke from this nightmare was an overpowering feeling of absolute horror and fear. This young boy was being torn to shreds right before my eyes, and I couldn't or didn't do a damn thing. This was one of those super-real dreams, and the emotions were so powerful nothing else mattered. This truly shook me.

On the next page is the quickly made drawing of the dream. In the upper left is the mad scientist and me looking at the boy encased in plastic and covered in earth. The lower left depicts the hands of the mad scientist crushing the eyes of the young boy as he blinds the boy by forcing the red and green stones into the eye sockets. In the center, the mad scientist cuts open the throat of the young boy with a skill saw. The upper right is what I imagine he is doing to the boy in the dream—he is making him into a Jesus figure, which I see floating with streaks of bright white light emanating from his head, like many pictures of Jesus.

Well, how do we work with such a crazy, horrible thing? I bring this to my dream group to work through. We start by addressing the deep emotion that arises with questions like: Can you describe this emotion? How did that make you feel? Can you express this emotion in words or gestures? If I were to locate that emotion in my body, where would it be?

The emotions I felt and still feel as I tell the dream again are fear, anger, and disbelief. I am afraid for the innocent boy, I am angry with the mad scientist for doing this, and I stand frozen in disbelief. I am about to say I'm angry with my dream self for not doing something, but that is an emotion from outside the dream. I express this emotion by tensing my body up completely, opening my eyes as wide as possible, and allowing the horror to pour into my eyes and down into my body. And the horror sits deep in the center of my body as I re-experience the nightmare.

I sit with this a while, a difficult but a necessary thing to do.

Finally, someone prompts, "Where else in my life have I felt this before? Also, is there something going on now in my waking life that is reflected or connected to this?" This is the beauty of dream work. Here I am, sitting deep inside a nightmare, and someone sees and understands that I am in an emotional state, so they gently bring me to the surface without losing the power of the experience. When they ask this question, it starts to transform the nightmare into something beyond the overpowering emotions that flooded me and still weigh here in my solar plexus. Sometimes nightmares are so overpowering it seems wrong to move out of the extreme emotion they produce, but the Land of Awes awaits us somewhere down the line through this process, and it behooves us to travel there if healing and progress are the goals.

Absolutely nothing comes to mind immediately about a connection to my past, so we have to look for clues in the dream and the drawing to help us locate the emotions somewhere in history. Someone asks how old the boy is. I tell them the boy is about nine years old, so naturally they then ask, "What happened when you were nine?" Aha. Nine-year-old Walter was baptized into the Mormon Church. That ball of emotions has moved now to my stomach. Thinking back, it was a time when I was forced to see things from a different perspective. In a sense, my eyes were replaced, and something removed my voice as I moved into the cultish world of Mormonism. So, something back that far and that deep is still at play in my life all these years later? Leave it to our dreams to humble us and remind us of our lifelong pursuit of balance and enlightenment.

In the bigger picture, if I think about my soul and its journey through this life, it may well feel horror at the silencing of my natural voice at nine and at the strange "rose-colored-glasses" that the stones may suggest that I put on during the Mormon years. As we move out from under the horror, perhaps we can find out what the nightmare wants us not only to feel, but also to *get*.

Looking closer at the drawing I made, two things really pop out, at least for me—the stones and the Jesus figure. Those red and green stones appear three times in the picture. Why red and green transparent stones? I mean, in the world of logos, if you were going to gouge out someone eyes, you wouldn't use stones, least of all colored transparent ones. So, it's likely the unconscious brings them into the nightmare as something symbolic. The sense in the dream is that these stones replace the eyes. Staying with that logic, the boy now sees life through a green stone in his right eye and a red stone in his left eye. Because I'm a lighting expert who uses all sorts of colored lighting in my work, this makes me think about the missing color, which is blue. With red, green, and blue light, you can produce any color. In that case, this nine-year-old boy is missing one-third of the necessary equipment for seeing his experience. But, you know, I am not sure where to go with that idea, so let's try something else.

Emeralds are green transparent stones, and rubies are red transparent stones, but nothing comes up right away thinking about that angle. This is the nature of dream work. There is no one right answer, so we get to try various ideas and see what sticks.

As I look at those red and green stones in the drawing, they suddenly remind me of the drawings of the chakras, the seven energy centers located in the body, which are each a different color. Red is the base chakra or Muladhara (in Sanskrit "Mula" means root and "Adhara" means support or base). It is located at the base of the spine and is the connection to the earth and the foundation for all the other chakras. It is about grounding and stability. Green is the color of the fourth chakra, the heart chakra or Anahata, located at the level of the heart. It is a place of love, compassion and empathy. Being the center chakra, it is indeed the heart of a being, bridging the physical and the spiritual. I should say here that you really don't have to believe in this whole chakra idea in order for the information or connection to be effective in dream work. As we work with dreams, the overriding factor is that evocative marker, clue, scenario, emotion, or story that draws an "aha" from the dreamer, indicating we are in touch with the underlying meaning or import of the dream.

In any case, let's go with the chakra idea for a bit. Putting aside the horror and imposing the chakra corollary on the dream, we can imagine the right eye of the boy seeing things through aspects the heart knows, and his left eye sees things through aspects the grounded, secure self knows. But what about that cut-open throat? How does that play in the chakra plan? The chakra just above the heart chakra is the throat chakra—the fifth chakra, known as Vishuddha, the chakra of voice, expression, and choice. Its color is blue, which throws us back to the missing blue light we need to complete the ability to use the three light sources—red, green, and blue.

In other words, we can look at this as a boy who is connected to the earth and grounded, who can see and participate in love and empathy, but who lacks the voice to complete the task. This clicks for me: I think that perfectly describes the nine-year-old Walter. He is a bit of a grounded visionary with no voice to articulate it.

But this nightmare happened when I was in my 50s, so why is it talking about all this childhood baggage? We always have to look at what the dream is trying to convey or reflect about our lives at the time we have the dream. The nightmare must be using the nine-year-old's experience of being silenced and his vision being replaced to key in on what is happening at the time I had the dream.

And that brings us to the third element of the nightmare that stands out for me: the mad scientist is making our boy into a Jesus figure. On the surface this makes no sense at all, but as we know, dreams speak a symbolic language, so let's look at the symbolism of a Jesus figure and see if that locates the nightmare in the present time, the time when the nightmare occurred. Jesus is the archetype of the willing sacrifice, a figure who gives up everything for other people, the ultimate empath in a way. And empathy is a huge part of how I function. My soul is always searching for ways to stand in a place of empathy and help others. The other aspect that Jesus represents is resurrection. This is when I get a deep "aha" that has to do with my life at the time of the nightmare. I can see how that soulful being who disappeared for a long period of time is now resurrected.

But what was going on in my life at the time of the nightmare to provoke such a violent overture for my soul to hear? It turns out that the nightmare was sent to kick my ass about backsliding on a personal achievement that I was failing to stay true to. I had finally come into my true voice, but I had let it be silenced.

On a warm summer night before the nightmare, I was at the annual Dream Ball at the end of the International Association for the Study of Dreams conference. Everyone attends the Dream Ball dressed up as a character from their dreams. I was dressed as Laura Bush's alter ego or shadow. I wore a black cat suit that covered everything, including my face, 6-inch red platform stilettos, a busty corset, and a pearl necklace. Except for the pain that I suffered in gaining a new appreciation for what women go through when they wear high heels, it was a magical night.

No one knew who I was, and they were all over me, touching, prodding, and asking questions of this mysterious, overly tall, figure that fascinated them. I kept silent, and it was in that place, believe it or not, that I realized I could connect with the deepest part of myself, a part that I had buried so long ago as a boy. Something about people looking at me as other than just the lighting guy who works with dreams freed me up. It allowed me to resurrect that quiet, powerful being I had carried silently all those years. As the music pounded and I attempted to discern things through the costume's limited field of vision, I stood in that place of revelry and awe that overwhelms me at times and fell into understanding my own voice in the world. Revelations can happen at the strangest times.

After the experience at the Dream Ball, I made a conscious decision to begin speaking from that deep place of soul, in my true voice. I was successful in doing so for a month or so, but then I began to doubt myself. I retreated back to my old lack of confidence, and that is when this nightmare came slamming into my world. Something in me liked the new way of being and was outraged about my retreat from it.

In this case the nightmare was a reinforcement device. The coating on the strapped-down boy was reminiscent of the way I was completely veiled at the Dream Ball. It showed me I had connected to an essential and important part of myself that had been buried for a long, long time, and it was imperative for me to stay the course and not cover it up again. It was a resurrection the dream gods did not want me to retreat from.

And I have stayed the course since then. This is what the Jesus figure represented. The resurrected Walter has reclaimed his voice that was silenced, removed the colored stones, and fashioned them into a pair of glasses made of rubies and emeralds. I now have a choice whether or when to place them over my reborn eyes to see the long path forward. With some distance from the nightmare, I have realized that the mad scientist forced me to look at the interior of my soul by forcing my vision inward.

What started as a horror movie ended up an adventure film with a moral tale. The horror has fallen away, and the clear message of seeing with new eyes and speaking with my true voice has been taken in. All this from what seemed to be a destructive, debilitating nightmare.

The important thing to remember when working with nightmares is that the process has to be moved through step by step. Moving from the horror of this young boy being destroyed to standing as a resurrected being with a new vision entails the same journey you can take with your own nightmares.

Oh, and in case you are wondering about the dream that brought on the crazy-ass idea of dressing up as Laura Bush in a corset—fear not, I will tell that tale when we talk about sex dreams.

CHAPTER 12

FACING THE DEMON

The Healing Power of Dreams and Dreamwork

GATHERING LEAVES

Spades take up leaves
No better than spoons,
And bags full of leaves
Are light as balloons.

I make a great noise
Of rustling all day
Like rabbit and deer
Running away.

But the mountains I raise
Elude my embrace,
Flowing over my arms
And into my face.

I may load and unload
Again and again
Till I fill the whole shed,
And what have I then?

Next to nothing for weight,
And since they grew duller
From contact with earth,
Next to nothing for color.

Next to nothing for use.
But a crop is a crop,
And who's to say where
The harvest shall stop?

ROBERT FROST

Our dreams can be instrumental in facing our demons. They capture both the darkness and the light, and thereby minister to the health of our souls. If we are open to them, dreams can be powerful catalysts for revealing and healing from trauma and loss. The following dreamers and their stories show how our dreams can help us move forward and create meaningful change in our lives.

THE ALLIGATOR AND KILLING THE FATHER

When you work with dreams, word gets around, so people often just walk up to me and ask me about their dreams. I was working on a TV variety show, and I became friendly with the costumers and the makeup artists. For frenetic, concentrated hours, things would get intense—makeup brushes flying, costumes being adjusted, hair being fluffed and sprayed, as I was fine-tuning lighting cues to give the right feel to each production number; then suddenly that would all stop, and we would end up with long stretches when we had time to talk.

A bubbly woman about 25 years old heard me talking about dreams, and during one of those long pauses she decided to tell me one of hers.

FETID WATERS

I return to my family home where I grew up, but it is different somehow. I am a younger me. When I get to the living room, there is a giant glass-walled tank with fetid water in it. There is barely room for me to slide around the edge. As I do so, I notice that there is a huge ugly alligator in the pool and he has it out for me. He lunges at me, and I barely escape out to the back yard. I run up to my mom, out of breath and explain that there is a giant mean alligator in the living room. She has no response, so I tell her again, and she still has no response. She doesn't even seem like my mom now. I am angry and frustrated. I start to cry and I wake up.

There is a dire feel to the dream as the woman presents it. We talk about the emotions inside the dream, the fear and the anger. I put myself in her dream shoes as we talk. We wander around in the landscape of the dream for a bit, then I ask her, as the projected dreamer, if I have suffered through something that my mom refused to acknowledge. She tells me no.

Then we talk about the fetid water. If we think of the water as emotions, it seems that there are fetid emotions about something at the very center of my family life (the *living* room). She goes silent when I talk about this, and has no real verbal response, but her body tightens, and she gathers her sweater around her protectively as she thinks.

Now it's time to talk about the alligator. I wonder out loud if the alligator has anything to say to me? Her eyes get big, and she tells me she is scared of the alligator and doesn't even want to think about it. I ask her if the alligator reminds her of anybody or any situation, and she shuts me down. She doesn't want to go any farther, so I honor that. She is visibly shaken, and so we lighten up the conversation. It seems like I have taken a wrong turn in the work here. I tell her to be on the lookout for another dream tonight. Often when we start listening to those voices from our own souls, more dreams will come to clarify the message that the unconscious is symbolically laying out for us.

Two days later, we are still stuck in the world of silk and sour notes as the variety contest drones on. My alligator-dreamer bursts into the room and drags me to another room to talk privately. I have a feeling that she might have had a follow-up dream involving something with her family and some trauma, but I am unprepared for what unfolds. She tells me the nightmare she had the previous night.

KILLING THE FATHER

I am in my childhood home-—the one that had the alligator in it from the other dream I told you about. Only this time the place is full of blood—human blood. I am knee-deep in blood, trying to find a place to hide. The entire house is full of blood.

It's my father. I am trying to hide from my father. My father has killed my two sisters and cut their bodies up into pieces. Oh, my god! He has killed them. Their body parts are floating in the blood. It is gruesome, and I am terrified. And now he is hunting for me to do the same to me. My father is trying to kill me and cut me up! I hide in a closet, I hide in other places, but I know he will find me. Somehow, I escape to the outside. I get in my car and drive away as fast as I can. When I look in the rear-view mirror, there is my father sitting in the back seat with a knife raised. Oh my god, he is going to kill me! He says to me, 'Go ahead, kill me. I know you want to.' He hands the knife gently to me and somehow while I am still driving, I plunge the knife into his heart and kill him. I scream and I wake up, with my heart racing and the pillow full of tears.

I am silent for a while, letting the powerful feeling this dream dumped into the room settle and take shape. I begin working on it by explaining that sometimes we don't listen or remember the message that the unconscious is trying to give us, dream after dream, so after multiple attempts, the dream gods up the ante in hopes that we will awaken long enough for the dream to be remembered and taken to heart. I explain the difference between the short-term memory center that activates when we wake suddenly and the long-term memory centers that take about ten minutes to become fully functional after waking; I discuss how nightmares evoke chemical responses that make the long-term memory centers come online faster, so the nightmare then gets remembered. I tell her about how dreams speak a universal symbolic language and remind both of us that we need to look at dreams symbolically.

Well, all of this theoretical mumbo-jumbo falls on deaf ears. This woman is enveloped by this nightmare, and I am not sure of my next step, so I close my mouth and wait.

She sits for a long while, twisting a makeup brush in her hands. Finally, she looks up and says, "Walter, you don't get it. This actually happened. My father molested me. I have never said that until this very moment, but it's true. When I told you the alligator dream the other night, it put me in a black mood for two days, I felt like I had told you a dark secret that I shouldn't have, and then when this dream came, memories of him touching me and touching me and touching me came flooding back. Oh, my god, why do dreams do this to us?" She sobs and sobs and sobs. We sit in that room together for a long time.

One of the great lessons I have learned in working in a field where emotions can burst forth like a broken dam is that, when it happens and the tears pour out, the best approach is not to say, "It'll be okay, I promise," but instead to shut up, listen, have empathy, and hand them tissues—but mostly just shut up.

So, I shut up and listen and feel deeply into the energy in the room.

When she is ready to talk again, and she asks my advice, I suggest she should see a therapist, and she agrees to do that. This is a huge passage she is entering, and doing it without deep personal help would be dangerous.

Then she asks me about the dream. "Why all the blood, and why did I plunge the knife into him and kill him?"

"Well," I begin slowly, "blood for me is life force, so in my dream we are dealing with something that has been sucking the life force out of me for a long time, which fits perfectly with what you are saying about your father here. As far as killing the father, let me ask you a question. Is blood involved there also? Do I see blood when I plunge the knife into him?"

"No." she replies. "I didn't see any blood at all, and he didn't seem upset that I had killed him either."

"Let me project something onto this dream from my perspective," I tell her. "Death for me is almost always a symbol of transformation in a dream. If we step back and look at a dream as a story, what better way to represent a change than having a death involved? Death is the end of something, but in my understanding, there is also always the other side of death, which is a new beginning. Something always rises out of the ashes of death. And this is MY dream, not my father's, so this dream, for me, is about my own death and resurrection. It is about plunging a knife into the memory of all that has happened that is so disturbing and horrid and allowing it to die, to transform. I actually see hope in this dream. In the end, it doesn't cost me my life force to put this to rest. No blood is spilled, no life force is given up in the transformation to a new life. There is a huge amount of work to go through here, lots to heal, but the dream gods are assuring me that I can make it, I can get through this and continue to move forward with my indomitable 'drive.' That is what the car in the dream is for me—my drive, my psychic drive, my will to live, my way to move on in the world, and I will one day soon be able to put all this in the rear-view mirror and move on."

That night we spent more time working this dream, including the aspects surrounding it, like whether her sisters had also been molested by him (I found out later that they had been). The dreamer was curious about her mother's role in all this, citing the indifference her mother had had in the alligator dream. We discussed how, given her mother's lack of response in that dream, it was possible her mother either had no idea about all this or was in a state of denial. At the very least, this was how she *felt* about her mother.

A can of worms was opened wide that night, and we did our best to stand in this place of awe without losing our souls to the darkness. I am so grateful to have been a part of something so important and transformative. She did go into therapy and was making strides when I last heard from her.

This tale illustrates how dreams come when we are ready to hear what they have to tell us. Sometimes, with trauma, it is fine to not face the monster and to hide. It can be a matter of timing. Sometimes molestation victims have no explicit memory of the molestation until the memories are triggered by something later in their life.

Jim Hopper, Ph.D., a nationally recognized expert on psychological trauma and abuse, refers to this on the page "Recovered Memories of Sexual Abuse" on his blog:

> . . . research evidence show[s] that it is not rare for people who were sexually abused in childhood to go for many years, even decades, without having (recognizable or explicit) memories of the abuse. (People almost always have implicit memories of the abuse, that is, memories they did not realize were memories, for example

physiological or emotional responses triggered by encountering things associated with the abuse, like being touched in a certain way).

The body and soul know how to protect themselves in such dire circumstances. The unconscious has a complete, explicit memory of all this trauma, and can hold it until the person is ready to deal with it.

When the time does come to deal with it, dreams can be instrumental in facing the demon. This brave woman was able to stand there and tell me that she had been molested by her father, saying it out loud for the first time. She could have fled and buried it again, but she chose to open that scarred old door and seek help. Moreover, while she and I were sharing her experience, we were transported to that incredible place of awe that this book is about. This was a moment of complete and utter aliveness. It is what life is about for me, living in these powerful places replete with soul and love and compassion—even, as in this case, a powerful place of severe trauma.

THE PAPER DOLL

Now, let's look at a dream in which the drawing plays a central role in the healing of a deep trauma. Things are a bit twisted here in this tale. The dream occurred first, the trauma happened eight months later, and the drawing and dream work was done five years after that.

The dreamer (her unconscious, really) felt compelled to draw and work this dream a full six years after having it, which is unusual; but with deep traumas the soul brings many sources together not necessarily in order, to attempt healing.

The drawing plays a key role here. It is the work of the unconscious trying to convey something to the dreamer about her current condition and what to do about it. If she had drawn this dream back when she had it, it would have been radically different.

SACRED STONE

A guru I worked with and respect in waking life offers me a sacred purplish stone with carvings on it. I accept and try to wrap it up, but am unsuccessful. She tells me I can take it without wrapping it up. I am not sure I can pick it up and carry it, but somehow I can. There is a wonderful feeling as I do this.

On June 13, 2013, the dreamer was working as a librarian at Santa Monica College. A crazed man armed with an AR-15-style weapon entered the library and started spraying bullets. He had already killed five people and wounded four on his way to the library. The dreamer and other employees barricaded themselves inside a storage room. This enraged the lunatic gunman, and he yelled for them to come out, or he would shoot them right through the wall. They refused and held the door shut. True to his word, the madman opened fire through the wall. Bullets were flying everywhere. Luckily, the police stormed the library and shot the perpetrator dead.

This life-altering event deeply traumatized the dreamer. She couldn't return to work and withdrew into herself. She has spent years in different therapies to deal with the aftereffects. She has felt that this monstrous trauma stripped her of her dignity, and she is reticent to be in a spotlight of any sort. This ordeal has also manifested somatically, producing aches and pains and extreme difficulties with her body.

Let's inspect the drawing. The very first thing that grabs our attention is that stick-figure drawing of the dreamer. Lots of people use stick figures in drawing their dreams, but this one is striking. It has a fully formed head with carefully articulated hair and even eyebrows. The body, however, is a deliberate creation of just five lines with hash marks to indicate fingers. The bottom lines for the legs bend outward slightly to show feet. The unconscious wants us to see and dwell on this stick figure. She is facing straight at us,

open to our view, but she is slightly off-kilter and floating on an undefined background. Both figures are off-kilter, bent slightly away from each other, and floating. The stone is also off-kilter. These factors invite us to feel that there is some unseen force bending these figures away from each other. And then we realize that these are mirror images. Both figures pose in exactly the same way, hands extended, feet turned out. The unseen power that pushes the two figures apart is the trauma the dreamer suffered.

Without her consciousness knowing, the dreamer has invited us to contrast and compare these two beings pushed apart by the trauma. They are both representations of the dreamer. It is also important that the guru is on the left and the dreamer on the right. If we look at this as a timeline, the past version of the dreamer is on the left. This is the dreamer before the trauma—vibrantly red, a guru—happy, wise, and giving. The figure on the right is the dreamer in her present state. She has been stripped of everything except her head, the source of thoughts. The therapeutic

work she has pursued has kept her head in the game. The stick-figure woman seems like a paper doll without clothes. By creating her in this way, the unconscious artist invites the conscious artist to add clothes to this traumatized figure.

And so, I invited the conscious artist to dress this almost invisible body in any way she wished. Here is the result:

She dressed the stick figure of herself in the same bright, lively color as the guru, gave herself a crown and a diamond by her heart, and added vibrancy flowing through her body. What a transformation! She even has feet now. Unlike the guru, we are privileged to see the inner workings of the soul who survived this huge trauma. She is strong and vibrant and ready to unwrap that philosopher's stone, which now has come alive with hash marks emanating spirit. Our heroine is now prepared to pick it up and take it on her journey to health and transformation.

This is another confirmation that our dreams create the framework of change we can flesh out in our waking lives.

THE TIGER MAN

Let's take a look at the life of one dreamer who epitomizes how the dream gods can guide us into the future. Much like Claude Monet as he painted those damned haystacks over and over (25 times) in order to say something, this dreamer worked fervently with her dreams to heal from a loss and build a new life.

Phuong is a regular participant in my weekly dream group. She is an impressive and resilient woman who cares deeply about her dreams and tries to follow their advice. She has given me permission to talk freely about her and this experience, although I have changed her name in case this book becomes a best seller and hundreds of tiger men go hunting for her.

Phuong was married for seven years. Unfortunately, her husband was the victim of a horrible mishap. He choked on a piece of chicken, and after a two-week struggle in the hospital, he died. It was a devastating experience for her. Shortly after his death she found out about my dream group. Because she was having disturbing dreams surrounding his death, she showed up to find out why.

In one dream, the departed husband starts talking to her, and she realizes he is dead and tells him if he is not dead to scratch her back, which he does, which freaks her out, and she wakes up. In another dream, she has his DNA, and from that he gets partially reconstructed—which also freaks her out.

As the dreams came, and we worked on them, she took what she discovered in the dreamwork and slowly built a new life. This wasn't just a casual look at her dreams. This woman took each dream to heart and used it to look deep within and change things, then looked to the next dream for more guidance.

It wasn't the only thing Phuong did to heal, but she made it an integral part of her journey. She took her husband's ashes to the Buddhist temple and dedicated herself to serving at the temple part-time in order for him to move on through the process of samsara leading to reincarnation. It takes at least 49 days to travel from one life to another incarnation in the Buddhist tradition, and Phuong was there, worshipping at the temple and using her dreams to help release him to the next life. On the day that she took his ashes and spread them in the ocean, she had the following dream:

SPECTACLES

I walk across a campus and see a hole filled with murky water. I accidentally drop one shoe in the water and the water suddenly becomes clear and at the bottom is treasure. I cannot take the treasure right now, I am afraid the government will take it, but I reach in and take out a pair of spectacles and put them on. I will come back later for this treasure.

In working this dream, we landed on the feeling that there was treasure waiting for her in the future. The murky water to me was reminiscent of when ashes are dropped into water. Dropping the shoe into the murky water clears things up, and a treasure is discovered. That seemed to relate to the idea of Phuong's having one foot in this world, where she lives, and one foot in the other where her husband had crossed over to. So, if I stand with one foot in this world and one foot in the other, accepting the passing of the husband into the other realm, I will be given a new way of seeing things (the spectacles) that will allow me to see a treasure that will soon come into my life.

Little did we know that the treasure was close at hand.

About six months after her husband's death, Phuong brought this dream to the group.

THE TIGER MAN

I am with my friend Van and we are at a club of some sort, but instead of men, there are animals there. The three I remember are a bear, a fox, and a tiger. The tiger stood out because he stood on his hind legs as though he were human. Van and I realize that this is a dangerous situation, and we run for our lives. This is very scary, but I am not too worried about myself, because I know that Van is a lot slower than me, so if someone will get eaten, it will be her.

I notice that there is a helicopter overhead following us and I think I see a guy in it, but I am not sure.

The dream shifts and Van and I are in a train car. We stand behind a velvet rope, the kind they use at clubs for lines of people. The rope is all that separates us from these wild animals. As long as I hold the rope up, the animals including that tiger that is standing on his hind legs can't get us.

Phuong presented the dream in a very subdued manner, but with a glint in her eye when she talked about Van possibly being eaten by the animals because she was slower. We had her tell the dream again after we taped up the simple sketch of the dream that you see here.

The drawing is sparse, but telling. On the far left is the only figure that is fully drawn (giving it more importance in the story). This is Tiger Man, who, oddly, seems to be moving away from our fleeing women. In the upper left is a helicopter, which is moving away from our heroines. To the left of center are Phuong and Van being chased through the woods. On the right is the train car with the faces of the three animals waiting just right of the vertical line that represents the velvet rope. From top to bottom they are the bear, the fox, and the tiger. To the left of the velvet rope there are three stick figures. One is Phuong, one is Van, but who is the third one? Also, it appears that Tiger Man is drawn twice inside the train car.

Well, we all jumped in on projections about this dream. I went to the place of accepting my own animal nature. We looked at the three animals. Where am I being a fox in my life right now? And why a bear? What do bears symbolize? Is there some place in my life where I am hibernating? And then there is the tiger. Tigers are dangerous predators. But this one stands and moves like a human. Is there some way I am being a predator somewhere in my life, or do I have someone in my life that is acting like a tiger right now?

When I asked that, Phuong's body tightened and her eyes got large, but she said nothing.

And the train car, what about that? That seemed to us like the beginning of a new journey. She leaned forward, smiled, and agreed with that as her body loosened up, almost like doing a subtle dance.

Phuong's responses were interesting and led us back into the idea of our own animal nature. We all have tigers inside us, and sometimes we need to drop the rope of convention and restriction and let them loose. The idea we ended on was that we had that velvet rope in our hand, so why not drop it and see what happens? Why not allow our animal nature a chance to overwhelm us and just see what happens?

We ended the work, but there was something still unfinished in the air. There seemed to be something she was not telling, but it is always the dreamer's choice not to go further than is comfortable.

Then, as Phuong was taking down the picture she had drawn of the dream, she offhandedly mentioned that she had had two dates with a new guy, and he was born in the year of the tiger. She wondered out loud if that could have any significance. We all roared with laughter, and asked why she hadn't mentioned this earlier. She told us it was embarrassing. She explained that it seemed disrespectful to be interested in someone so soon after her husband's death. She didn't want to bring it up but felt compelled to say something because we had hit so close to home with the comments about men and tigers and dropping the rope.

This was one of those moments when things come together in the damnedest way. I realized that what I had observed in her body's reaction had been a body "hit," where the symbol breaks into consciousness, and then her comments and our laughter opened the door wide. The dream now makes sense on a different level. That her girlfriend Van might get eaten by this tiger is a secret wish that the tiger would eat her, since Van is another version of her in this dream. And then there is the tiger that stands like a man, and she happens to be dating a man born in the year of the tiger? Not hard to figure that out.

Other things came into the discussion. The helicopter is possibly her husband, who is watching over all this but is headed away now. The Tiger Man seems to be headed in the wrong direction, so he is really not a threat on one level. On another level, it could be a subtle way of telling Phuong that it is time to step up her game and do a little pursuing herself. The third figure in the train car is possibly the new Phuong, ready to face and be consumed by the tiger waiting patiently in the wings.

Well, at the end of the day, all this projection led us to encourage her to drop that velvet rope and allow the tiger in. Grrrr.

She did exactly that. She dropped that rope, kicked it aside, and embraced a new life. She allowed Tiger Man inside her heart and ended up falling in love with him. Many of us from the dream group attended the wedding of these two lovely beings at a Buddhist temple in Orange County, California. The woman who had dedicated herself to making sure her husband moved on in the process of samsara and had listened to her dreams was rewarded with a new life of her own. Phuong and The Tiger Man now jump in their jeep with their two dogs and head out into the wilds and explore together.

Dreams are damned amazing, no?

PART 6

MYSTERIOUS WISDOM

When Dreams Reveal Our Inner Knowing

CHAPTER 13

PRECOGNITIVE DREAMS

How a Pair of Red Shoelaces Saved a Life

No, there was nothing unusual in any of these dreams as dreams.
They were merely displaced in Time.

J.W. Dunne
An Experiment with Time

The word "precognition" comes from the Latin *prae,* "before," and *cognito,* "acquiring knowledge." According to *The Cambridge Dictionary,* precognition is: "Knowledge of a future event, especially when this comes from a direct message to the mind, such as in a dream, rather than by reason." Precognitive dreams are those dreams you have that end up being actual events or facts later in waking life.

Is this even possible? Precognition can be a wild and provocative area to explore. We are up against some pretty heavy opposition to the idea of seeing into the future from many rational, brilliant people and beliefs. The broadly held scientific principle of causality—the idea that an effect cannot occur before its cause—dismisses the idea of precognition. Also stuffed in that same can of worms is the clear lack of much scientific evidence of precognition. Since no one can predict the winning numbers of the lottery or the one stock that will soar tomorrow, the firm reasoning is that precognition must be bunk, and that makes perfect sense. When people say they knew intuitively something would happen *after* it occurs, is that really to be trusted? Couldn't they just be lying or fooling themselves or bending things around a bit to fit? Proving that precognition exists is a long, steep road strewn with generalities and unreliable information, but at the end of the road there is a small pot of gold of truth to be found—if you are patient and open.

As sentient beings, we have a persistent desire to know what is in the future. It has been the subject of novels, movies, and endless speculation by religions, philosophers, and drunken yahoos hanging out at the bar. The desire to know about the future is so strong, it moves beyond science—into the world of emotion and belief. And guess what? That is not a bad thing. It is wonderful to have an open attitude about all the strange things in the world of predictions, and to sift through them for resonance and truth. They can remind us that we don't have all the answers about our world and our existence and inspire us to keep our minds open to new ideas, information, and experiences.

A note of caution here, however. We mustn't let our needs and projections overwhelm us to the point where we fool ourselves, as we lurch about looking for something to give us meaning.

I had one client who had multiple precognitive dreams (at least she thought they were) that a famous movie star came to her and made love to her over and over, promising to take her away from all her troubles. This was obviously symbolic, but the dreams were so real to her, and her state of being so fragile, she became convinced that this well-known, handsome man would actually run off with her, and all the scenes in the dreams would happen in the future. She even went out and bought the clothes and lingerie she saw in the dreams. Yikes. I could not persuade her to even consider the idea that the dreams were speaking a symbolic language. In waking life, she started stalking the star, showing up at every event where she could find him, trying to make the prediction come true. Needless to say, it didn't turn out the way she imagined. This is one reason stars have security details. We must take any and all predictions of the future with a giant grain of salt, and keep our feet planted firmly on the ground.

Indeed, I sincerely doubt that most of the predictions of soothsayers, psychics, seers, fortunetellers, prophets, palmists, tarot readers, or oracles come true. Those who do this predicting tend to speak in vagaries, betting that their subjects will ignore the massive number of predictions that don't come true. But you know what? Every now and then something is right on, so we have to make room for that fact too. And even if the generalities and predictions don't hold water, in the process of thinking about them, we investigate our lives and our feelings, and that is not bad medicine. What really matters is whether what we come across in our journey adds a little more understanding to our life.

Most likely, you have experienced a déjà vu moment, or several, in your life. Most people have. This is that bizarre sensation you get when the guy in the blue shirt brushes your arm as he retrieves his Venti Apple Pie Frappuccino at Starbucks. As his shirt touches your skin, something registers in a flash that this has happened before. The guy, the blue shirt, even the kind of coffee drink, it all feels so familiar. It gives you pause, and you wonder: does it mean you really knew it was going to happen or does it mean something else, like you should talk to the guy? Well, of course, be friendly if you want to. Don't look to science for explanations; they're still debating and researching this phenomenon. But the main point here is that the déjà vu experience wakes us up to experiencing life. It makes us feel like we are in contact with something deeper and more exciting than the humdrum noise of life that often engulfs us.

This flash of depth, of synchronicity, happens with dreams as well.

We are, after all, in search of that glorious Land of Awes that appears whenever the true Self stirs and gives us a nod, and if a dream correctly predicts something, it's an invitation to the place where awe dances with destiny. If a dream comes with what appears to be something that will happen in the future, it is another opportunity to look inside these magnificent souls of ours, whether or not the event comes true.

HINDSIGHT DREAMS

Just like déjà vu moments, we may have precognitive dreams with no idea that they are precognitive—until the same event happens in waking life. I call these precognitive hindsight dreams. The realization that the event has happened before in a dream doesn't occur until the event is in progress or concluded. I once had a dream in which I saw dead, bloated, black human bodies floating in the water near New Orleans after a huge storm. In the background, white lifeguards were leading a parade of Mardi Gras-masked people down the beach. When hurricane Katrina hit a few months after this dream, I was watching the news, and I saw the exact image I had seen in my dream—bloated, dead bodies floating in the water. There were no lifeguards or Mardi Gras revelers, but those bodies were the same image from my dream. This is probably the most common type of precognitive dream—when something appears in waking life and syncs up with a dream you've already had.

And the purpose of my having this dream? I don't really know, except it brought to mind that we are all connected in so many ways on this planet. When I was in that moment of recognition, my soul dropped into a deep sense of mourning and loss, which I believe may not have happened so profoundly without the dream. On such an occasion, we realize we are involved in something much larger than just our own myopic view of the world. There is a fabric of society and soul that connects all of us, and every once in a while, those connections flare up with recognition.

Let's look at a few examples of other types of precognitive dreams.

PREDICTIVE DREAMS

Remember the dream I had that led me into dreamwork, the one about my brother having dipped "into the till"? At first, when the phone call came two weeks later and had such a similar theme, this looked like a precognitive *hindsight* dream. But once the conversation started, things got even more intense. So much of what was said on the phone was the exact same script written into the dream. And I could verify it because I had written the dialogue of the dream down right after I had it. Because I knew what was about to be said, that moves the dream into the world of precognitive *predictive* dreams, where you know the outcome in real life before it occurs, because it already happened in a dream. This precognitive predictive dream was a huge turning point in my life. The events and the words spoken were fairly mundane; nothing much changed in my world because my goofy brother somehow avoided being arrested. But knowing what was about to be said based on a dream changed my life, driving me into a deep, lifetime relationship with dreams.

In this same vein, another dream makes an even stronger case for precognitive prediction. This was something I knew and predicted long before the event took place, as opposed the more common scenario where you look back and only see the connection to the dream when the event occurs. In this instance, I knew well beforehand that something would later occur.

On November 15, 2006 I had this dream:

CARRIE IN THE DEEP SOUTH

I travel to New Orleans where my close friend Carrie lives and I drive up a very muddy dirt lane that I am not supposed to drive on. I get out of the car and squeeze past a tree that others have also had to squeeze past. So many people have done this that they have worn the bark off. Oh, my, this will not be easy. I get my head easily through the opening, but my shoulders get stuck. I writhe and push and get farther, but I have to twist my hips back and forth to get through. I finally succeed and I realize why Carrie told me not to come this way. I arrive at her address. I look at the numbers comprised of old destroyed numbers from houses destroyed in Hurricane Katrina. Her address is 212.

When I wake up, I absolutely know for sure that 2:12 is the time that my grandchild will be born. Oddly, there is nothing I see in the dream that directly signals this, except the barkless tree I have to shimmy past, which reminds me of a birth canal. I am so sure of what this means that I call Carrie and tell her the child will be born at 2:12.

My daughter Audrey was eight months pregnant at the time, so I had a month to wait to find out if this was just a hair-brained idea that I couldn't get out of my mind, or the truth.

Audrey went into labor the evening of December 15th, and I got the call to come to the hospital at UCLA around noon on the 16th. My son Philip and I went over to witness the birth, and I set my digital watch to the atomic clock time so I could accurately record the time of birth and see if my prediction was right.

We sat in the room with Audrey's mom, her cousin, and her aunt as the labor progressed. Putting aside the arduous and harrowing aspects of giving birth, I found the entire event of childbirth heavily steeped in the deepest and strongest magic I have ever witnessed—palpable and overwhelming. This was also one of those moments when, selfishly, I was thankful for being a man. I cannot imagine going through this process.

However, 2:12 PM came and went, and Audrey was still in labor. So much for my crazy prediction. The nurse told us to go home, and that they would call us when things got closer.

Around midnight, we got the call to come back in. We rushed back to the hospital room, where the music Audrey had chosen to have playing during the birth was playing for the umpteenth time. It was the soundtrack for *Ashes and Snow*, an art installation by Gregory Colbert about animals and people that we had seen on Santa Monica beach. My heart went out to her. She had endured 36 hours of labor.

And finally, it happened. Out came this lovely, beautiful baby girl. Birth is something so mystical, with a presence, a feel, a sense of awe that fills the space at the moment, and it will bowl you over. You can feel the passage

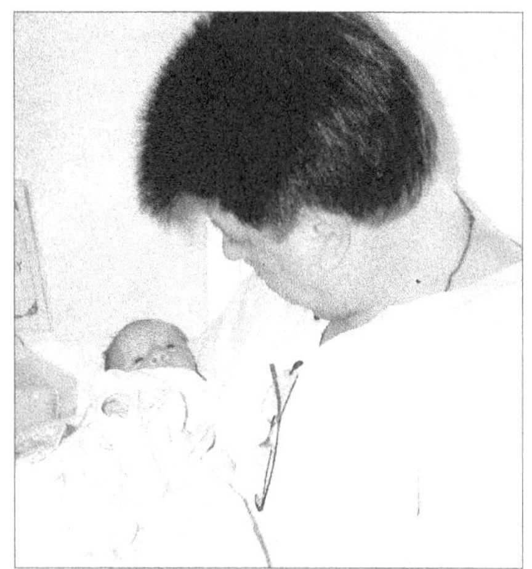

of something from another place into the present. In this rare moment, this world and the other world are connected via the door of birth. Talk about a visit to the Land of Awes.

So, being me, I looked at my watch—and to my mild disappointment, it read 2:13 AM. I had missed my prediction by a minute. Damn.

But then the doctor announced loudly, "Time of birth, 2:12."

Close enough! In the time it took for me to bask in the magic of the event, the minute on my watch had rolled over. But I was satisfied; my provable prediction came true.

And what does this mean? Am I a clairvoyant who sees into the future? Should I open a tarot-reading shack where I predict people's lives? Oh, hell, no. This was a personal moment when I was in touch with something deep and meaningful, a connection to something beyond my own understanding—and not controllable.

As I held that wondrous being for the first time, moments after she was born, she looked into my eyes and smiled. I know babies are not supposed to be able to focus on things just after birth, but this little creature looked into me, saw me, and melted me. She has been my deep abiding buddy ever since. Perhaps a bit of that connection she and I have is enhanced because I listened to some intuitive thing that bubbled up out of a dream about New Orleans.

WARNING DREAMS

Also in the canon of precognitive dreams is the warning dream. Yes, dreams can sometimes save us from something. I do not understand how this all works; I just know it does.

Let me give you an example of a precognitive warning dream, the most powerful example of such to come out of my dream group to date. This comes from my friend Deborah Dutilh, who allowed me to tell her story here.

WEARING J-F'S SHOES AT SEAL BEACH

Jean-Francois did a painting of a seal at the beach. A man sees the painting and wants it. He tells me my paintings are just as good, too. I put on Jean-Francois's hiking boots with red laces and go to the beach. I'm pushing a shopping cart to the store at the beach. It looks like a hardware store. Jean-Francois is still there.

Then at the beach, I see a blonde woman who has a boat. She brings the boat to the shore, jumps off and comes up to the man who is sitting there with his penis out. She flips his penis and says it's not such a big deal. This makes the man very mad. She jumps on the boat and then a huge seal jumps on the boat behind her. The seal is very friendly and she pets him. They both leave on the boat.

Then J-F and I are walking on the beach. We stop and sit down and he sits in front of me and leans back against me. I still have his boots with the red laces on. It's a very affectionate moment.

J-F and I are in his car in the store and are leaving the store. We drive all the way down to the last aisle, turn down the aisle, and that's the end of the dream.

Deb brought this dream to group not long after having it.

We worked it extensively, having fun with the sexual content—the blonde boldly flipping a penis—and the idea of a car going up and down aisles in a store. But there was something else here underneath the seemingly pleasant romp on the beach. For one thing, I was aware that Jean-Francois, the dreamer's husband and father of her children, had died two years before the dream. Although he had been a mountain climber, interestingly, Jean-Francois paints an ocean animal, a seal, and then the seal shows up later in

the dream, as though to indicate the seal has some important role to play. This emphasis by the dream on the idea of the "seal" stands out.

If the sea symbolizes the unconscious, and we consider that seals are one of a handful of creatures that live both in and out of the sea (of the unconscious), that makes them natural messengers from the unconscious. Their black coat possibly symbolizes the shadow side, or unconscious thoughts arising. What dark, unconscious message is Jean-Francois trying to give to us?

This is also a visitation dream, since Jean-Francois is not only present, but in an intimate moment, he sits against Deb. It feels like something big is afoot here.

The drawing is dominated by the three Jean-Francois images. I get the feeling that this guy has something to say. When we talk about that as we project on the dream, the group is moved by the affection of this man, and we talk about that and what Deb's relationship to him had been.

Lucy from the group looks at the store and asks, "What does the future hold in 'store' for us?"

I notice that the lower right picture of Jean-Francois, where he is sitting up against Deb, has a ghost-like quality, as though Deb is a ghost being absorbed by Jean-Francois. This adds to the thought and feeling that she and this deceased man are still tied together somehow, and it feels slightly ominous to me.

For some reason, I key into the part of the dream where she is walking on the beach with her late husband. Oddly, she is wearing the hiking boots that he always wore, with their long red laces. I immediately think about "walking in the shoes" of someone else. We work further on the dream, talking about her relationship to her husband, to the sense of loss, addressing the presence of the swift currents of water that appear in the drawing and what they could mean, and so forth. But the "walking in the shoes" thing keeps hanging in my soul as being really important.

What I don't want to say is that as soon as Deb described walking in his shoes, I immediately jumped to the horrid fact that Jean-Francois died of brain cancer—Glioblastoma multiforme (GBM), the most aggressive and almost always fatal form of brain cancer (the same cancer that killed John McCain). I wonder if that is the piece of "walking in his shoes" that should be addressed. I don't want to say anything, and try to dismiss it, but it won't retreat into the unconscious. It is the "elephant in the room," but I feel like it is too ominous to say to someone—"Hey, Deb, maybe you have that same cancer Jean-Francois had. You ought to have it checked out." But, I feel like I need to bring it up in some subtle way.

With this in mind, I launch privately into another projection. Jean-Francois starts the dream, in a sense, by "sealing" the dreamer's fate when he draws that seal. That seal of fate then shows up incarnated as the giant mammal that jumps into the boat with the blonde woman. The seal must have a connection with this woman. The blonde woman who jumps into the boat with the dark seal suddenly reminds me of the angel of death, sailing off with the shadow messenger in the form of a black seal to the land of the dead, to return later.

I keep quiet about that projection, but I keep steering the discussion back to her relationship with her husband, asking in different ways, "So, are there ways that I am walking in any of the paths that my husband walked?" We talk about the children she had with him, and her relationship to them, and then finally she says, "You know he died of brain cancer two years ago." Ahh . . . I am relieved. We now have enough light in the room to see the huge elephant with hiking boots on. We go on to talk about that, saying nothing outright, but my intuitive sense feels relief that we have allowed a warning about cancer to at least enter the room. So often in working dreams, an entire subtext sits invisibly floating in the air.

Later, keying on the double seals in the dream, I thought about Deb and Jean-Francois being "sealed" together somehow. I also thought it significant that she titled the dream *Wearing J-F's Shoes at Seal Beach.* This dream was most likely not about her having cancer, but we had at least touched that base and allowed it to rise to the level of consciousness. We may not have had a definitive understanding of the dream, but by the end, the clear elephant in the room was the cancer that had killed Jean-Francois.

About two weeks later, as Deb tells it, she started having horrible migraine headaches that became debilitating. She went to the doctor, and he gave her medication for it, but Deb started thinking about that damn dream. Deb is a highly intuitive dreamer who really gets the depth of dreams and has spent a huge amount of time digging deep into their psychology and meaning.

She started wondering about that elephant-in-the-room question of whether she might have the same cancer that her husband had suffered. It was really outside the world of reason, but Deb and her sons had already been through this experience with her late husband. She asked the doctor if he believed in the power of dreams to predict illness. When he said he did (I am amazed by that), she requested an MRI, which he scheduled.

What they discovered was Deb's greatest fear, the thing that her intuition and dream had told her. She had that same brain cancer that had killed her husband. It was in its early stages of development and would not have been detected until much later if Deb had not insisted on looking for it. The doctors were astounded. They operated, opening up her skull and removing the tumor. Deb then went through chemotherapy and radiation therapy, losing her hair and living through the nightmare of chasing the cancer demon. The life expectancy of survivors of this most aggressive form of brain cancer is about 18 months, and Deb knew this. When she returned to our group, she was weak and scarred from the experience, but my god, this woman was alive like you have never seen someone alive. When you looked into her face, you could see all the way to the back of her soul.

Everything changed for her. She became involved in the GBM community of survivors, sharing her story and listening and learning in this dire yet life-filled place of people facing life fully armed with such knowledge. She wrote a one-woman show about her experience and performed it in Los Angeles, then took it to the Edinburgh Fringe Festival. And she has been inspiring people ever since. As I write this, it has been seven, count them, seven years since her diagnosis. Only five percent of people in her age group make it to five years. Deb is alive and going strong, beating the odds so far with no recurrence of the cancer, and she is living a full life because she listened to a dream.

Gotta love that, no?

Where do these warnings come from? I don't really know. In this case, I would look to a deep somatic connection for the answer. When she had the dream, the cancer was there, and the body on some level knew that. The body and the unconscious have a relationship we understand little, but here, they conspired to bring to consciousness a warning about a fatal illness. Dreams are connected to that deep, unseen knowledge the body has.

And there is a follow-up to the precognitive dream that helped save her life. In September 2018, Deb brought another dream to the group, from July of that year, which she titled *I'm Done!*

I'M DONE!

I'm lying in bed and the bedroom door is ajar. There's a pair of leather hiking boots not far from the door. Suddenly the boots quietly slide or walk around and behind the open door. Then the door closes with the long well-worn red shoelaces stretched out flat underneath the door. And then, as if being sucked up like spaghetti, the laces disappear behind the door. I can't recall if I felt a presence or just knew the boots belonged to Jean-Francois, my late husband.

So here are those hiking boots again, so distinctive with their red laces. Only this time, five years after the first dream, they come not as a warning, but as an agent of release.

Deb writes this just after waking from the dream: "I wake up very much in the present, ready to start my day. This feeling has been unusual lately, so I am pleasantly surprised to have it. I had wanted to write a sequel to my one-woman show and even signed up for the workshop. But honestly, I have not been motivated at all to go backwards. I'm drawing myself away from any desire to inspire others with my story. I want to focus freely on my life in the present moment, create something new. This attitude feels so good and healthy. The laces are worn-out and frayed, untangled as if I've milked this story for all it's worth."

What an inspiration this was to all of us in the group. There was not much we needed to say or work on with this dream. Deb was powerfully present on this night, and the feeling was that it was time for her to start living for herself, to let this story walk out the door on its own and let the frayed, old laces be sucked up into history like spaghetti. And she is out there now, charging through life, torpedoes be damned.

Something else has to be said here. In this last example, you can see the long-term effects of working with your dreams. This French mountain climber and his iconic boots with red laces is a dream figure that has stayed closely aligned with Deb and her dreams and her creativity for seven years. They are the same boots that she first walked in and that led her to discover her illness, and they appear again in this last dream to tell her it is time to move on. Dreams are not just "one offs" that come to tell us something and then disappear. An entire inner world inside us functions at night, and it stays ever so closely attuned to our psyches, our souls, delivering up guidance every damn night for around two hours or more per dream. And some part of us hears it and benefits from it.

Dreams—the entire world of dream figures and everything surrounding them—have a life of their own. They seem to benefit and guide us, even if we do not recall everything. With what we do recall, it is good to track repeating themes, characters, and objects. We all have some form of frayed red laces that tie us to the deeper part of ourselves and contribute to the flow of our beautiful life up here in the conscious world.

CHAPTER 14

VISITATION DREAMS

The Grief Eater Meets and Eats the Dad

No man is an island,
entire of itself;
every man is a piece of the continent,
a part of the main.
If a clod be washed away by the sea,
Europe is the less,
as well as if a promontory were,
as well as if a manor of thy friend's
or of thine own were.
Any man's death diminishes me,
because I am involved in mankind;
and therefore never send to know for whom the bell tolls;
it tolls for thee.

JOHN DONNE (1623)

Relationships are essential to our well-being. Even bad ones. Where we stand on issues, how we feel, how we think, what we are passionate about, how we balance our lives—all are deeply influenced by our relationships. When something traumatic happens to us, it is that trusted friend or family member who gets to listen patiently as we explain, project, and emote. Such listening not only helps us clarify our thoughts and emotions, it also enriches the listener as they practice empathy in relating our experience to their own. In this exchange between imperfect beings, we find direction and purpose stumbling through the dark maze of life together, sharing thoughts, emotions, and ideas.

And sometimes we lose one of those important connections, someone who has been a candle of enlightenment, helping us find our way along the road that inevitably concludes in death. When such a loss happens, it leaves a gap in our life, as we battle against being engulfed in the darkness without this precious connection. Our unconscious is also affected by this loss and seeks a way to deal with it. That may be at least one reason why visitation dreams happen. Visitation dreams are when someone, usually an individual who has passed on, visits us in our dream.

I used to think visitation dreams were just wishful thinking—the soul trying to make sense of someone's passing. Losing someone close to us is so profoundly difficult and unsettling, our soul craves connection to what it has lost permanently. So, it is natural that our unconscious might make up an image of the person and present it to us in the form of a dream.

However, after working with many dreams in which a loved one has come back, I have changed my view on such things. It just feels like there is something else going on here, and I can't really explain it. Visitation dreams move us into that place of awe so easily. It may be true on one level that we are inventing something that gives us closure, but does that really matter? Ofttimes, magic is afoot when someone visits from the other side—and in that magic, life renews. Having a visitation dream can give us a way to continue a relationship that has been essential to our own enlightenment. It reminds us that the relationship still resides inside our soul, and we can access it there when we need it.

SLIDING INTO PARADISE

Here is an example of a visitation dream I worked recently. The dreamer, Laurent, is a 60-year-old Frenchman who lives in Paris and works worldwide in social and economic development. He is married to a French novelist named Ana who is originally from Vietnam. Laurent developed a good relationship with Ana's father, who lived into his 90s. When Laurent's father-in-law reached his last days and it became clear that he was about to pass, Laurent and Ana hopped on the next plane to see him.

When they arrived at his bedside in Los Angeles, he recognized Ana, but not Laurent. Laurent was deeply saddened that he didn't have a chance to reconnect one last time before this man passed over. They had had a relationship that engendered joy and respect. Several months later, Laurent had the following dream.

THE CABLE

I walk into my bedroom, which is on the second or third floor, which is pretty high up. It is my bedroom, but not one I am familiar with. I am about to shave and I look over and I see my father-in-law, Kha, resting on the bed in the center of the room. I am surprised to see him since he had passed away nine months ago, but here he is. It is a joy to see him! He starts to get up from the bed and says, "I am sorry, I am disturbing you." I insist that it is fine, perfectly fine and he is not disturbing me at all. He insists, though, "I am disturbing you. I will go." I tell him again, more insistently, that he is not disturbing me at all, and that in fact, it is so good to see him. He gently smiles at me.

He walks over to the window and looks down to the garden below. He looks back at me, then takes a harness and puts it around his waist and hooks it into a black cable that runs from the window down into the garden. He leaps out the window and slides down the cable to the enclosed garden below. I go over to the window and see him down below in the garden. He is smiling and yells up to me, "Tu vois, c'est rien!" (You see, it's nothing!) He waves and moves on.

This is a simple but powerful visitation dream. As Laurent and I talked about it, he was focused first on the exchange with Kha, who was so apologetic

about disturbing him. Laurent's feelings were wonderful, almost overwhelming, as he reconnected with this man, which he hadn't been able to do in waking life.

Then Kha goes to the window and stands in it, looking back at the dreamer. The feeling we both got from this was that it was the window that separates this world from the other world, the window of death that we will all stand at one day.

Now the dream does something strange. Kha doesn't leap out, he doesn't float out, he doesn't sprout wings, he doesn't just disappear—he puts a harness on, clips it to a black metal cable, and slides down it. I asked Laurent about his associations with such a thing, and he related that he had recently watched a 1979 French movie thriller titled *Flic Ou Voyou (Cop or Hood)*, where the hero, played by Jean-Paul Belmondo, escaped from certain capture by doing exactly this, sliding down a cable to freedom.

This method of moving from the high spot quickly down into the earth beneath is a bit scary, and the dream makes sure we see this. Death is a scary thing, and this reminded both of us that at some point in the future, we will have to stand between worlds and take the plunge into death and beyond. But Kha lands in a walled garden, which is curious. Why a walled garden? Well, a bit of digging turns this up:

> Curiously, the literal meaning of the word Paradise is Walled Garden, but it has long since lost that meaning. The word "paradise" entered English from the French *paradis,* inherited from the Latin *paradisus,* from the Greek *paradeisos,* and ultimately from an Old Iranian root, attested in Avestan as *pairi.daeza*. The literal meaning of this Eastern Old Iranian language word is "walled around" + "to create, make."
>
> PAUL AMERIGO PAIO
> on StackExchange.com

In the biblical tradition, this is the Garden of Eden, which was a walled garden, and a paradise. So, Kha slides down into "paradise," that place of death and renewal. When we die, each and every one of us slides down into a walled garden of paradise: our ashes or our bodies end up back in Mother Earth's garden, whether we like it or not.

In this dream Kha, our intrepid daredevil, shows us how to cross over, sliding swiftly down into the walled garden. This is a curious approach and seems carefully specific. The dream visualizes this strong connection between the two worlds, as if wanting the dreamer to know that the sturdy cable will be there when it is time for any of us to take the plunge into Mother Earth's garden "paradise," where life not only ends but renews.

And then comes the touching ending. He looks up at Laurent, smiles, and declares, "*Tu vois, c'est rien!*" (You see, it's nothing!), telling us that death is just a slide down a cable, and with a final wave, off he goes. This simple visitation dream has done its work—Laurent and I are certainly in a state of awe as we finish the dreamwork, for the dream has worked its magic on us. The next time someone asks me if I am afraid of death I will declare, "*Tu vois, c'est rien!*" Well, to be honest I will probably say, "You see, it's nothing!" because my command of French is a bit dubious.

THE GRIEF EATER

Not all visitation dreams, however, are as benevolent as this one. Many times, people have deeply unresolved issues with those who pass on, and their dreams will reflect that and sometimes offer up help in resolving those issues. When someone passes to the other side, it doesn't fix our deep-seated anger, disappointment, or sense of abandonment unless we do the work necessary to resolve our own feelings.

Here is a dream from a 35-year-old woman whose father committed suicide when she was 17 by shooting himself while talking to her mother on the phone. It is not only a visitation dream, it also has an element of lucidity.

WELCOME HOME

I'm in my childhood home. My mom and brother are there. We're all just doing chores around the house, when my dad comes home. "Oh, no," I think to myself. "Here he is again." He does what he often does in these dreams, which is to lurk around the edges of the house. This time he's especially sulky and the productive energy in the house has shifted. Everything becomes tainted with his presence. This has happened so many times before, and I just hate it. Then I make a conscious decision in the dream; I do what I have never done in a dream before. I look at him and say, "Well what? You obviously aren't happy and have something to say. Instead of just sitting there like you always do, why don't you tell us what's wrong?"

He looks at me with that deeply depressed countenance he always has in every dream and then dematerializes. He has disappeared in other dreams, so I am not surprised that he would disappear again, but this time it is different. He doesn't just disappear, he dematerializes and rematerializes inside of me. In order to answer my question, he possesses my body. My senses are sped up. My breath and vision are double speed and I feel intense emotion. I feel rage, and sadness. This is scary and yet fascinating. I am feeling everything that my father felt before he committed suicide when I was 17. As him, I am furious with my awful wife. She has this plot to ruin my life! Not just ignore me or hurt me, this woman is hell-bent on ruining my life. What is the point of living if my life is ruined? I want to kill her. It is the only way I can move forward. I have to kill her. I will figure out a way to kill her. (Note—my father actually did plan to kill my mother near the end of his life.)

I become aware that I'm feeling everything he felt before he ended his life. This is overwhelming, distressing and fascinating at the same time. I am not sure I can handle any more of this. He leaves my body.

I think to myself, "Damn, that was intense. I need to get grounded and I need help to do it." I ask out loud if any of my animal spirits are willing to come and help me. I look down and there is the black panther, the one from the underground tomb and the wild turkey dream. I'm happy and surprised to see her.

I wake up.

The dreamer brought this dream to the dream group, drew a picture of it, and shared it. We were so bowled over by it we were speechless. Just sharing it and laying it out in visual form brought us down into that place of awe and dread and wonder that something like this elicits. Everyone in the room felt their own version of this malevolent spirit as the dreamer reexperienced this harrowing event.

We had heard other dreams of hers where the father had appeared, but this one crossed into new territory. The dreamer had actually experienced the father's feelings inside herself, and so had we. And in that empathy, there was healing. The dreamer was quite calm and resolved about the dream, even during the telling, which allowed us to let the experience wash over us instead of becoming something that we had to work through.

I wondered about this, and I voiced my opinion that it seemed like a lot of work had been done already on the dream before she got here. The dreamer explained that she had continued the process of the dream by doing some active imagination. Active imagination is a process Carl Jung dreamed up, so to speak, which can be used to bridge the gap between the unconscious and the conscious. In a meditative state, you employ imagination, and even fantasy, to enable the unconscious to yield illuminating images and narrative elements.

Here is what she did: "I brought the panther, my father, and I together. The panther began eating my father bit by bit. Starting from the head all the way to his toes. She ate him bones and all, like a gingerbread cookie. At one point the panther looked back at me and told me she was a grief eater."

She used this powerful predator animal that had been a companion in other dreams to eat the grief. Wow. What a potent tool to help heal the extreme grief of such a monumental and debilitating trauma. This speaks volumes.

The main point about visitation dreams is not whether people live beyond this life as we know it or not. The importance is in how these dreams affect the dreamer. Whether the wisdom and comfort or the discomfort and haunting come from the other side or from our own souls doesn't matter. When someone who has passed on appears in a dream, it is an invitation to stand in the Land of Awes and use the past and this experience to see forward in our lives.

CHAPTER 15

AFFIRMATION DREAMS

Twelve Steps Can Be a Long Journey

This whole creation is essentially subjective, and the dream is the theater where the dreamer is at once scene, actor, prompter, stage manager, author, audience, and critic.

CARL JUNG

General Aspects of Dream Psychology (1928)

WHEN DREAMS SMILE AT US

Dreams usually come to show us something we don't know or aren't aware of. They want us to see our foibles and follies and how to deal with them. They usually offer up new information about our lives. When I work with a dream that seems to exclusively tell us things we already know, a dream that is rosy and positive, I do so with suspicion. I look deeper for something that has been left out, and more often than not we find something lurking there.

But that is not always the case. So many of our dreams deal with things that need correction or speak to our difficulties, shortcomings, and missteps that it is refreshing sometimes to have a dream that is just a joyous celebration of the dreamer's life or attitude. I call these affirmation dreams. They are also called mastery dreams.

Affirmation dreams come to confirm that the course we are on is right and true. Even though we are consciously aware that we did indeed divorce that jerk, and it was clearly a good thing, doubts and regrets can linger subconsciously. An affirmation dream sometimes comes to reassure us that, yes, moving on from Mr. Abusive is the correct course—and we may need to hear that in this moment in order to move on or move deeper. Just like good friends, our dreams can give us that reassurance we need.

You can imagine that the unconscious has an absolutely huge list of things it wants you to deal with and prioritizes things to send you via symbolic messages in your dreams. The dream gods probably fret there every night in the dark trying to figure out whether to send you a dream about your relationship, your work, your health, your misplaced priorities, your book you are writing, your bad feelings towards your sister, your obsession with dark chocolate, your insecurities, or a hundred other things. Sometimes, though, an affirmation dream gets bumped up the list, because you need to know how great you are. Sometimes we just need a really pleasant dream to lift our self-assurance and place us on a small pedestal for a moment.

SINGING WITH MOTHER EARTH

Here is a dream that I awoke from smiling and singing:

SINGING INTO THE DEEP

I am at church. It is a church on two different levels at the same time. It has the feel of the Mormon church from my past, and also the feel of a cathedral, like Chartres Cathedral. As I look about, I realize that this is indeed Chartres Cathedral with its distinctive "Chartres blue" stained glass. The church is full and a service is in progress, which feels Mormon. I sit in the middle of my family. We are all dressed in black and white and all nine of us are lined up in the pews like little penguins.

Just as services are about to start, a large Black family comes in and they want a funeral. They have the body with them in an open casket, which they carry down the aisle. They, of course, take precedence over the boring old service that was about to happen. Oh, this is something exciting and meaningful, at least to me. Having a Black family here displeases my family, and they all sneak out en masse.

The mourning family is trying to figure out the logistics of things and they head down into the crypt under the Cathedral, carrying the casket with them. I notice that the guy in the coffin looks a lot like me, only Black. I am now sitting at the back of the Cathedral with this huge woman. She is part of this group that came in. Somehow, she just magically appears next to me. How strange. She sits on the bench next to me, but these are no longer stone benches, but are made of earth. This woman is extremely large and I am leaning into her left side, as her body molds around me. Damn, this feels warm and comfortable. We rock together, and she starts singing this wonderful song about "… going down into the deep … Going down into the deep." I love this, and start singing the chorus of this song about plunging to the deepest part of the ocean, which I also know has an echo of the carrying of the casket down into the crypt. Perhaps this is the song we are rehearsing for the funeral service. As I sway back and forth with this wonderful woman with the deep pleasing voice, that vibrates through my body, I am reminded of the summers in North Carolina in my youth where we would drive past the "Black church" as my mother called it and the most wonderful sounds would come out of the open windows. I would ask why we couldn't go to church there and my mother would look at me appalled saying, "Because it is the Black church, that's why."

Some tall man with muscles sitting next to me tells me I shouldn't do this, that I will just get involved and this is not right . . . I scoff at him and pointedly increase my joy and enthusiasm for this, raising my singing voice further. He suddenly sees and feels my enthusiasm and I win him over. He moves closer to me and joins in the singing and swaying. I feel so good, rocking and singing with this huge Black woman, and the people in the pews start enjoying this. The three of us are vibrating with joy and we start laughing in delight.

There is a whole lot in this dream we could go into, especially about the shadow figure in the coffin, and the fact that, in waking life, unbeknownst to me (until Jeremy Taylor pointed it out), there is a Black Madonna in the crypt in Chartres Cathedral, which takes the dream down into a place I hadn't anticipated—but we will confine ourselves to talking about this huge Black woman.

For me, this is Mother Earth. I mean, we are suddenly sitting on the earth, and she envelopes me, and I feel like I am back in the womb, so, yep, I am going with Mother Earth here. What the dream says to me is that in moving away from my family's Mormonism (they all march out like little penguins when the Black people show up), I chose the right path, and now I have this wonderful relationship with the earthy mother and know how to sing from the soulful depths of my being. When I awoke from this dream, I felt such a deep sense of affirmation of my soul at peace. Don't tell anyone, especially my neighbors, but sometimes on warm summer days I sit quietly in my yard and sway back and forth softly singing, "Into the deep, into the deep." I don't know why, but it just feels so damn good to do that.

TWELVE STEPS

Here is another affirmation dream, from someone I work with in the movie industry. It seemed at first glance to be a distressing mess but turned out to be a delightful affirmation dream.

MONKEY POOP

The dream begins where I am wandering around in an Asian market in China or Japan or some such place. There are outdoor stalls filled with produce and goods, with sellers and people busy shopping and talking. It is a lively place. I am a bit confused, but I wander down through the market and notice that people ignore me, and are downright disdainful of me. Also, every person I meet points in a direction where I need to go. So, I go there. If so many people are pointing for me to go to this passageway, I guess I will go. I enter a passageway off the marketplace, passing under an arch. When I do, monkeys appear from everywhere and start shitting on me! Holy crap!

They are relentless, and I end up covered head to toe in monkey shit, and, god, it smells horrid. I cannot escape this. I cannot go back through the arch, so I run forward as the monkey shit continues to rain down on me. I am exhausted by the end of the gauntlet, and I stand at the end of the passage covered in monkey shit, disgusted by my own smell.

Finally, I exit the passageway through another archway. To my delight, there is a wonderful shower that is given to me, water appears from everywhere and all of the monkey shit is washed off. Every damn bit of it. And now, I notice as I walk through the market, drying off, that people greet me and smile and interact with me. I think these are the same people from before, but now I am part of the foreign place.

This particular drawing on the next page is a bit of a cipher, but still an essential part of understanding the dream. With its simple stick figures and words, this should encourage people who are reticent to draw their dream. When the dreamer drew the picture, certain elements changed

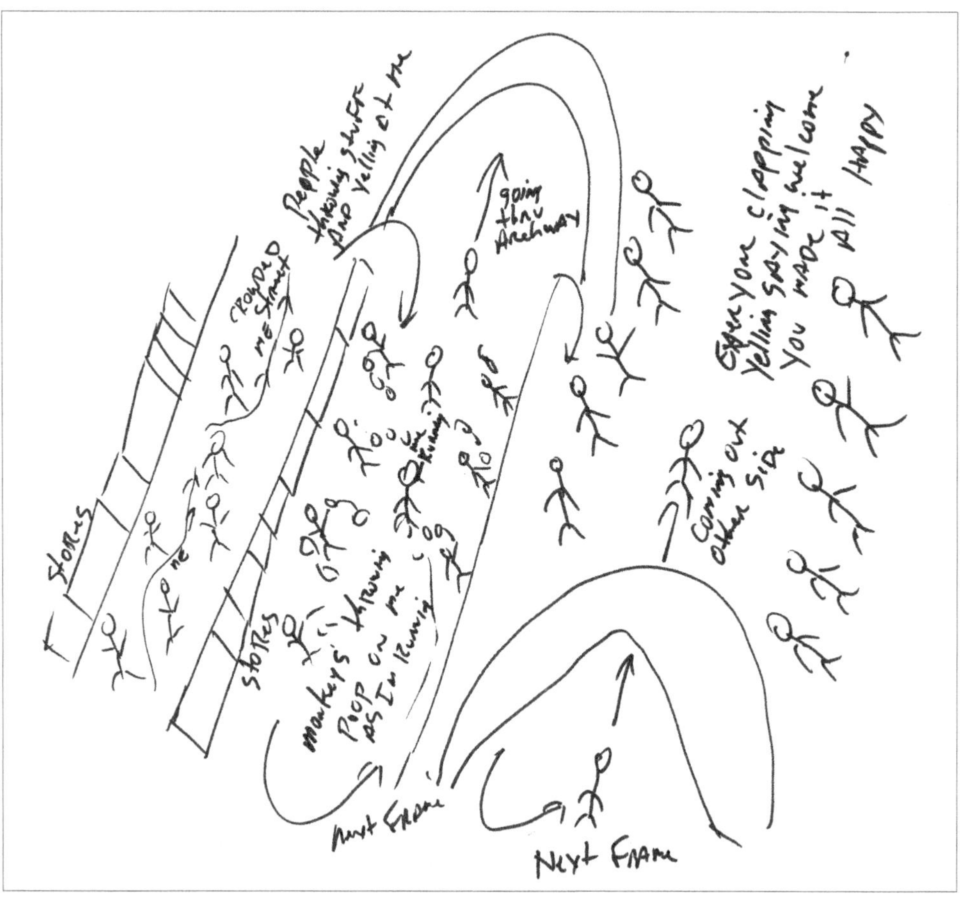

from the dream report, and new elements appeared. In the picture, when the dreamer enters the crowded street full of stores (on the bottom left), the people are not just ignoring him, they are also yelling and throwing things at him, something not in the dream report.

The dreamer drew the dream in three sections, starting to reading from left to right, each time restarting from the bottom. The first section is the people throwing things at him and pointing him to move into the second section. The second section is the gauntlet of monkeys throwing poop on him (I count 12 balls of poop being thrown). The poop-throwing ends as he passes through an arch at the end of the second section (at the top). The third section brings the arch down to the bottom to start the "next frame" and makes it even larger, where we start again from the bottom.

The arch is a wonderful delineation of a clear symbol of passage. It is not just a blank space, or a door or a window, but an arch. For me it relates to the feminine both in the sense of the curved shape and because it echoes the shape of the vagina, that wondrous place designed to bring forth life. The dreamer is being reborn into a new life, through a new birth canal. This idea is further supported by what the dreamer wrote here on the drawing—"coming out other side." The use of three panels also conforms to the classic fairy tale trope of "the third time's the charm," as our hero finds success in the third attempt. Another addition not in the dream report but included in the drawing is the reaction of the people at the end-—"Everyone clapping, yelling saying welcome, you made it."

It is important to remember that this dream is the dreamer's, and the context of his life is paramount to any possible understanding of the dream.

So how is getting shat on by a bunch of monkeys an affirmation dream? Well, it turns out that the dreamer is an alcoholic about four years into recovery. One day his wife pulled out a huge bottle of booze, slammed it down in front of him, and said, "It's this or me. Make your choice." He had heard about Alcoholics Anonymous from people who had been through the program (think of the people pointing to the passage in the dream), and that very night he called up a guy who had been in AA and went to his first meeting. It was a difficult and humbling undertaking, but he went to meeting after meeting—and by sheer determination and lots and lots of help from others in the program, he stayed sober and focused. He chose to save his marriage and himself and hasn't touched a drop since that day. He went from being consumed with drinking to being the guy they call to speak at various AA meetings—where they consume his wisdom instead of booze.

So, this dream, on one level, reflects this journey. He starts out in a "foreign" place where, like the people in the dream, everyone basically ignores him except to throw things at him. People throwing things is a physical manifestation of the verbal insistence to go down a different path. I mean, who wants to be involved with someone whose real love is a bottle of booze? They don't really want to have a relationship with a drunk except to point out the path to sobriety. And that had happened in his waking life. People around him became more distant and kept giving him subtle and not-so-subtle hints about seeking help for his drinking.

Once he decides to enter the passage of sobriety, what appears? Why, none other than the monkey on his back, of course. One doesn't just waltz into sobriety. Those monkeys that are the years of drinking and ignoring others now come to torture him on his hero's journey through the gauntlet of recovery. When I asked him how long the passage in his dream was, he explained it was short, maybe only like 12 steps or so.

"You mean like the 12 steps in a 12-step program like Alcoholics Anonymous?" I asked.

"Oh hell, you're right!" was his response. He was bowled over by this—a huge "aha" moment.

And then there is the ritual shower of emotion that comes after completing—well, it is never complete, now is it?—the 12 steps it takes to get through the passageway of monkey shit. At some point in the recovery, there is a baptism, a renewal of soul, an opening of the eyes. After a great deal of soul-searching and difficult work, our dreamer was baptized into a new passage where his friends and family cheered on the new man. He renewed relationships to the people who, before sobriety, were simply foreign to him.

So, this dream comes to remind him of how far he has come and how remarkable he is. It affirms his journey into sobriety. And in affirming, it helps keep him moving forward with a clear eye to the future and a remembrance of what it smells like to have monkey shit all over him.

When affirmation comes in a dream, grab it and cherish it. We are unique and powerful souls pushing through the muck and mire of life, and now and again our dreams want us to know how wonderful and awe-inspiring we are, no matter what other detritus and toxic impediments surround us. Think about the last time someone told you how wonderful you are. Maybe you didn't hear them. Perhaps your dreams are telling you what an amazing being you are, but are you listening?

PART 7

SEX, DEATH, AND OTHER FACTS OF LIFE

When Dreams Speak to Life's Big Themes

CHAPTER 16

BIG DREAMS

Finding Venus and the Elixir of Life

"Big dreams," as originally conceptualized by C.G. Jung, are rare, extremely vivid, and highly memorable dreams that people experience as being dramatically different from the relatively mundane and forgettable contents of "little dreams."

KELLY BULKELEY, PH.D.
Dreaming in the Digital Age

What constitutes a "big" dream? In my experience, it is not necessarily a long dream or one with angels and gods and flying camels who quote the *Kama Sutra*, but one that has a deep, lasting impact on the dreamer and often is a portal to meaningful change.

For instance, I had a client who reported a simple dream:

I am standing inches away from my mother's face. She takes my face in her hands and smiles.

Simple enough, and it just seems like a small, pleasant dream, but during the telling, there was electricity in the room, and the dreamer dissolved into tears. When it evokes such a strong emotional response from the dreamer, this moves the dream to a different level of significance. However, the fact that it triggers this deep emotion doesn't necessarily make it "big" either.

This is also a visitation dream because of the presence of the mother who has journeyed to the other side, but that also doesn't in and of itself make it a "big" dream.

This is a "big" dream because of the context and the quality of the connection to the Land of Awes—that deep interior place where real magic happens. Big dreams carry such power that they often herald or initiate a turning point in the dreamer's life.

The dreamer's mother had passed to the other side about six weeks prior to the dream. She and her mother had been on god-awful terms for most of her adult life, which the dreamer had struggled with and tried to reconcile, but that effort had failed. Her mother always scowled and berated her for her failures, which sent the dreamer into a spin every time it happened. They had a miserable relationship that always depressed her.

For the dreamer, the smile and touch in the dream made a sincere connection to her mother (and via projection, the mother within herself)—something she had always wanted and now could have. An abiding sense of genuine awe accompanied this visitation, and it shifted the course of this woman's life. It didn't happen overnight, but the dream was the touchstone for the dreamer's work on her relationship to the feminine—work still in progress. From that point forward, she carried that image of her mother smiling into her attitude towards others. She brought that smile and connection into her personal relationships, and her life expanded significantly. That's what makes it a "big" dream.

SEX WITH ANGELINA JOLIE

"Big" dreams can come in many forms, but often they are like myths or fairy tales in that they have some quality that rises above the personal into the stratosphere of magic, or transcendence. When someone tells a "big" dream, an inner door opens and invites us into our own souls, the soul of the dreamer, and the maelstrom of the collective unconscious.

Let's look at one of my own big dreams, one that invited a true change of course in my life.

BLACK HORSES

I am at a beautiful retreat like Esalen in Big Sur. It is a place of healing. There are a dozen of us around this heavy wooden table covered in a white cloth; we're eating a banquet and there are deep conversations going on. I strike up a conversation with Victor Garber, the actor. I tell him that I really admire the character that he played in a television show about spies titled Alias. We talk about how incredible it is that he drops into this dark, angry, controlled character so easily. I tell him that I know what that is like, to be a hardened person with great depth. We have a good connection. Suddenly, without warning, he morphs into Angelina Jolie.

Oh, my god, Angelia Jolie is standing in front of me, and double oh my god, she is looking straight at me, and her eyes light up. She smiles, cocks her head just a bit and moves towards me. Her body moves poetically as she comes over to me. She stands solidly in front of me, places her hands on my shoulders and looks straight into my eyes without blinking. She looks deep into me and insists that we go outside and make love. "Well," I think, "If Angelina Jolie insists we make love, who am I to say no?"

There is a sloping sidewalk on the outside grounds, and we lay down there. There are people all around, walking and playing and reading on benches. She takes off her top and exposes a brown, wet see-through T-shirt made of just a few pieces of thin vine fiber that has hieroglyphic writing on it. We have sex. Oh my god, this is incredible, this is astounding love-making, my spirit soars, my senses heighten, I am in heaven.

Now I take my hand and reach into her chest and make love to her heart. As I do this, I can feel my own heart and the emotions exploding from it. I am making love with my heart, and it is wonderful. I listen closely to her heart as I make love to it with my hands. I sync up our heart rhythms and we are one in this glorious adventure.

Suddenly a UPS guy in his brown uniform pushing a brown package on a dolly down the sidewalk runs into us. He smashes right into our bodies and gives us a look, like, "You're blocking the sidewalk, you idiots." He asks me: "Aren't you working?" And I reply, "Am I working? Can't you see that I am making love to Angelina Jolie?" He shrugs and moves on.

We continue making love for a long time, and the longer it goes on, the more I relax into my body and the more heightened my spirit becomes. This is truly beautiful, and it makes me feel in touch with myself and very self-confident and as though I am moving in a new direction inside myself. Wow. There are images of horses that appear while making love. Moving black horses. The entire experience moves into the experience of watching these powerful black horses move poetically across the sky. I feel the rhythm of the powerful horses in my body.

Now it is after the lovemaking and it is time for me to leave the resort. There is a large open seashell about five feet across filled with tea, and I take a small seashell and dip in and drink it. Victor Garber is drinking some too. A woman joins us with her half shell of tea and mentions that you can't taste the Echinacea in the tea, and I tell her I can taste it and also there is the very distinct smell of the mint in it, and I am sure it is a healing tea. I am attracted to this pleasant woman with long flowing hair. There is something magical about her. We all drink and smile. My body feels enlightened as the tea courses down through it.

Do you get a sense of magic or awe when you read this dream report? I do—it gives me shivers—but this is *my* dream. I can only hope you feel some of the awe that screams out at me.

So, what are we to do with such a dream? Is this a fantasy that tells me in waking life I should recognize that I have a passion for Angelina Jolie, and either be ashamed and beat myself up for such thoughts, or see if I can find some way to actually pursue her like my client who stalked the movie star? I doubt it. Or perhaps I should simply lust after her but just leave it there to bubble and stew? Don't think so.

So, if I don't get to hang out with Angelina Jolie in waking life, how do I approach this powerful dream? As I usually do when working a dream, I start with the emotions I recall having during the dream. Inside this dream, the first thing that pops up is a feeling of "healing"—not an emotion, strictly, but this feeling of healing comes over me. I take that as the theme of the dream; often the first thing that appears or the first emotions that arise are an indication of the dream's possible theme.

Next in emotional territory is a pleasant sense of comradeship with Victor Garber, a pleasing feeling of connection with him. Then my emotions shift to embarrassment as Angelina eyes me, then into acceptance of the connection, and then into joy and love and connection as we move into a sexual encounter. There is definitely sexual energy here, but inside the dream it feels like a deep and abiding spiritual experience that is about discovery and love and awe. Then there is the moment of the UPS guy, which is irritating, so a tinge of anger enters here, but it also clarifies the other emotions. It is as though I was getting too far out with my emotions and was brought back to earth for a moment. The UPS guy is a touchstone, which then makes the emotions even more heightened. And now the emotion we launch into is ecstasy, as I fall into a beautiful rhythm with both the horses and the lovemaking.

In the aftermath of this incredible ecstasy, the theme of healing from the beginning recurs. The re-morphed Victor Garber and a mysterious woman drink the magic elixir of life with me. I take this as an indication that I am to take this experience with me and use it in my life, to drink from the healing collective unconscious. At the very end of the dream, I drink the elixir and feel enlightened as it courses through my body. I am not sure how to describe the emotion here. The closest I can come is joy, confidence, a sense of completion, a sense of love and endearment—all these and more. So that is the emotional sense of the dream.

CELEBRITIES AS ARCHETYPES

Now onto the Angelina piece. Since this dream is not only a sex dream and a healing dream, but a celebrity dream, I have to ask the dreamer what this particular celebrity means to them. What is Angelina Jolie to me? I have worked in Hollywood for 40 years, behind the curtain of glamour and fame amongst stars like her, so my view of them is different than most people's, I suspect. Most celebrities are people just like you and me, and are fairly unexceptional when they are not performing. Some of them are even downright dopes or arrogant fools. But the great ones have a honed skill that most of us do not. They know how to climb down into the deep caves where the archetypes dwell and clothe themselves in what they find there.

These stars elicit from us a measurable response and adjust their performance according to that response, until they achieve a sort of communion with the audience. This is easier to see in theatre, where the response is immediate, and actors can do things to elicit bigger laughs or more emotion. In film they can rely on the director, as she responds and helps shape their archetypal projections.

In order for this to work properly, I believe the archetypes the stars project also have to be part of who they are at the core. Tom Hanks is a genuinely wonderful human being, and he puts on the cloak of Mister Nice Guy easily. But his niceness is only a piece of it. He also has a deep-seated, angry archetype that he can access when required for his work, and that makes him not just a good guy, but a complex being and an intriguing actor who keeps us guessing which archetype is dominant.

Back to Angelina. I find Angelina very sexy, of course, but in a bad-girl sort of way. She is a portal into a place of sexual abandon for me. She knows how to stand and look and evoke the archetype of sexual love. When I watch her acting, I find myself crossing into a place of abandon, where I soar and feel pleasure and self-confidence. The dream addresses that part of me that needs to release inhibitions and be present with my own love and passion. She invites me into her spider web, and I go willingly, like a hypnotized fly.

This archetype she embodies is a Siren of *Odyssey* fame, part bird and part beautiful woman, her song so seductive that no man could resist. In that form, Angelina is, for me, a possible symbol of addiction. And just in case I don't get that this is completely symbolic, the dream gods include hieroglyphics on her skin to remind me to stay on Earth as I enter this very consuming world of sexual encounter. It is as though the dream is screaming, "You do see that this is symbolic, don't you? Hieroglyphics are symbols, Dreamer Boy." And when the clear appearance of symbols emblazoned on her chest in brown is not enough to keep me centered, we have the intruding UPS guy dressed in the brown of earth to symbolize a grounding.

So, the Angelina part is (on one level) a healing reminder to be self-confident and to revel in the joy my life offers every day, on every sidewalk I tread. The Angelina archetype also begs me to be aware of falling too much under my own spell and losing touch by becoming addicted to love or sex. Oh, and by the way, the name Angelina is derived from Greek and means "messenger of God." Interesting.

What about the piece where I reach inside Angelina's chest and make love to her heart? We can't just let that pass. I think this makes it a truly loving dream, not just a sexual fantasy. I plunge my hands into the very center of this love archetype and experience a connection to the collective unconscious. The feeling in the dream while this goes on is nothing short of magic—a feeling so powerful, I am overwhelmed just writing about it.

Words fail in trying to describe the experience, but I think you get the sense of its power. When I sync up her heart and mine into a single rhythm, my soul crosses the threshold of magic, and I stand in the Land of Awes.

And what about Victor Garber? He is as important as Angelina and reinforces the entire message of the dream. This is my male version of the Angelina archetype, and astoundingly, he morphs into her. When a morphing happens in a dream, it shows there is magic afoot that needs to be acknowledged and examined. So, the character who is a wonderful nice-guy but who also has a dark side as a spy and is not so innocent morphs into the seductress and then morphs back into his male form. Wow. What a wonderful opportunity to see how my anima and male-self interact. In a sense, while I am making passionate love to the Angelina character, I am also making love with the Victor Garber character. And I don't think that it is coincidental that Victor Gabor portrayed Jesus Christ in *Godspell.* Together with Angelina, we have two messengers of God, one morphing into the other. I am always thunderstruck how intelligent dreams are if we look deep enough into their exquisite poetry.

I have always thought that I have an innate ability to cross back and forth easily between my male and female selves. I think I see things from a feminine perspective easily and have always been intrigued by the idea of how it would feel be to be a woman. (Haven't you wondered how it would be to be the opposite sex at some point?) This dream reminds me to use that empathic capacity to understand my own abilities and use them in conjunction with others. As I make love to Angelina's heart, I feel like I have become her.

While I am lost in the long and wondrous pleasure of making love to this archetypal beauty, another image appears to heighten the experience even more: flying black horses. At that point, my lovemaking syncs up with the rhythm of my animal self, represented by these mighty, poetic wild animals. They create harmony with my animal self, that part that is unbridled and instinctive and black, a symbol to me of the unconscious and also the shadow part of myself.

Mounted on horseback, heroes and dreamers ride upon very close but unknown raw powers of their animal self and intelligence, challenged with quickened libido and pulsing drive. They must tune to these and hold them well if life is to be lived as a fully embodied spiritual adventure of heart and mind.

The Book of Symbols: Reflections on Archetypal Images

What a wild ride this dream has become, no?

HEALING TEA

Let's move to the end of the dream, where we are drinking healing tea out of seashells that we dip into a giant half seashell. Why seashells? The first thing that comes to mind is the fact that seashells wash ashore onto the sands of a beach. And the beach is that place that separates the sea and the land. In Jungian terms, the sea is a symbol of the unconscious, and the land is a symbol of consciousness. Wouldn't it be wonderful to have a drink of

The Birth of Venus by Sandro Botticelli

some sort that would allow us to connect or see into both those worlds? In this dream, we do.

And now we have another character who appears for the first time in the dream. Who is this woman drinking the magic elixir with us? The answer lies in the giant half shell. And to ensure that I don't miss this reference, we three all have miniature versions of this giant seashell, which we dip into the vessel to gather our own elixir—the elixir of life. For me, this is the half shell that Venus—goddess of love, beauty, desire, sex, fertility, prosperity, and victory—appears on at her birth in Botticelli's painting *The Birth of Venus.*

The woman in this painting looks almost exactly like the woman sipping tea with Victor and me. Wow. The dream gods worked hard to make sure I got the connection between Venus and Angelina. For my money, this new woman, this simple Venus, is a new form of my anima.

We have passed through a wonderful ritual that brought me deep inside my own desires and projections and now has me standing in a new place with my own male self and my anima. We three are one. Victor is my male self, Venus is my anima, and I am both.

From the depths of the unconscious, the dream now brings something I had to research to get an "aha" from.

In my experience, the two senses least experienced in dreams are smell and taste. Very rarely do I hear anyone mention the taste or smell of something in a dream. And since both taste and smell are present here, it is a signpost for me of deeper and subtler meanings. This is not just conjecture; it is brain science.

Chemoreceptors are the basis for both smell and taste, and the two senses are closely related (as we have learned during the coronavirus pandemic, with some people losing both taste and smell as an initial symptom of infection). When you eat something, the molecules of food move through the back of the throat and reach olfactory nerve endings in the roof of the nose, and so in a sense we taste things with our noses. Smells are taken in by the olfactory bulb, which starts in our nose and runs along the bottom of the brain. It has connections to the hippocampus and the amygdala, which are associated with memory and emotion. The senses of touch, vision, and sound do not pass through these areas. So, the science points to a direct connection between the senses of taste and smell, and emotion and memory. It could be 50 years since you were in your grandmother's house, but if you walk into a space that has that identical smell, you will recognize it immediately, and memories and emotions of your grandmother and her house will flood your consciousness. People who lose their senses of taste and smell describe an emotional debilitation, not just an irritation due to some innocuous anomaly.

As to why taste and smell are rare in dreams, I speculate that the connection of taste and smell to the hippocampus and the amygdala takes more effort on the part of our sleeping brains to execute than free-moving touch, vision, and sound—but that is a guess. I have not located any research on the matter yet.

It's also worth taking a look at taste and smell from the perspective of symbology.

Taste and smell are processes that occur when we take something inside and experience it internally. When I am in France, experiencing a wonderful meal of intense tastes, I eat slowly, savoring the subtle flavors that delight, taking in the pungent smells, building a clear and concise memory of how these tastes and smells make me feel, and depositing them in an archive that I can recall when someone offers me these same tastes and smells again. When we fall in love, it inevitably includes the deeply sensuous and unique smells and tastes of our lover, which we catalogue, so that when we encounter those same smells and tastes again, deep emotions are accessed and reexperienced, even if we are not consciously aware of it.

Since taste and smell are so closely connected to memory and emotion, when they appear in dreams, they naturally evoke a unique response from the dreamer. Taste and smell are deeply personal, and I think the dream gods use them to prod us into an emotional place or to dredge up a memory that we need to look at right now. That they use them so rarely only underscores their importance.

Now back to our dream, where we are sipping fragrant tea from a seashell. Two herbs are mentioned as we sip our tea. The first is Echinacea, which the Venus woman mentions she cannot taste, but I can. Echinacea was used by Native Americans for treating infections and wounds, and it is taken now to prevent colds and promote immunity. The three of us are drinking something that gives us immunity. Immunity from what, you ask? Why, death, of course. Since I am here now with an immortal goddess named Venus, it only makes sense that we are drinking the elixir that gives immortality. And the reason she cannot taste it? Well, she is already immortal, so it is just like water to her now. On the other hand, I can taste the healing power of the tea, because I am still mortal. So, here is a deep message about life and death for me. In the obvious department, I am going to die, but for this short time on this side of the veil, I am able to access something eternal. In a way, I am tasting death here, and it is a good thing. And death in dreams is symbolic of change or transformation.

(I have a strange little association with Echinacea. I have always had difficulty pronouncing the word Echinacea, I tend to pronounce it as "euthanasia." The standing joke I make to cover up my embarrassment when I mispronounce it is: "I am just *dying* for a cup of *euthanasia* tea." That reinforces this whole association with death again, with the immortal Venus not being able to taste "euthanasia.")

The healing feeling of this dream is so huge, it gives me access to the archetypal world that goes on beyond the horizon. It is as though the collective unconscious hovers right here, flowing out of that giant seashell, and I am one with the collective memory of all humankind.

THE RIVER NYMPH MINTHE

And now to the second herb: I can smell the mint in this elixir, I tell my Venus. It turns out that in Greek mythology, a naiad, or river nymph, named Minthe rules over the River Cocytus. She is extremely beautiful, but the life of a water nymph is a bit lonely. Water nymphs are assigned to hang around and watch over their watery domain and inspire poetry from those who come to visit. Her particular venue, one of the five rivers encircling Hades, doesn't get a lot of visitors. The River Cocytus is not on most people's travel lists. Lonely Minthe presides over her river, but what a bore it is. Like most water nymphs, or maybe more so, she is a bit mischievous and dangerous, and she takes to visiting the god of the underworld, Hades, from time to time—especially when his wife, Persephone, is not around. Persephone is Hades' longtime wife, who spends six months in the underworld with him and the other six months above with her mother Demeter.

Well, Minthe, our little vixen—who I must say is a lot like my version of Angelina Jolie—knows how to open that door of seduction and use what's inside. Using all her nymph powers, she spins her spider web of seduction and entraps the willing Hades. The affair goes on at length, and they have a rocking time in bed when the wife is away.

Needless to say, Persephone eventually catches the two lovers doing the horizontal mambo in her bed, and she goes into a huge rage. She chases Minthe, and when she catches her, she steps on Minthe with all her might, crushing her. Minthe somehow survives the onslaught, but each time she arises, Persephone pounds her back down, crushing her into bits. The pounding, instead of killing her, transforms her, bit by bit, into the fragrant herb that is named for her—mint. And that is the origin of the fragrant herb, which was used in funerary rites in ancient Greece to mask the smell of the decaying body.

Which in turn brings us back to the strong associations that run through this dream: sex, death, and transformation.

The website OurHerbGarden.com offers this:

> Mint history is colored by stories from ancient mythology. Proserpine, Pluto's wife, was said to have transformed a hated rival into the mint plant. Both the Latin, Metha, and the Greek, Minthe, have come to be associated with metamorphosed beauty.
>
> Note: Proserpine and Pluto are the Roman names for Persephone and Hades.

My elixir contains mint, or "metamorphosed beauty," which happened in the dream not once, but twice! Victor Garber morphs into the beautiful Angelina Jolie, and Angelina morphs into the beautiful Venus.

Moreover, to add to the mix, mint was used in a fermented barley drink called the Kykeon, an essential preparatory entheogen taken by the participants before beginning the Eleusinian mysteries of ancient Greece. This was a super-secret initiation rite, and those who passed through it achieved certainty of some form of afterlife.

In the final act of my big dream, I am drinking a healing tea comprised of metamorphosed beauty and Echinacea, which brings immunity from the things that have made my soul weak in the past. It grants me immunity and immortality.

But I cannot let myself off so easy. There are additional deep personal lessons here in this big dream. For a very long time I saw women through the lens of the Angelina archetype, that sex siren who will suck your blood as she gives you pleasure and pain at the same time. My dance with this mysterious feminine archetype of pleasure and pain has followed me most of my life. It started with that glorious/horrible experience as Judy Garland turned into a succubus in my arms, followed years later by my first sexual encounter, which was, to be honest, a profound trauma filled with angst and deception. This dream comes once again to address that deep distrust of both women and the feminine within myself developed from these soul-shattering events. I am still a work in progress it seems, but I have developed through years of hard work and reflection a strong relationship with my own feminine, which has moved from my greatest weakness to possibly my greatest strength.

These are my own projections onto this "big" dream, which would certainly have gone a completely different direction if it were yours. Digging deep into it, seeking things that would resonate with my own soul, this is what I came up with. This transforming dream invites me to be willing to see things in a non-linear way, and to heal myself and help others heal.

That is what I do with my dreamwork. With each dream I work, some part of me is healed, and some part of me is given to those who also seek healing. It is my task to reach inside those I work with and make love to their hearts, one dream at a time. We are in this life together, even perhaps beyond, and my job is to open the door to the Land of Awes and allow those who venture into that space to stand dumbfounded and gobsmacked in the presence of their own souls.

I would add that this dream stays present in me as I move forward in my life. When I think about this dream, "big" magic wakes up, fills me with awe, and gives me the chance to look into the dreams I am working for that same magic. I use this dream, in a way, every time I work a dream with someone. Sometimes just before my dream group begins, I brew a tea with mint and Echinacea and sip it out of an old seashell. That often brings me into the golden place of awe where I am more open to the powerful forces that arise when someone pours out their soul in the form of a dream.

If you have a "big" dream—and you will usually know when it happens, for the dream will speak to you loudly—spend some time with it and see what it has to say. And don't be afraid to work through it more than once, from many angles and with other people. Cherish it, and it will yield support and wisdom to you for years to come.

CHAPTER 17

SEX DREAMS

Frolicking with Laura Bush Dressed as a Dominatrix

I once had a thousand desires,
but in my one desire to know you
all else melted away.
The pure essence of your being
has taken over my heart and soul.
Now there is no second or third,
only the sound of your sweet cry.
Through your grace I have found
a treasure within myself.
I have found the truth of the Unseen world.
I have come upon the eternal ecstasy.
I have gone beyond the ravages of time.
Now my heart sings,
"I am the soul of the world."

Rumi
from *All My Youth Returns*

SEX AS A METAPHOR IN DREAMS

When working with a dream that includes sex, it is good to step back for a minute and look at it in a strictly symbolic way. Sex can be about the union of the male and female parts of ourselves, or about loving others, or about balance between ourselves and others, or second chakra aspects, or penetrating something new, or letting go into beauty, or many other things. And every once in a while, sex in dreams is about sex.

Carl Jung discussed the aspect of metaphor in dreams concerning sex:

> Further researches, expressly referred to by Maeder, have shown that the sexual language of dreams is not always to be interpreted in a concretistic way—that it is, in fact, an archaic language which naturally uses all the analogies readiest to hand without their necessarily coinciding with a real sexual content. It is therefore unjustifiable to take the sexual language of dreams literally under all circumstances, while other contents are explained as symbolical. But as soon as you take the sexual metaphors as symbols for some thing unknown, your conception of the nature of dreams at once deepens. *Collected Works, Vol. 8*

In my experience, sex appears in dreams very, very frequently. As a matter of fact, I think most sex dreams never get reported or recorded. I say this because I am in touch with myriad people and their dreams, and when I either get familiar with a person or am just bold, I ask what they dream about most often. The replies vary from being chased to being naked to flying to work and various other things. They rarely mention sex dreams. But when I ask directly about sex, many—not all, but many—reply with something like, "Well, yes of course. I dream about sex all the time, but let's not talk about that." Although this means we are missing a key piece of the dreaming world—a loss to the dream canon—it is totally understandable. We here in Western civilization are rather repressed as a society when it comes to sex, and talking about it is a social no-no. Our conscious selves are great at making huge judgments, so much so that we often suppress dreams that involve sex.

We also often feel some embarrassment about sex dreams. I am not dismissing the embarrassment. If experienced in the dream, or even after, it is something to be looked at in a symbolic way; it can even be a factor in working the dream. However, I have found that the embarrassment is usually felt after, not during the dream. Usually inside a dream like this, we don't have guilt or bad feelings. It is a joyous, soul-embracing experience. However, soon after awakening from such a dream, instead of recognizing it as a wonderful symbolic event, the judgmental conscious mind jumps in. Instead of embracing the powerful positive message of this spiritual experience manifested in a sexual way, we take on a feeling of guilt. Our conscious mind doesn't like it when we wake in the middle of the night next to our beloved just having had a long encounter in a dream where we were kissing, caressing, and dancing naked with anyone besides that lovely creature lying next to us fast asleep, unaware of our "infidelity." The pesky, puritanical part of ourselves berates us, and we tuck that dream away somewhere and let it fade from memory, if we can.

This is counter-productive to what the dream is trying to do, at least most of the time. If the dream is trying to talk to us about new ways we need to connect with our animus or anima, it would be natural for our unconscious to pick a symbolically appropriate sex partner to express the desire some part of us has to connect to new energies. In that case, a feeling of infidelity is most likely imposed on the dream rather than being integral to it.

However, sometimes infidelity in a dream is actually about infidelity, and for a good reason. Infidelity in a dream may indicate something we really need to hear about our relational life, something we are not facing. What if we are in a relationship that is not healthy for us, and we dream about wonderful sexual encounters with other people? In that case, the dream may be a way for the unconscious to guide us towards healing the relationship or finding an exit from the situation.

Once I had a client who kept dreaming of her companion having affairs, and she was convinced that he was secretly seeing someone. She was really agitated about this. We worked on it, and she finally talked to her lover about her fears and dreams. When she did, he assured her he wasn't seeing anybody else, but offhandedly asked her if she had a desire to have an affair. She went silent as she realized she was the one who had this compelling lustfulness. She had no idea how to deal with that feeling; fortunately, she ended up with some good counseling, and they worked through this as a couple.

In other words, dreams have to be considered individually; there is no standard answer for what sex means in a dream.

Sex is so personal and revealing that we guard it ever so closely, at least in the society I live in. We hide our thoughts about it lest we be revealed and ridiculed, or shunned. And we rarely talk about the actual events of sexual encounters. Because sex is such a deeply personal and usually hidden aspect of our lives, sex in dreams often points to deeper and hidden aspects of our psyche. For that reason, sex in dreams can be seen as symbolic of deeply held emotions that are repressed or misunderstood.

When you find yourself having sex in a dream with someone you don't like, perhaps you need to connect on a deep level with the shadow part of yourself represented by that person. You may have had sexual dreams about an ex, but they are not necessarily about getting back together. They are, on one level, about connecting with and integrating the shadow of your own anima or animus that they represent.

And if you identify as heterosexual but have sex with someone of your own sex in a dream? Does this mean you are gay? Well, maybe, but more likely it is symbolic of something deep and meaningful. These dreams can be about loving the male part of yourself if you are a man and embracing your feminine if you are a woman.

And what if you are non-binary, bi-sexual, asexual, gay, lesbian, polyamorous, or any of a variety of other approaches to sex, gender, and life? Each person's dreams have to be considered individually, of course. Life offers such a complex cornucopia of choices and possibilities, and our dreams will deliver up the right symbols and emotions for each of us across the sexual spectrum.

One client came to me privately because he kept having erotic encounters in his dreams with his roommate from college, a man he hadn't seen in 10 years. When we dug down into the dreams, it turned out the college roommate had become successful and deeply spiritual. These were both characteristics the dreamer saw lacking in his own life, but which he was making attempts to engender. The dreams were, in a way, encouragement to him to continue his attempts at success and spirituality. He came to the idea that he was making love to the spiritual and successful part of himself. That was an "aha" that came out of the work on the dream.

What about sex with objects? This is probably easier to see as symbolic, since it does not involve other people to muck up our understanding. I have listened to dreams of people having sex with trees, flashlights, statues, and a church steeple. One woman had a series of dreams where she masturbated on a closet doorknob. When we investigated the contents of the closet, it turned out it was where she stored all her fine jewelry and best clothes that she would wear on dates. Her "aha" was centered in loving that woman who looked damn good in the mirror after she dressed up. And it wasn't just that—it was the sensual feeling she possessed about herself at that moment.

Sex with a student, a family member, or your lover's best friend are all stand-ins for learning some lesson about what each of them represent. Sex with a student might be about getting in touch with something that went awry sexually or spiritually when you were a student. Sex with a family member has us looking into family dynamics. Sex with a lover's best friend may call for an awareness of what beautiful, sensual aspects of your lover you are missing at that moment.

And sex with yourself? Well, you don't need help with that one.

The dream world does not have the same rules that we impose on ourselves here in the waking world. Dreams are always trying to find the best way to use their poetic narratives to show us the path forward. Sometimes that involves erotic encounters that are totally (and often rightfully) taboo here in the land of consciousness.

In my understanding and experience, sexuality in dreams and in waking life is truly a spiritual matter. Just like other awe-filled experiences of my life, sexual interaction is a wondrous portal to a deeply spiritual experience. It is a place of vulnerability, of connection, of letting go, of caring and sharing not just your body, but also your spirit that soars and your soul that dives into the deep caverns of psychic echoes. When sex goes right, other beautiful worlds appear. It is real magic. It reinforces who we are and our mystical connection not only to our naked, soulful self, but also to another exposed soul with whom we share something beyond the sum of the parts. When approached as a spiritual experience, sex is no longer just about base desires; it becomes another door that opens into that glorious chamber of ecstatic awe that this book is about.

But you know that, don't you? If you have been fortunate, you have had more than one of those experiences when a tender or raw passionate moment has grabbed you and thrown you to the ground, split you open and released the various parts of your soul—allowing them to soar and dance in poetic cadence with the rhythms of life right there just beyond our seeing.

SEX AND TRAUMA

I have been talking primarily about sex as a positive aspect of dreaming. There is also another side to this, and that is sex and trauma.

I've worked many dreams where the underlying driving force was some form of traumatic sexual encounter. In working with such dreams, it is most important to listen carefully, be empathetic, and honor the fact that this is something extremely personal and sacred. It is important to realize that these types of traumas require a lot of work and help from professionals. The tools we talked about when working nightmares apply to dreams brought on by sexual trauma.[3]

---

3. For more insight into sexual trauma and dreams, I recommend *Trauma and Dreams,* edited by Deirdre Barrett.

CORSETS, A WHIP, AND SIX SUITS FOR $673

To return to the broader aspects of dreams and sex, let's look at a comic and sex-filled dream of mine I had back in 2006, in the middle of President George W. Bush's second term. I do have reservations about sharing this dream, but that is my conscious ego talking, so here goes. This tumultuous dream was a wild adventure I will never forget. I did edit out a few nasty details to save you (okay, me) from blushing too much.

LAURA BUSH AS DOMINATRIX

Laura Bush and I are standing on a huge, round, ultra-white bed in the middle of the White House. I am in a tight-fitting black corset and she is wearing a silver and black corset, black stockings with dragons on them, and red spike heels. We circle slowly in some sort of mating ritual. She strips the corset off me and tosses it to a Secret Service agent. George W. Bush has just finished addressing the nation and now joins us. Laura stands tall on the center of the bed and slaps a whip in her hand. The sound of it makes me shudder. This woman is in charge and I just bet she is going to have her way with me, whether I like it or not. Yikes. She starts jumping up and down, and George W. leaps on the bed and does the same. They are acting like a couple of wild monkeys, so maybe I am safe. Perhaps I can slink away and find some clothes. But, no. Suddenly, her demeanor shifts and she locks eyes with me, causing me to freeze in my tracks. George W. is still jumping up and down and making monkey sounds, so she lifts him with one hand, all the while staring unblinking at me, and tosses George W. off the bed. Her eyes blaze as she approaches me. When she gets to me, she places her whip behind my knees and pulls up hard, throwing me down on my back. There is no escaping her. She is a sexual tiger as she has wild crazy sex with me. I am tossed about like a rag doll as she commands me to pleasure her in a multitude of ways and I comply.

Meanwhile George W. is suddenly on the side looking at the new suits he bought.

He laughs and tells Laura (as she pauses for a moment), "Hey, Laura, I got all six suits for $673." She says, "You mean one suit?"

"Nope, nope, nope, all six and for $673! What a bargain! Only $673!" he replies.

The suits look kind of cheap for the president, I mean why would he buy cheap suits? And those ties, they are cheap polyester.

He watches Laura and I continue our romp as he eats an overstuffed peanut butter and jelly sandwich. As he does, the red jelly gushes out and drops all over his new tie. But not to worry, he licks it off as he moves around the bed checking out all the cool positions Laura and I are getting into.

I now chase her around the bed in a circle, which makes me realize that all this is being recorded somewhere. I wonder what effect that will have if it ever comes out. Laura takes a break and works on her nails. Wow, there are secret service agents watching us right now, and they seem nonplussed about all this, how weird. I have to find some place to hide.

As I awake from the dream I realize the sex doesn't feel sexual in the dream, but with George and I and Laura jumping around on the bed and frolicking, it must have been a strange sight and I laugh out loud.

Well, that is a wild one, no? When I was inside the dream, all of this seemed quite natural and wonderful. However, my conscious mind is mortified telling it. The titillation has to be stepped over (not dismissed, just stepped over) and the symbols seen for what they are in order to get anything out of this dream. It is so easy to allow our sexual instincts to make this dream a joke, a political cartoon about George W. Bush being cuckolded. However, the fact remains that this is my dream, my symbolic message from my own unconscious, and must be approached with an eye to what I can learn from it. What is such a brash, comical dream about?

It is not necessarily about a desire to have sex with Laura Bush. More likely it is about connecting to the strong part of my feminine and looking at my passive male self at the same time. (Remember, dreams exaggerate!) In the tradition of Gestalt work, all parts of the dream are parts of myself. With that in mind, let's look at the three main figures as parts of me.

Some part of me is like George W. Bush, I fear. As president, he is the ultimate authority figure, so this is Walter in his most authoritative mode. I am not too thrilled by that, but the dream speaks truth to the soul. George W. Bush is an authority figure who always delegated his authority (to Dick Cheney, amongst others). If I accept him as part of who I am, the Walter who is in charge of his life, I see someone who is distracted and hands over his authority to others.

And then there is the dream ego. The naked Walter is a receptive being here, exposed completely in his nakedness, so the entire world sees him as he is. Indeed, there is no escaping exposure here. The cameras are rolling, and this wild frolic will eventually be broadcast across the globe. He is clearly submissive and a wide-eyed participant in all of this. There is also something joyous about him. He is having a damn good time in this wild, back-and-forth, crazy sex. There is some part of him that revels in the submission.

In waking life, I think of Laura Bush as a meek and mundane woman, the last person in the world I would think of as a dominatrix. If she is symbolic of something in me, it is the mundane female within, who is really a tiger ready to be let out. She is the only one of the three here who is truly an authority figure. The woman with the whip is to be obeyed.

When we put these three figures together to see a better of picture of what Walter needs to be and do, things start making sense to me. When my disowned authority figure (George W. Bush) is distracted and not in control, my strong female (Laura Bush) roars to life and connects with my male self that is willing to be dominated by the feminine, and what a ferocious union of fantastic energies that is. In short, we are talking about aspects of dominance and submission. That brings on an "aha" for me. The dream wants me to look into that area of my life, that place of dominance and submission. Where am I dominating at this moment in my life and where am I being submissive, and what is the relationship of the two in my life?

This opened a Pandora's box of questions that I am still working on. Since having this dream, I have been on the lookout for moments where my dominance and submission appear and how I deal with them. I have been looking at my relationships with family, friends, and co-workers, and shifting the dynamic of my submissive and dominant behavior ever so slightly to see what happens. It is a part of my journey, another marker on the road to individuation that Jung talks about.

What about those very specific numbers? Six suits for $673. The dream is very specific about that amount, and even repeats the numbers so they are not missed. As the dreamer I feel compelled to consider it. When something like a specific number comes up in a dream, and it stands out like it does here, I encourage the dreamer to roam around in their memory and look at ages, dates, or anything the numbers seem to portray. What jumps out at me personally is a date: June of 1973 or 6/73. When I look back carefully, memories appear. In June of 1973 I was dating six different women at Brigham Young University (six pur*suits* you may say). One of these pursuits that I tried on led to my first sexual encounter. That gives me an "aha" as I think about it. That first sexual encounter was full of angst for me, wrought with intense conflict about submission and dominance. I was completely submissive, and that partner was dominating and controlling. Could this dream in 2006 be about something so far back as that? Why, yes. I am a work in progress, just like you, and my unconscious is still full of things I am straightening out from those deeply personal, hidden experiences and traumas from so long ago. And I thought I had worked all this male/female angst out with the Angelina Jolie dream which came roaring up from my unconscious six months before this dream! But hell no, here we are again. Evidently I still have work to do on all this.

And the round bed? The roundness is emblematic of the feminine, and is also the shape of a mandala, which, in Jungian terms, is a place of centering the self. The invitation is to center myself as I explore the concept and experience of authority.

We could do so much more with this dream, but let's leave it there as an open door that invites more dreams to give further wisdom and healing. On some level, this dream is just downright funny and outrageous and something fun to wake from. And this discussion—my take on the dream, with some help from other dreamers I shared it with—is not the only meaning or approach. The important part is how the dreamer feels about it, and I feel pretty damn good about it.

That said, I don't want to ignore sex dreams that are actually about sex. Sometimes a cigar in a dream is a cigar. I had one client, a delightful, full-of-life woman, who for a time would dream about having delightful sex with various men. One week it was a badass biker dude, the next it was a sexually repressed businessman, the next it was her erudite college professor. The encounters always started out quiet and innocent but ended up in screaming, orgasmic sex. The sex was filled with abandon and joy—and often with humor, as she had sex in every position imaginable. Each time she awoke from these encounters, she would talk to her life partner, and they would recreate the sexual positions and the wild sensual dialogue she had experienced in the dream. It became a hilarious and meaningful experience that drew them together. In this case, sex in the dream was actually about sex. It was also about other things, I suspect, but the overriding experience engendered a new, deep love of sex and her partner.

Here is another sex dream of mine that blew me away and which I think gave me insight into sex, but from a completely new perspective.

FEMALE ORGASM

I am sexually aroused as I stand in a room naked, alone. As I look down my body, I notice I have large beautiful breasts. Wow. I like that. I look lower, looking for that erection I am feeling, but nothing is there. I bend down wondering what is going on here. Then I see it—instead of a penis, oh my god, I have a vagina. I suddenly realize I am a woman, or more succinctly, I am still me, a man, but I have a woman's body. I have always wondered what it would be like to be a woman. I explore my vagina lightly with my hands, and out of nowhere there is a man pressed up against my body and he enters me. Oh my god. What the hell is happening? We develop a rhythm to this sexual encounter as I feel things I have never felt before. My sexual experiences have always had the feeling of something moving from deep inside of me and transferring that energy into my partner and then that energy returning. This is different. The energy comes into me through my throbbing vagina and swirls inside of me and spins upward through my body, to my complete delight. This is so strange and I cannot control anything. This powerful force explodes out of the top of my head, rendering me dizzy. And then it starts all over again. Something is building inside of me that starts with each successive sensual experience. Although that energy launches up through my body and out the top of my head, some of it starts to stay swirling through my midsection. This builds and builds until something cannot be contained any longer. My body shakes uncontrollably as these energies go off like depth charges, and I climax as I raise my hands high over my head. All of the resident energies that have been building quiver up through my body and explode out of the top of my head as I scream in delight, which wakes me up.

What a wonderful—and also embarrassing—experience. Luckily there was no one else in the house when this dream occurred. I cannot fathom explaining to someone that the reason I screamed at the top of my lungs and jumped out of bed was that I had just had an orgasm as a woman. I have no idea if this is what women feel when they climax, but if it is, sign me up to be a woman in my next life. This dream, as strange as it is, has given me a chance to think deeply about how sex can be so different and wonderful for each person. Perhaps I can learn how to be a more sensitive and caring lover.

Sex is an intimate experience where we are both figuratively and literally naked and connected to not only another human (or two) but to our own deep desires and drives. Because of that, when sex appears in a dream, it is good to look at the vulnerability and depth it may be trying to get us to see and feel. Dreams know what they are doing when they bring sex in. When that happens, step inside it and allow the intimacy to affect you.

Oh, and I am dying to know if my experience of a female orgasm is anywhere close to what happens to you mysterious female beings. Would someone let me know? I am too shy to ask.

CHAPTER 18

DEATH DREAMS

Of Death and Dragons

My armor is like tenfold shields, my teeth are swords,
my claws spears, the shock of my tail a thunderbolt,
my wings a hurricane, and my breath death!

J.R.R. Tolkien
The Hobbit

Death appears frequently in dreams, and it has many forms. Most often when death occurs in a dream, we are the observer. We watch as the police shoot and kill the "bad" guy. We see hundreds consumed by a tsunami as we are rescued by a helicopter. We observe from behind a blanket as a teenage girl hangs a woman who looks a lot like us from the ceiling. We wince as a one-eyed ogre crushes an entire family of turtles. We stare hopelessly as an airplane catches fire and bursts into flames, killing everyone onboard. We are horrified as we turn with the knife we just used to make a peanut butter and jelly sandwich, and it accidentally stabs our best friend, and she dies before our eyes.

Although death in dreams is common, the actual death of the dream ego (that character in the dream we identify as one's self) in a dream is rare. Most of the time when we are about to die in a dream, we wake up just before our death; often because it is so shocking that we are ripped out of the dream at that moment.

There is an old wives' tale that says that if you die in your dream, you will actually die. That is hogwash. I have died many times in dreams, and I have always found something magical on the other side of death. I was once beheaded in a dream, and then I passed into another realm where two old men were playing chess. In another dream where I drowned and felt my soul pulled through a wall, I found myself in a room filled with liquid light that I could breathe into my lungs.

SUICIDE IN DREAMS

Here is a dream of mine where I not only die, but the death is in the form of suicide, something that in our conscious lives is usually totally abhorrent. But in the dream space, it is a place of wonder and beauty.

TAKING THE PLUNGE

I am walking along between two rows of houses, all attached. I notice that all the doors are closed and no one is present, except this light-filled woman in a flowing blue dress who stands next to this ominous hole in the earth. I look down into the hole at her invitation and see that it is filled with bubbling red-hot deadly material, and I know that I have to plunge into it and die. I look into her eyes and it confirms what I know I have to do. I hesitate for a minute, then jump in feet-first, committing suicide. I am completely aware that I am dead, and a wonderful feeling sweeps over me. The place I stand in after dying is a brighter and clearer version of the same world I had just left, with the doors open and people peeking out at me. I wave at the people and they wave back. I am where I am supposed to be.

When I drew this dream, I felt compelled to only depict that moment of transition when I plunge into the ominous hole and die. As I worked on the dream, I kept staring at the picture, trying to recreate that feeling at the instant of death. I slowed down the action, reentering the dream, trying to feel the transition. It became a meditation, as I moved back and forth between fear and death time after time, slowing down the transition each time, until I was able to stop the experience at that point where things changed. I focused on that subtle point of transformation for a long time, breathing into it. In that meditative state, I let go of thoughts, and I was transported into a place of bliss and awe. Just like in the dream, I fell through into a beautiful place of self-knowledge and understanding.

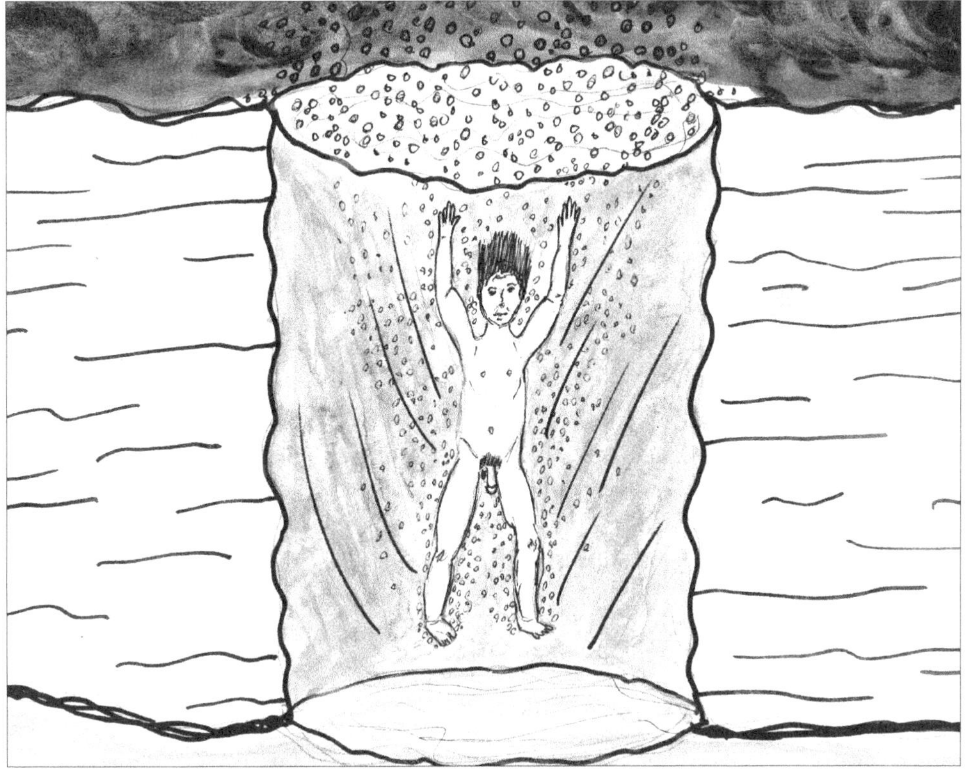

DEATH AS A SYMBOL OF TRANSFORMATION

In studies of death dreams, almost all of the dreams where the dreamer dies end up being positive, uplifting dreams as opposed to threat-of-death dreams, which are almost always distressing and often end as nightmares.

As a symbol, death in dreams is about change or transformation. It is one of the few symbols in dreams that seems to be constant. I don't think I have ever encountered a dream with death in it that wasn't about some form of change or transformation. Something is ending, and something new is appearing. As to the form and meaning of that change, that is wide open. Drowning to death in a tsunami may be about being overwhelmed by my own unconscious or emotions, and being beheaded may speak to a need to get out of my head and start anew from some place not so involved in the thinking process.

When I kill someone else in a dream, on one level they are a stand-in for me and thus invite change. When I grab a huge rhino horn off the wall and run it through that guy who just won't shut up about himself, on one level that is my armored self trying to silence the open part of myself.

Our conscious minds really hate this sort of thing, though. Who wants to admit that they killed their own father in a dream last night? Killing my father, however, may be about moving on from the wounds given to me as a child. In order to allow such a dream into our conscious awareness, we have to get past the horror of killing someone we have deep feelings about and recognize it as a symbol of our growth.

But why the radical difference between the euphoria experienced with actually dying in a dream like our suicide dream, and the distress and fear that arise with a death-threatening dream like the tsunami dreams? The answer may be as simple as the fact that the death-threatening dream is about transformation that has not yet occurred, and the actual death dream is about transformation completed.

As the mustached, smiling villain—who looks a lot like my ne'er-do-well cousin with the giant addiction problem—starts to plunge his curved knifed into my chest, I wake with a start, clutching the covers. And with that awakening, the dream has done a number of things at the same time. It tells me that change is imminent. The knife is about to plunge, and this focuses my attention on some aspect of my life that is up for a huge change. Also, as the dream presents me with that ne'er-do-well cousin with addiction issues, perhaps this refers to some addictive behavior in my own life that needs to change. And if that were not enough, the dream has turned into a nightmare, which is often an unfinished dream, so it invites me to continue or finish the dream. In a movie, if the hero is about to have a curved knife plunged in his heart, could that possibly be an ending to the story? Hell no—and it is the same with dreams.

How would you continue this dream? Perhaps the villain/cousin plunges the knife into my heart and I die, but then what? That's not really an ending to the movie, so what happens then? Perhaps I step out of my dead body and watch the cousin collapse into tears for what he has done. Or perhaps just as he starts to plunge the knife, I grab it and fling it in the air, and it spins and spins and turns into a blackbird. Or because the blade is curved, it rolls off my chest and kills him instead. I am making things up here, but magic can happen through actively imagining what follows at this moment of transformation. You can throw all sorts of ideas and scenarios up in the air and see which ones land an "aha."

What about when others die in our dreams? I watch as hundreds of people are sucked up into a funnel cloud. Their dead bodies end up strewn across the pasture, and as the sun comes out, all of them turn into dairy cows grazing on thick grass. What do we do with that? Well, pretty much the same thing we always do—we think symbolically, and we own the dream. What part of my life is in such turmoil that it needs to be sucked up into the upper reaches of my atmosphere and then killed (changed) and transformed into a gentle, milk-producing creature? Perhaps it is time to give up all the swirling tumult in my life and take refuge in the simple things, like absorbing fresh green growth from the earth and turning that into life-sustaining sustenance for others. And that is my projection on this dream, because of where I am in my life at this moment: I am writing a book about dreams and awe, hoping to turn the tumult I have experienced into something that will help others. Your projection will be completely different, no doubt.

When you find death in a dream, think of it as a symbol of change, transformation, remodeling, reshaping, or metamorphosis, and see what happens to your understanding of the dream.

DREAMS AND ACTUAL DEATH

There is another very important aspect of death in dreams, and that is when dreams are about actual death—the passing from this mortal existence that all of us will experience. Just like some sex dreams turn out to be about sex, some dreams about death are actually about death. Death is also a transformation, of course, but we are talking here about dreams that foreshadow death itself.

If there is a place where dreams have importance, the ones surrounding death are right at the top of the heap. Death is one of the great questions of life that we all face and carry with us every day. Our lives can be a richer place if we allow death into them. Michael Meade talks about how in life we come in one door, walk across the stage of life, and go out the other door; and the sooner we stop walking backwards to the second door and turn around and walk towards it, the better we will understand who we are and what we are about. The better we will live.

Dreams of the dying are unique, special, and sacred. I would recommend the book *Dreams and Death: The Benefits of Dreams Before, During and After Death,* by Nicole Gratton and Monique Séguin. These two delightful French-Canadian authors, who have worked amongst the dying in hospice and within their families, talk about the dreams they have witnessed from this unique perspective. Sometimes they are as simple as the man who dreams of being on the last lap of a car race, or as complex as a black dog that appears not only in the dying woman's dreams, but also in the dreamworker's dream the night the woman dies.

One summer night I was conducting my weekly dream group when three charming, rather mature women showed up. I have no idea where they got the information about the group, but there they were. They explained that they had come together because one of them could see well enough to drive at night, and the other two acted as co-pilots. The youngest one was 86, but all three had the energy of teenagers.

The young one jumped right in with a dream. She explained that it seemed like an important dream, but she wasn't sure why, except that it just felt really big, and it had stayed in her memory clearly every day since she had had it, a month or so before.

THE FRIENDLY DRAGON OF DEATH

I am on a giant cruise ship and we are in the harbor about to embark on a cruise. I am with three other people and we stand on the fantail of the ship, but somehow the part we are standing on is sticking out of the black underside of the ship. We see an old wooden gate at the end of the place we are standing. It looks like those gates they have on ferries.

Suddenly there is a deafening roar and a menacing colorful dragon bursts out of the water. We see his huge face as he shakes off the water and then he looks straight at me, then dives back into the water and disappears. The four of us look at each other in shock. We have to tell the others on the boat about this!

We rush back to the entrance to the ship, and tell the young men there that are in charge of letting people in about the dragon and they give us this condescending look and then nod at each other, "Sure . . . a dragon . . . you all saw a dragon . . ." They obviously don't believe us. As a matter of fact, on the rest of the voyage, the word gets around to avoid the four weirdos who think they saw a dragon.

I now walk into the dining room of the ship, and there, at table 4, is my husband and two of his friends. There are four chairs at the table, so I go to sit down with them in the fourth chair. My husband tells me that I can't just sit anywhere I like. All the places are reserved and I have to go talk to the concierge to find what table I am assigned to sit at.

I go to this long rounded clear hallway that light pours in on and I find the concierge. He has a clipboard and looks up my name on it. "You are assigned to table 4," he tells me.

So, I return to table 4 with my husband and his two friends. The problem, though, is that I can't seem to get seated right. When I sit, I am at an odd angle and can't see my husband or the other two. I keep moving and trying, but no matter what I do or what angle I take, I just can't get seated at table 4.

We dive into this dream. The feelings she talks about are centered on the shock she felt when the dragon appeared, but not fear. There is a warm and friendly feeling to the dragon, she says. She also is pleased and annoyed to see her husband, who in real life has died.

I have her go over the sketch and tell the dream again, using a laser pointer. There in the center are the four people (stick figures) looking out over the ferry gate at the dragon (the object in the drawing that draws our focus most). Part two of the dream is drawn in the upper right third of the paper with table 4 and the husband (the central figure at the table) and friends, and the dreamer talking to the concierge with the long, rounded hallway behind him as he tells her to go to table 4.

I have an immediate "aha" from the dream, but I recognize it as my projection, so I hold fire for a bit.

I ask her about the husband and the two other men at the table. She explains that her husband and one of the guys are dead, and the other guy is very close to death at this moment. "It's what you get when you get this old—everybody dies," she explains, as she and the other two women cackle. I begin wondering if these are three magical witches that have invaded and taken over the dream group.

Something in her voice as she talks about death grabs me, though—something both cavalier and painful—so I pursue that. "This dream seems, on one level, to be about death. Is it okay if we talk about your husband's death?"

"Sure," she responds. "He had horrible dementia and was in a nursing home when he died. I visited him every day and read to him. It was not so easy, because I am not sure he always knew who I was. But I read to him. Every day I read to him. He would say all kinds of crazy things, just crazy things. As a matter of fact, I will tell you about the last time I saw him before he died. I was about to leave and he grabbed my arm and very loudly yelled, 'I see the gate! I see the gate! I see the gate!' I settled him back into the bed and left soon thereafter. He died later that night when I was gone, but that is the last thing he said to me."

"And what did that say to you, this gate reference?" I ask.

"I think he was just saying things, but I guess I took it to mean that he saws the gates of heaven or something like that. At least that is what I would like to think," she responds.

"Would you mind if I hijack your dream for a minute and project some things on it that I am thinking and feeling? I promise to give it back and you can ignore any or all of my projections."

"Go right ahead," she says.

"My dream is about the ship of death. I am about to take a cruise on the ship of death. I say that because of a number of things. First there is the dragon. The dragon you drew is a Chinese dragon, which is not usually associated with death, but there is some connection here, I think."

Her eyes light up. "Oh, I know this dragon, he has been with me in my dreams before. He is my friend, and I know him very well. He came to me before my husband died. He comes often, so yes, he is my dragon, and someday he will come for me. I don't fear him. He is the dragon of death, and my friend," she tells me.

I am taken aback by this, but I continue with my projection. "Now let's look at that moment when I am standing on the fantail looking out at the dragon. You mentioned that it looked like a gate from a ferry. The ferry, for me, is the ferry across the river Styx from Greek mythology where Charon, the ferryman, transports the dead across to Hades, or the underworld. And the gate? Didn't I just tell us that that was the last thing my husband saw before he passed? 'I see the gate' is what he said. In my dream, I also see a gate."

She hadn't made that connection at all, but she now got a big "aha" from that. It was a poignant moment, and we sat with the feeling of that for a minute. She opened her eyes wide and glanced at the two other benevolent witches and all three of them cackled again.

I went on, "Now let's go inside and deal with the table 4 business. What this tells me, in my hijacked version of the dream, is that it is not my time to die yet. My husband, who has passed, his friend, who has passed, and his other friend, who is about to pass, are all onboard and settled into their places on the ship of death. They insist that I go and check with the concierge as to my place here on the ship of death. The concierge, for me, is the angel of death. He guards the tunnel of light where people pass to the other side. The angel of death directs me back to table 4, where I will one day sit, but no matter how hard I try, I just don't belong at table 4 right now. It is not my time to be on the ship of death, but when my time comes, my husband, my dragon, and my friends will be there with me. This is sort of a rehearsal for my passing, and my god, what a cruise it will be!"

Well, there were no words for a bit after that. Her face produced this engaging, beautiful, magical smile, as tears rolled down her cheeks. It didn't matter what we said after that, we had landed deep inside a place of awe, and the room was filled with the soul of that wonderful dragon.

That was a night to remember. Death was in the room, sitting right there in the form of a dragon, and it felt good. As she took down the drawing and rolled it up to take home, she said:

"He's my dragon, you know, he's my dragon. And I look forward to seeing him again."

And what are we to conclude from all this? First, I would say that somehow, death is magical. It sits all the time just under the surface, and if allowed into our consciousness, it can benefit how we live here in the temporary existence of awe and love and pain. This delightful woman with the dragon dream had a relationship with death that was accepting and healthy. As I basked in her presence and felt what she felt as we worked the dream, death served as a touchstone for experiencing life in a state of awe.

Second, I would say that death in dreams is an invitation to transform. If you seek to understand death as a symbol of change and transformation, you will open yourself up to new and beautiful paths, to keys that will allow you to change jobs, heal your wounds, find a new relationship, heal family adversities, recognize your worth in a new world, and in a positive and magical way, move gently towards death, as we all must.

I will never forget the night the three witches of death came to visit us and imbued the room with extraordinary magic.

CHAPTER 19

THE FERRYMAN'S DREAMWORKER

We Are All, Without Exception, Unique, Glorious, Beautiful Souls, Each with Our Own Genius

THE MERCY OF THE FALLEN

They have left us clues,
those merciful souls
who have passed beyond the gates of reason.
Embedded in the scorched wet tracks
left by Charon's immortal transport
lie the echoes of their sensuous sun-drenched lives.
Stand naked in those muddy ancient tracks
left here for us,
reach your arms to the darkened sky.
The shooting stars that fall from the grasp
of those untethered souls who ride with the ferryman
will land in your dreams
and fill you with awe.

WALTER BERRY (2020)

A JOURNEY TO THE OTHER SIDE

One of my most recent dreams encompasses a myriad of themes and images:

THE FERRYMAN'S DREAMWORKER

In the middle of a dream. . . I am in an old amusement park that has been shuttered and has rusty old rides everywhere. It is the middle of the night and the only light is from a full moon, which pours in at an oblique angle from the horizon, making huge shadows on everything from everything else. I hear creaking metal and look up and see the rusty Ferris wheel buckets swaying in the wind. As I look past the Ferris wheel buckets, I notice the stars are out tonight in full force.

I have been talking with The Ferryman, this guy who reminds me of a young Tom Hanks. He is the one who carries people to the other side when they are dead. He is smiling and friendly and we strike up an immediate friendship. We sit and talk for hours amongst all the rusty old thrill rides.

He suddenly lights up with an idea.

"Hey, do you want to go with me tonight when I make my run to the other side?" he asks.

"Hell, yes! Sounds like fun. I'm in," I reply.

We walk over to this long line of thrill-ride buckets laid out on the earth, one behind another and attached with a sparkling silver chain between each one. Their sides are oval-shaped with swirls of blue waves that surround a white center area that is shaped like an egg. They are like old biplane cockpits with a round hole in the top you climb into. The cockpits are lined in black velvety fabric. It reminds me of the linings of coffins. There are 12 sets of these buckets laid out 2 by 2 and attached to each other, so there are 24 of these strange-looking things lined up perfectly behind each other on the earth. They are attached to the lead car, which is a double car where two people can sit. That is where the Ferryman and I will ride. Our double bucket is different. It is oval like the others, but scorched and worn on the leading edge as though it has passed through a thousand sandstorms or meteor showers.

Each bucket has a single person in it, all are anxiously attentive to our presence. The Ferryman takes his seven-foot-tall walking stick made of old gnarled wood and slaps the side of each car with it as we head slowly towards the front of this strange brigade of vehicles. As he strikes each car, he listens to the sound each one makes and then looks the person in the eye and holds that gaze for a moment. There seems to be a strong emotional connection between this pleasant man and all the people. This seems so odd and new to me. It's as though he can see through each of them and everything they think or feel. He also checks to make sure the doors are closed and everything is ready. After it satisfies him that all is in order, he stands at the front of the lead car and raises his knurled walking stick high over his head parallel to the earth and shakes it. The 24 people raise their hands high over their heads in response. Everyone is committed and ready for this monumental journey. This gives me goosebumps. The Ferryman climbs into the driver's side of the double bucket at the front and I climb into the passenger's side.

I look back at all 24 people and they are all smiling, but they look spooky because of the way the cars are directly lined up facing the moon. Because of this, the full moon throws the shadow of each person onto the face of the person behind them. It's an odd sight as the shadows dance on each face all the way to the rear. There are people of all ages. I am surprised there aren't more old people here, but, hey; I am just a visitor.

We lift off into the dark night sky. Strung out behind us are the 24 people in cars and we are pulling them as the silver chains clank and strain. There is a sense of music to this clanging of chains, an eerie melodic mesmerizing sound. The Ferryman gets that Tom Hanks twinkle in his eye and does a few twists and turns over the amusement park for my benefit. This must look pretty damn cool from the ground, this string of old buckets flying over the old park.

We travel out into the night and gain speed. The moon has disappeared, leaving only starlight to see anything by. The journey is silent for a long time as we push deeper into the darkness.

Suddenly the guy directly behind me, an older guy, maybe mid-sixties, yells out, "Stop! Stop! The stars are showing me something. I see the numbers 2 and 1! Wait, I also see a whale and a squid and something else out there!"

Sure enough, all of us look out where he is pointing and we all see a formation of stars in the shape of the numbers 2 and 1. Then he points lower, and, yes, there are stars that form constellations of a squid and a whale and something else.

The Ferryman stops the car and looks at me.

Why is he looking at me?

Then I realize that he has tricked me. He didn't bring me along just to let me experience this. I am the Dreamworker who has come along to work dreams!

Well, okay, I am always up for a challenge, so let's do this.

Out here in the dark, on the way to the other side, everyone's life is easily accessible to anyone who wants to tune in. I look at the guy behind me and read his life telepathically somehow. His name is Frank. The guy is dead, of course. He died at 22 or 24, but he also died at 8 or 9 years old at the same time. Somehow that knowledge comes to me as I look at him. I ask him what happened when he was 21, because the first thing he saw out here were the numbers 2 and 1, in that order. He talks about how joyful his life was at that moment, and then how everything changed when he died at 24. He talks extensively about how that death drastically changed the rest of his life. Everyone on the ride is silent, totally engaged and listening to Frank and his story as we stand perfectly still here in outer space.

As I am unpacking this dream with Frank, I suddenly realize something. The Ferryman has brought me here to teach me something. When people die, they travel with him, and as they do, the unfinished and bereft images that represent parts of themselves that they haven't healed will appear along the way. When this happens, he stops the ride and a Dreamworker—which is me on this trip—will work through every unfinished, unhealed event. The Dreamworker does this with each passenger until everyone has cleared their soul of every damn one of these wounds and all the unfinished business of their life. Once we have completed that, The Ferryman can finish the journey and disembark his passengers, who will then be ready to go onto the next part of life, which is death and life again. Now, how cool is that?

Suddenly the dream shifts and I am at a dream conference. Jeremy Taylor, my mentor, has just finished talking and we break up into workshops. A woman with short grey hair approaches me. She and her group applaud me for my work with the dead guy on the thrill ride bucket brigade. I am slightly embarrassed, but also thrilled that they witnessed it and wanted to hear the story. She brings me a drawing of the whale and the squid and the other something that the guy talked about. "You know, this is an angry fish, don't you? And this is an angry squid, don't you? And this is an angry other thing, don't you?" she says with an angry tone. "Yes," I say humbly, "I know that."

As we move towards the workshop, I confide in a guy who looks similar to The Ferryman and quietly tell him the entire tale about The Ferryman and the Dreamworker. I wonder for a moment if this is something too sacred to speak aloud, but from the twinkle in his eye I know I needed to tell this thrilling tale.

As I am telling my story with deep passion, out of the corner of my eye I notice an intriguing door off to the left with a black doorknob. The instant I focus on the door, there is a powerful rush of deep emotion that sweeps over me, paralyzing me. I realize suddenly that The Ferryman and the 24 passengers are in the next room behind that door. It is a completely dark room. A room so dark, no one could see anything if they dared to open the door and look in.

Waiting there are my people, and emotion wells up in my throat. They are waiting, patiently waiting for me to return and join them in the journey to the other side. I am their Dreamworker and it is my job and privilege to open each of their dreams as they go. They may have to wait a long time for me to finish what I am doing, but time is not a problem with them. Knowing that, I relax and continue my saga with my new friend. But suddenly the love and the sense of belonging these wonderful people have for me chokes me up.

Oh, my god, this entire group of people, all 24 and The Ferryman to boot are right in the next room waiting patiently for me. The Ferryman and his smiling face and my new companions that are dead are watching and smiling and just waiting patiently for my return. It makes me realize that I am not alone in this life, or in this death—I am not alone. I wake up, tears streaming down my face.

This is another "big" dream of mine, and I thought it appropriate to end this book with it. This is definitely a dream from the Land of Awes, so let's use the skills we have developed in our adventure together and open it up.

I was struck by the universality of this dream and enamored with the concept that dreamwork is exactly the solution to the unfinished business that appeared inside the dream. All 24 of those people probably represent parts of me, and I just bet they all have a ton of things that need clearing up before completing the passage to the next life. Isn't this something all of us need to accomplish? We need to look deep into the center of our souls and clear up all the things that are still bothering us, things that stand in the way of our individuation and enlightenment. And why wait until we are sitting in that rusty old amusement park ride bucket on the journey across the ether to the other side? Let's look at our whales and squids now, and face and incorporate all of who we are, good and bad, into a life that is lived without reservation.

By now in the process, you know that we are going to plunge deep into this big dream. You could probably do it by your lonesome, but I will help. Let's look at the various aspects of the dream and see where the ride takes us.

THE UNIVERSAL, THE PERSONAL, AND BEING BORN IN A CIRCUS TENT

This dream seems lofty and deals with the big questions of life and death, but it is also extremely personal, which I didn't see until I worked with it both by myself and with my insightful dream group. It is easy to look at dreams as metaphors for everyone and slide over the fact that this is my dream—that I need to look at my own soul and at what I need to celebrate and also to fix. On one very important level, it is about what I am doing in my life and what I will do. This dream invites me to take on the mantel of the Ferryman's Dreamworker, and I gladly accept that job. It is my greatest joy to journey alongside all these perplexing and beautiful dreamers and their soul-laden dreams that I get to live inside of and learn from.

Let's dig deeper and see what this dream holds.

Here goes. First, what emotions does the dreamer feel in the dream? The overall feel of the dream is extremely pleasant. I strike up a new friendship, which is joyful. In this dream I get to go on a sacred journey that few people experience more than once in their lives, and that is also a joy. I am surprised that I get to do dreamwork, but that too turns into a joy as I slip into a genuine place of awe in the dream. Another emotion arises when the gray-haired woman confronts me about how everything Frank saw is angry. This makes anger rise in me.

At the end is another emotional piece, as I realize that all those people are patiently waiting for me. I am deeply moved by that, so much so that the sense of connection spills over into waking life as tears of love and joy stream down my face. That final, powerful emotion seems to be the key to the dream. When I tell that part of the dream, my body shakes and I am flushed with emotion, caring, and a sense of love that somehow overwhelms me and connects me to my own soul.

That is the landscape of the emotions in the dream. It can be the principal purpose of a dream to allow us to feel things, to be emotional, sad, joyous, angry, loving. How often do we get to express our emotions in this difficult life of ours? Not enough, says I, so let it roll when you work a dream—it can only make you healthier. Besides, your inner self—your soul—wants to express itself, to show its genius, strengths, weaknesses, and hurts, so look deep into the emotions in a dream—you will never regret it.

Now, let's move on to the narrative of the dream. The first thing that appears is an amusement park with old rusted rides. Amusement parks like this harken back to my early childhood. The memories are fuzzy, but I remember that our family used to go to a lot of the carnivals and amusement parks in Southern New Jersey, and those rides were a place of magic for me. My stomach churned and my spirit soared with delight as I was flung high into the air inside an old metal spaceship that spun around and around, or I got to crash into my brothers in the bumper cars.

Where this line of thought leads is to this: My mother was born in a circus tent in Sarasota, Florida because her father was in a traveling Wild West show, and I wonder if that fact has any bearing here? That may be a side step, but that happens when you open up to the powerful influences of a dream. My friends tell me that my mother being born in the circus fits perfectly with how they see me—the Trickster Clown.

Perhaps the dream is using these thrill ride objects and the entire idea of the amusement park as a reminder of the magic place we start from in life, and saying it is only appropriate that we leave this existence in that same magical way. Or, perhaps it is a reminder that the magic in my life has become rusted and unused, and it's time to climb back into it and soar again. I think both things are correct for me.

THE FERRYMAN CHARON

On to The Ferryman now. The Ferryman we are talking about in this dream refers to Charon, the dour Greek underworld god, who reports to the master of the underworld, Hades. He is the son of Erebus (Darkness, or Shadow) and Nyx (Night), and his task is to ferry the souls of those who have departed across the five rivers surrounding Hades.

Interesting here is that Charon in the Greek myths is the polar opposite of our young Tom Hanks Ferryman. When the psychopomp Hermes shows up with the souls of the dead on the shores of the river Acheron (the river of woe), certain rules apply. When the souls are buried, they must have a single silver coin in their mouth—or Charon, the grisly god, will leave them on the banks of the river Cocytus, the river of lamentation. (This is the same river that Minthe, that vixen from my Angelina Jolie dream, ruled over.) There they will wander as ghosts for a hundred years. Charon, using his ferryman's pole, forces the sinners who have paid into his ancient skiff. They then travel to the river Lethe (as in "lethargy"), the river of forgetfulness, where they are instructed to drink the water, which makes them forget their earthly lives and prepares them for reincarnation.

This is not at all like our Ferryman or the journey in the dream. The ride in our dream seems magical and joyful compared to the doleful and harrowing experience in the Greek version, even if it is wrought with difficulties that have to be ironed out. Our Ferryman does have a long walking stick reminiscent of old-school Charon's paddle, which he uses both as an oar and as a cudgel in herding the dead into and out of his skiff. As we see in this detail of Michelangelo's Sistine Chapel fresco *The Last Judgment,* Charon swings his oar at the damned as he forces them off his skiff into the waiting maw of Dante's hell.

Detail of *The Last Judgment,* 1535–1541 by Michelangelo Buonarroti

But our Tom Hanks Ferryman uses his oar to make the people secure in their ride to the other side.

Why such a difference between the two stories—how do we reconcile them? We can explain the difference if we take a step back and look at the Ferryman as an archetype who moves us from one reality into another. Thus, he is an archetype of change and transformation. The symbology is clear in both cases. But there is no avoiding the glaring fact we are talking about actual death here, at least on one level.

The dream gods want to talk to the dreamer, me, about his death, the crossing-over that will occur in the not-so-distant future, and how to work with his own shadow figures. In my dream, that message is far more effective if delivered by a trickster Tom Hanks than a dour Charon of Dante's ilk. This is not Dante's dream, so whatever went on in his life may not apply here in Walter's. The dream gods use the story of Charon and the crossing but infuse that tale with the memories, joys, difficulties, and needs of dreamer Walter. Dreams deliver up the tried-and-true tales, myths, and folklore that carry universal messages, but they are tailored in content to affect the dreamer they are designed for.

The dream confirms that my job is to help people see within their own dreams the help and answers they need to live their beautiful, unique lives. If you see that your own dreams are tailor-made for you by your own unconscious in pursuit of wholeness and individuation, then the Ferryman and the Dreamworker have done their job.

I think there is a Ferryperson or two in each of our lives—not just the guy that takes us on our final journey to death, but the force that moves us from one stuck place into a clearing where we can move more freely and follow the threads of our lives forward.

The Ferrypeople in my life have usually been actual people, not just concepts. My friend and colleague David Jenkins illustrates how a Ferryperson can function in our everyday lives. David is a dreamworker who has worked extensively with me in dream groups, workshops, and personally. He and I have collaborated on dream workshops where I work from a visual angle, and he works from a narrative angle, with terrific results. Over time, he noticed I was conducting myself during workshops in a self-effacing way that just didn't sit well with him.

Sometimes as I work a dream, I become a trickster. I pretend to not understand something or get it wrong on purpose so the dreamer can correct me or inform me, and then often they'll get an "aha" or express something that can lead to a new angle on the dream. Well, David watched this self-effacing trickster humor I sprinkled broadly into the dreamwork for quite some time. But he perceived that, in using this technique, I was putting myself down. I wasn't just pretending not to understand something; I was extolling my shortcomings.

He confronted me and told me that although the dreamers might get something out of my doing this, they also lost some respect for me. Indeed, David told me in no uncertain terms that "putting myself one-down" as he phrased it, affects my self-esteem and thus the work. He actually glared at me, like Charon holding that cudgel. He told me if I wanted to succeed as a dreamworker, I would have to stop such nonsense.

In other words, without my realizing it, this clever little trick had held me stuck in self-doubt. David grabbed Charon's oar and whacked me upside the head, launching me out of the conundrum. So, I changed how I used the trickster approach by eliminating the self-effacing piece. I still become the trickster when working dreams, but Ferryman David significantly changed how I do it.

But my Ferryman dream still has much more in store.

What about the design on the sides of the cars in the Ferryman's flying caravan, which feels somehow mystical? Blue ocean waves surround a white egg. I had to draw this part of the dream in order to contemplate its significance. Once I did that, I realized that these cars are a symbol of renewal, of resurrection, of reincarnation. As Charon forces us to drink of the waters of forgetfulness, the egg of new life arises, parting the waves of death to give us new existence, a new birth. Thus, in my dream, each of these 24 souls has a symbol of renewal emblazoned on the side of their bucket transport, symbolizing that every one of them will live again.

LET'S BE FRANK

Let's turn to the man who caused the Ferryman to stop the journey to the other side, the man who excitedly saw the 2 and the 1 and the squid and the whale in the sky. Frank, that 60-something-year-old guy sitting directly behind me in the line of buckets—who in the early part of the dream sits in my shadow from the moon—is "frankly" me. He is the right age, and I have projected onto him the shadow parts of myself. In fact, as I look back at him, I bend side to side, moving my shadow on and off him, watching how the light and shadow play on his face (something I do a lot in waking life, being a lighting expert obsessed with light and shadow).

And just in case I don't get that this is about being "frank" with myself and casting my shadow on my frankness, the first thing Frank sees are the numbers 2 and 1. In the dream I jump immediately to making that 21, but what he says is 2 and 1, and if I twist that slightly, it comes out, we 2 are 1. So, my frank self lets me know that we are in this together. Let's stay with the numbers, since this dream has quite a few that call out for attention.

Frank has died several times in the dream, first at eight or nine, again at 22 or 23, and then "actually" when he was 24. And you don't think the dream will let me get away with thinking this is actually about someone else, like I did at first, do you? Nope. I have to look at my life at eight or nine and again at 21 through 24.

Let's start with eight. Of course a story comes to mind when I think back on my life at eight. This particular story is archetypal, and very revealing of my childhood.

THE FACTS OF LIFE

I am the second of seven children, and when I was eight, I remember my older brother Bob talking about something he quietly called "the facts of life." He was talking with his friends, and when I overheard this, I asked him about it. His friends snickered and left. I asked him again, and he turned bright red and told me it was a secret, and he had this appalling look on his face. Yikes! What was this "facts of life" secret? I really wanted to know, but I had a feeling that it was a secret so deep and dreadful I shouldn't know it. I tried to let it go, but I couldn't. Facts are things that exist; they are indisputable truths. Life—well, that is all the things that move, like humans and animals. So, they must be talking about some indisputable truth about *my* life, my eight-year-old-self thought.

After waiting a week, a week in which I had nightmares of monsters and robots chasing me, I went to my parents and asked them.

"Mom and Dad, I heard Bobby talking about 'the facts of life,' and he says it's a secret. What are the facts of life? And why is it a secret?"

Well, you can imagine their response. They looked at each other in disbelief, and there was silence while they exchanged glances, as if to say, "You tell him!" "No, you tell him!" back and forth.

Finally, my mom said, "Yes. It is a secret and you are not old enough to know about it."

"What? Why? Why can't I know? How come Bobby gets to know and I don't?"

They both got this look, the same appalled look I had seen on Bobby's face. Oh, my god, I had stepped into a dark place unmeant for me to tread. My heart raced. My young mind raced about in panic. Maybe I was adopted. Maybe I would die soon. Maybe there was no god.

Then my mom said, "Bobby is different from you. We are all different from you. We are all unique, and when the right time comes, you will find out about the facts of life, so don't ask again."

My dad then chimed in loudly, so loudly that everyone heard, "Who wants to go to McDonald's?"

Well, that was that. The gaggle of kids piled in the station wagon shrieking and howling, and off we went to the one treat we always loved. I never asked again about "the facts of life," but you can well imagine how the whole thing stuck in my craw, as my mom would say, and silently turned me inside out. The forbidden question needed an answer, no matter how dark it might be. That look on their faces was so horribly distressing. My god, what was going on here?

So, I was different, and that seemed to be the key. My mom had once told me I differed from all the other siblings, that I was more sensitive than all of them put together. And it stuck in my soul that when I confronted her about the facts of life, she said it again.

I became obsessed. As I would drift off to sleep in my lower bunk bed, counting the number of wavy lines the metal springs made, the nightmares with monsters and robots came back. Then it dawned on me: *Oh, my god, I am not real! That's what they meant! The facts of life are that they are human and I am not! I am a robot. Oh, god, I am a robot!*

I turned cold and cried, lying there in my bunk. I have never felt so all alone in all my life as I did at that moment. My mind conjured a horrid thought: *When I am older, they will tell me I am not one of them, that I am a machine, not a human. If I took a knife right now and cut myself open, I would see that there was machinery under there, not muscles and flesh. All this time I have thought I was a boy, a human, with a soul, but I am not.*

But wait—I had severed a toe earlier that year, and there was lots of blood, so I must be human. I remembered that when we finally got to the doctor who would operate on me, he had these enormous, black-rimmed glasses that made his eyes look like giant saucers with chocolate doughnuts in the center—he was downright scary. He looked into my eyes and smiled and then said to my mom that I was a very "special young man" and he would fix me up like new.

Well, looking back from my eight-year-old self to my seven-year-old self, the realization dawned that the five hours those doctors spent putting my toe back on wasn't so much a miracle of medicine as an engineering feat. They had to call in a doctor who specialized in robots—so no, just having blood didn't make you human. I was a robot. No wonder I was so "different" and "special." "The facts of life" were that I was not human, but a well-constructed robot—with blood.

If this had been a movie, it would have been a really cool thing, but it was not. I became closed and quiet, resigned to the inevitable moment when I would be exposed at the unveiling of "the facts of life." I trudged through life that way for a long time (well, months, which is a long time for a kid), carrying this deep, alienating secret.

TWO TOTALLY HOT GUYS AS ANGELS

So, Frank, our character in the dream, talks about dying at eight or nine, and this robot scenario qualifies as a death at eight—but what of age nine?

Two huge things happened when I was nine. The first had to do with my mother and her libido.

One sunny afternoon in Brookfield Estates, our quiet little housing development in Southern New Jersey, two young men from Utah and Idaho dressed in white shirts and ties were "tracting" (a term for leaving religious tracts at people's doors) for the Mormon Church. This was an unusual sight in those days—no Mormons lived in Southern New Jersey. My father was a lapsed Catholic and my mother a Southern Baptist, so the state of religious beliefs in our family was a pot of confusion. None of us had ever heard of the Mormon Church. When my mother opened the door to reveal these two tall, lanky, beautiful men, it took her breath away. They were like two angels sent from heaven. They struck up an immediate conversation, and she invited them in for glasses of water.

They came back later when my dad was home and presented this bizarre "lesson," using a small black flannel board to tell their story. They put figures of Jesus and the apostles and Joseph Smith and the "Angel" Moroni and golden plates on the flannel board. It looked like a two-dimensional version of Punch and Judy, but my mom was totally digging it. They told the story of how the true church had been taken from the earth and then restored in 1830 through Joseph Smith meeting God and Jesus and then this angel who gave him golden plates to translate into the Book of Mormon.

Say what? Well, my dad was baffled about the entire thing, wondering why my mom had invited these guys over. My mom, on the other hand, was all-agog and loved the whole event. Not only was she all a-flutter about these friendly, smoking-hot men, I think the visual presentation was just what she needed. It turns out, believe it or not, that my mother had never learned to read. She had left school early and worked as a child in sock factories to support the family of eight kids while her alcoholic father drank himself into oblivion.

And so, the Mormon Missionaries came back time after time with lesson after lesson. Their trusty flannel board had more stories to tell. Soon all of us were getting baptized into Mormondom.

Now remember, I was a robot, so all this religious dogma meant little to me; I just went along with the program. Watching all this made me long for the simple days when I thought I was human, but I was dead to that now. I was an unfeeling hunk of machinery waiting for the dreaded moment when my robotness would be revealed and I would be removed from my family and put into service like a vacuum cleaner or combination blender/calculator.

And then that same year, two remarkable dreams changed everything. The first was this very strange experience I kept silent about until my mid-forties.

THE BALL OF ENERGY

I am in the backyard on a sunny summer day sitting silently watching the leaves in the trees sway in the breeze. Suddenly this magnificent gold ball with strange marks on it magically appears about six feet in front of me at eye level. It seems alive somehow as it spins and stops and bobs and floats. It glows with an amber light from within, which pours out of the strange symbols on its surface. I get mesmerized watching it. It is about the size of a softball and it invites me to talk to it. I have no idea what to say. It asks me to stand and I do. The ball moves closer and closer, and I can feel this powerful energy pouring off of it, and I become afraid. I move fearfully backwards and end up slammed into a huge tree trunk. There is no escape, and the ball moves inside my chest, where a heart would be in a human. I try to scream, but nothing comes out. This is the end. I am done. This must be what humans call death. I accept that my robot self is dying.

And then I feel things. Oh, my god, I feel things. I feel emotions like sadness and joy and fear and love, and it confuses me. Robots don't feel things like this, so I must be human! This rush of emotions and energy coursing through my body wakes me with a start.

When I awaken, oddly, so oddly, the feeling is still there. I can feel this ball of energy inside my chest. And even stranger, it stays with me. From that day forward, I know that there is something inside me I can trust, some inner self that is the real me somehow.

After that, as I traipsed through life, enduring the Mormon indoctrination, high school, the pains of growing up, the bad marriage, and all the rest, the one thing I could rely on was that ball of energy inside me. The Judy Garland experience activated the ball of energy to a greater degree than any other time in my life, but it was always with me, vibrating silently inside. I could trust it to center me, so I felt connected to some deep place inside of myself and at the same time, to something powerful outside of myself.

I was hesitant to tell this story. It seems so strange and way outside the walls of reason, but it was what happened, and it is part of who I am, so I am compelled to put it down here.

Still, in waking life, this strange ball of energy dream didn't convince me that I wasn't a robot. Hell no. I incorporated it into the tale of being a robot and trudged on.

And then part two happened. I had a recurring nightmare that first appeared just after the ball of energy dream, and it visited me every week for months.

BLOWING THE WHISTLE

I am standing in the center of a huge gymnasium. I am dressed in bright white shorts and a bright white t-shirt, and there is a silver whistle hanging around my neck on a black cord. On either side of me, there are 50-foot-high rippling red human muscles that stretch the full length of the gym and reach all the way to the top of the ceiling. They are wet and slimy and pulse and ripple with power. They are identical, and somehow I know they are here to fight and I am the referee.

I place the whistle in my mouth and blow it loudly. When I do, the two muscles surge to the center and fight, pushing with all their might at each other. I am stuck in the center, and I am being crushed to death. My body is being pulverized and the worst part is that I cannot breathe! I am about to pass out when I somehow blow the whistle again. The muscles retreat immediately, back to the edges of the brightly lit gymnasium where they started. I catch my breath, brush off the slime, and believe it or not, I blow the whistle again. The same thing happens all over again—I am crushed in the center until I almost pass out and then I blow the whistle again. This same scenario repeats five times. I wake from the dream in a panic, trying to catch my breath.

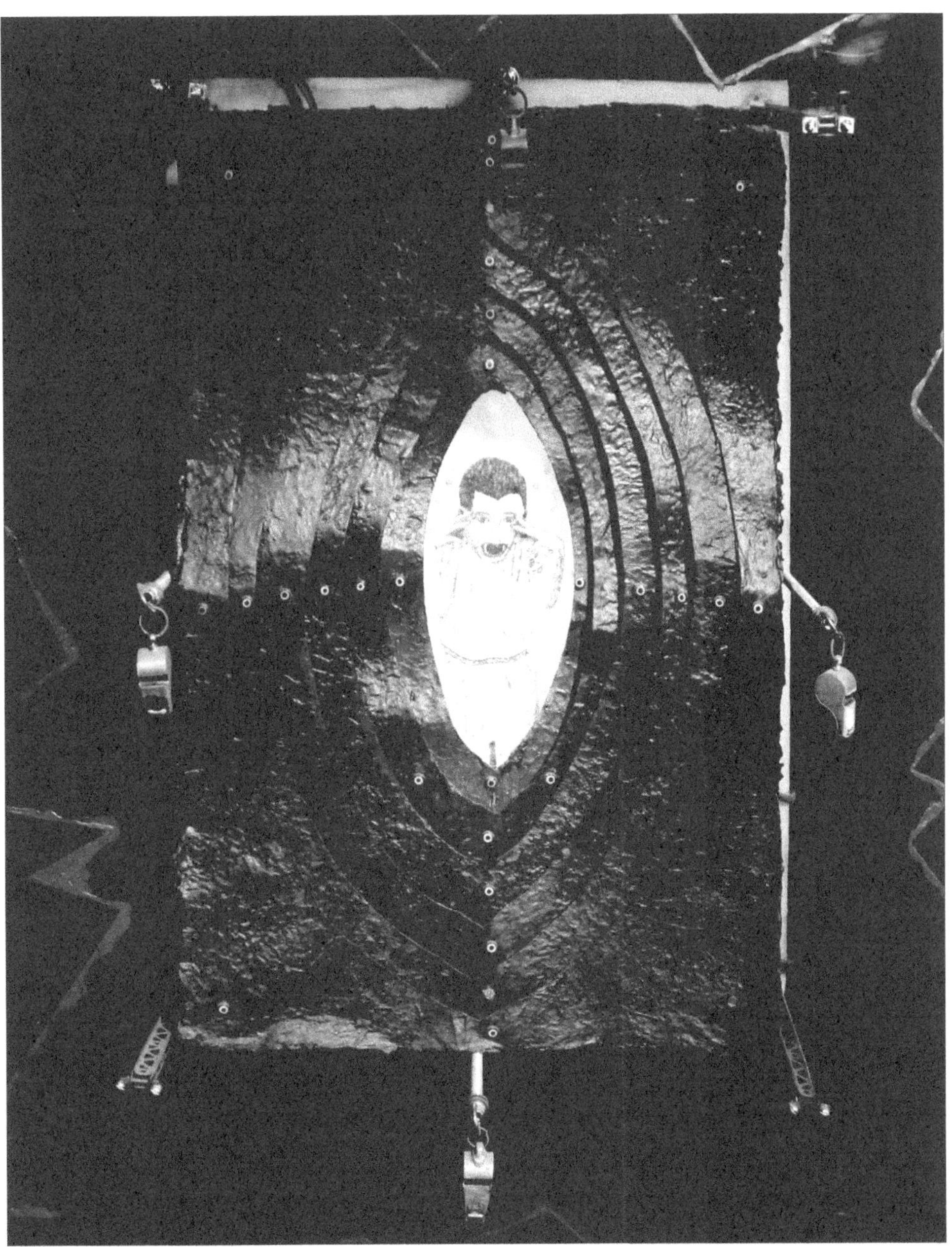

Blowing the Whistle Walter Berry (2015)

My first thought upon waking was: *What an idiot! Just stop blowing the damn whistle!*

But then it dawned on me. If I couldn't breathe, but I was really trying to, I must be human. I was not a damn robot, I was a human! In that instant, the robot era terminated itself.

It was an ignoble end to the robot theory, and I had to rethink all sorts of things. It really threw me. I went out to the shed in the backyard and sat on the lawnmower, and in that solitude I put things together. And strangely, the nightmares of the muscles stopped after that.

It wasn't until I was in my 50s that I realized that the crushing muscle dream was something besides a nightmare of no importance. I told it to a woman who promptly informed me it was probably a birth dream: those crushing walls of muscles were the vagina contracting during birth. What a revelation that was! Why had I never thought of that? Vaginal walls crushing in on me? Sounds absolutely delightful from this place in my life.

As a child I was back to being human, and I slowly accepted that fact. That ball of energy stayed with me, which still somehow maintained my secret robot status, at least to myself, so the robot idea didn't completely die. The ball of energy is the touchstone for me in detecting a moment of awe. You probably have something similar in another form that speaks to you in moments of joy or awe or warning. I suspect that those of you who know me will say to yourselves, "*Now* I get him."

So, that was my eight- and nine-year-old self and how those events fit into Frank's "dying" at eight or nine. At eight I died into becoming a robot, and at nine I died into becoming a Mormon. These were big changes, or deaths, which the dream wanted me to look at.

BEING FRANK ABOUT MY TWENTIES

In my big dream, we still have to unpack Frank at 21 through 24. Frank tells me he was full of joy at 21, and that all changed when he died at 24.

When I was 21, I was in my sophomore year at Brigham Young University, after returning from my two-year mission for the Mormon Church in California, and it was a joyous time. I took my first theatre directing class that year, and I created a one-act play based on two Dr. Seuss stories—*The Big Brag* and *Yertle the Turtle*. When it was performed, I was shocked out of my gourd at how successful it was. People absolutely roared and jumped up and down with joy and laughter. It was a seminal moment of awe for me. I felt real worth at that instant, and this cemented my love affair with the theatre. It was probably the most "successful" moment of my life, and it changed me forever. It immersed me in the Land of Awes. And so, it seems that Frank and I were on the same path at 21.

Which leads us to age 24. What sort of death occurred then for me? In working dreams, brutal honesty helps, and the brutal truth is, that was when I met my future wife. It was to turn into a difficult marriage and a painful experience that was death-like in so many ways. And yet, standing in the place I am now, I am thankful for that transformative experience. It is part of who I am.

And just like Frank, who has to work through his unfinished business before he can land on the other side, I too have unfinished business having to do with my long-ago marriage, and this dream is the moment to work through it.

A WHALE AND A SQUID IN MORTAL COMBAT

What else does Frank see in the sky during our journey to the other side? Frank sees a squid and a whale and something else. The "something else" was distinct, but by the time I recorded this long, clear dream, it had fallen from memory. I suspect that slice slipped back into my unconscious and may appear in some future dream. We shall see. But the other creatures Frank saw in the sky, I saw too, as I sat there next to the Trickster Ferryman with his Tom Hanks twinkle.

There they were—bold as can be—a giant whale and a squid composed of points of light or stars, like constellations. A whale and a squid? Sometimes in working dreams, symbolic forms like these defy meaning. They seemed important, but for the life of me, I didn't get them. I was pretty set on letting them fall into that special mental bin marked Factos Obscura, but then something came to me. "Wait a minute! Didn't I see a film called *The Squid and the Whale?*" Sure enough, I had seen that film in 2006. I didn't remember much about it except it was about a divorce and two kids.

I ordered the DVD on eBay and watched it again, and that whale and squid in the sky in the dream fell surprisingly into place. The movie is about two boys aged 16 and 12 whose parents separate. The younger one takes the mother's side and the older one takes the father's, as they go through a painful coming-of-age scenario while the parents slug it out in the background. The younger one masturbates in public all the time, and the older one is a trickster who tries to pass off Pink Floyd lyrics as his own and is attracted to his father's new girlfriend. Identifying with the two boys, I see how the younger brother is my robot self, and the older one stands in the center of the gymnasium being crushed by a vagina. The roles of the parents are dead matches for my marriage struggle in my twenties.

The title *The Squid and the Whale* refers to the moment when the older boy goes to the American Museum of Natural History in New York with his mother and sees the giant diorama of a sperm whale in mortal combat with a giant squid framed in black (reminiscent of our dark sky in the dream). It frightens the boy so much, he can only look at it through the gaps of his fingers, which resembles the sketchy way the squid and the whale appear in my dream. It also suggests the terrible struggles of the four characters as they face powerful forces, and their lives transform.

The film's final shot (spoiler alert!) is of the boy, previously frightened of the squid and the whale, now standing tall staring at the diorama, much like our Frank in the amusement car bucket gazing at the squid and the whale made of stars. And if all this weren't enough—guess what the two boys' names in the film are? The older boy is Walter, and the younger boy is Frank. Wow, what a "coincidence," no? This is how smart, accurate, deep, complex, and profound our dreams are.

THE LAND OF AWES STANDS WAITING

This "Big Dream" exemplifies the vast, knowing expanse of the unconscious, both personal and collective, that awaits our understanding. Not every dream is as life-changing (or as clearly decoded) as this one, but each dream can give us such clues about ourselves. I now stand ready to see who amongst those 24 souls traveling to the beyond is next to tell the things that need to be seen in their life and mine. I am prepared to hear and feel and understand the dreams of others—as well as my own—to launch each one of us, one soul at a time, into the Land of Awes.

I hope you will take from this book the affirmation that we are all, without exception, unique, glorious, beautiful souls, each with our own genius. Your psyche, your soul, your true unadulterated self waits for you to see, hear, and experience the incredible being that you are. I urge you to embrace your own genius by digging deep inside your soul and allowing the poetry to appear.

Find some words that feel like they just need to be expressed, and tell someone in a poetic way that you love them. Then in that same poetic voice, tell yourself your own value. Allow yourself to dance in rhythm with your life. Really. You know you want to—just allow your body to move to the song of self now and then. Allow artful creative forces to overwhelm you and put some marks on the world with your hands. Wax philosophical as you think of the life lessons you have endured. Find wisdom in the folds of life that only you know—voice it, or write it. Listen to those powerful voices of your child, your adult, your unvoiced god who speaks through your dreams. You are the most delightful and important person in your life, and your dreams will affirm that.

Yes, dark images do arise from these bubbling cauldrons of self-realization, as we traverse nightmares and unpleasant dreams that bring to our attention the missteps and travails laid upon us. We have dark periods and losses that seem so destructive that we will never recover. But these dreaming souls of ours never give up. They stand in the dark every night conjuring magic potions that even in their darkness are elixirs brewed from the primordial soup of our own unique souls, offering up what is needed to rise above the din of ego and self-doubt that surround us in our conscious world. The Land of Awes stands waiting, its old, scarred door standing ajar, beckoning us to step on in. The map needed to find that door is written on your soul every night in your dreams.

I invite you to dwell often in the Land of Awes by following the archetypal pattern your dreams create for you. It is a place we all deserve to stand in, live in, and rejoice in. Join me there.

Blessings,

The Ferryman's Dreamworker

PROSPERO

Our revels now are ended. These our actors,
As I foretold you, were all spirits, and
Are melted into air, into thin air:
And like the baseless fabric of this vision,
The cloud-capp'd tow'rs, the gorgeous palaces,
The solemn temples, the great globe itself,
Yea, all which it inherit, shall dissolve,
And, like this insubstantial pageant faded,
Leave not a rack behind. We are such stuff
As dreams are made on; and our little life
Is rounded with a sleep.

William Shakespeare
from *The Tempest*

SOURCES

Opening epigraph

Jalal ad-Din Rumi, "The Guest House," *The Illuminated Rumi.* Translated by Coleman Barks. (Broadway Books; 1st edition, October 13, 1997).

Preface

Albert Einstein, from *Living Philosophies.* (New York: Simon and Schuster, 1931).

Introduction

Carl Jung, *The Spirit in Man, Art, and Literature.* 1930. (*Collected Works of C.G. Jung, Vol. 15*, Princeton University Press, 1971).

Chapter 1

Rachel Carson, *The Sense of Wonder.* (HarperCollins Canada. 1998).

Chapter 2

William Stafford, *The Way It Is: New and Selected Poems.* (Graywolf Press, 1998).

Chapter 3

Antoine de Saint-Exupery, *The Little Prince.* (Reynal & Hitchcock, 1943).

Chapter 4

Emily Dickinson, "The Soul should always stand ajar." *The Complete Poems of Emily Dickinson.* (Little, Brown and Co., 1960).

Carl Jung, "General Aspects of Dream Psychology." *Collected Works of C.G. Jung, Vol. 8.* (Princeton University Press 1970).

Chapter 5

Carl Jung, *Collected Work of C.G. Jung, Vol. 8.* (Princeton University Press 1953–1979).

Chapter 6

Rumi, *The Essential Rumi.* Translated by Coleman Barks. (HarperCollins, 1996).

Melissa Dahl, "People Who Can Control Their Dreams are also Better at Real Life." (*New York Magazine*, September 11, 2014).

Clare Johnson, Ph.D., *Llewellyn's Complete Book of Lucid Dreaming.* (Llewellyn Worldwide, USA, 2017).

Robert Waggoner, *Lucid Dreaming: Gateway to the Inner Self.* (Moment Point Press, 2008).

Chapter 7

Carl Jung, "Good and Evil in Analytical Psychology," *Collected Works of C.G. Jung, Vol. 10. Civilization in Transition.* (Princeton University Press, 1970).

Amy Newmark and Kelly Sullivan Walden, *Chicken Soup for the Soul—Dreams and Premonitions.* (Chicken Soup for the Soul Publishing, 2015).

Chapter 8

Henry Wadsworth Longfellow, "Nuremberg: A Poem," *The Complete Poetical Works of Henry Wadsworth Longfellow.* (Nabu Press, 2010).

Robert J. Hoss, MS, *Dream Language: Self-Understanding through Imagery and Color.* (Innersource, 2005).

Rubin Naiman, Ph.D., "Dreamless: The silent epidemic of REM sleep loss." (*Annals of the New York Academy of Sciences*, October 2017).

Agnes de Mille, *Martha: The Life and Work of Martha Graham.* (Random House, 1991).

Chapter 9

C.G. Jung, *The Red Book.* (W.W. Norton & Company, 2009).

Wikipedia, "Awe." en.wikipedia.org/wiki/Awe, retrieved April 25, 2021.

Carl Jung, "The Structure of the Psyche." *Collected Works of C.G. Jung, Vol. 8.* (Princeton University Press 1953-1979).

Devdutt Pattanaik, "10 best mythological tales from around the world." *Hindustan Times* (October 2016).

Chapter 10

Michael Meade, *Fate and Destiny, the Two Agreements of the Soul.* (Greenfire Press, 2010).

Michael Meade, "East and West Must Meet," Living myth podcast #26, Mosaicvoices.org.

Chapter 11

Jimmy J. Fraigne, et al., "REM Sleep at its Core – Circuits, Neurotransmitters, and Pathophysiology," Ed. Patrick Fuller, Harvard Medical School, *Frontiers in Neurology.* (May 29, 2015).

Brigitte Holzinger, Bernd Saletu and Gerhard Klosch, "Cognitions in Sleep: Lucid Dreaming as an Intervention for Nightmares in Patients With Posttraumatic Stress Disorder." *Frontiers in Psychology.* (August 21, 2020).

Antonio Oliviero, "Why Do Some People Sleepwalk?" *Scientific American.* (February, 2008).

Chapter 12

Robert Frost, "Gathering Leaves." published in 1923 in New Hampshire, public domain.

Jim Hopper, Ph.D., "Recovered Memories of Sexual Abuse." jmhooper.com, retrieved April 7, 2021.

Chapter 13

J.W. Dunne, *Experiment with Time.* (Faber and Faber, 1927).

Chapter 14

John Donne, *No Man is an Island.* (Souvenir Press, 1988).

Paul Amerigo Pajo. StackExchange. (May 2011) StackExchange.com.

Chapter 15

Carl Jung, "General Aspects of Dream Psychology." *Collected Works of C.G. Jung, Vol. 8.* (Princeton University Press 1970).

Chapter 16

Kelly Bulkeley, Ph.D., "Dreaming in the Digital Age." *Psychology Today* (February 2016).

Ami Ronnbert, Editor, *The Book of Symbols: Reflections on Archetypal Images.* (Taschen, 2010).

Anonymous. "History of Mint: Folklore and Medicine." OurHerbGarden.com.

Chapter 17

Rumi, *Rumi: In the Arms of the Beloved.* translated by Jonathon Star. (Tarcher, 2000).

Carl Jung, "General Aspects of Dream Psychology." *Collected Works of C.G. Jung, Vol. 8* (Princeton University Press 1970).

Deirdre Barrett, Editor. *Trauma and Dreams.* (Harvard University Press, 2001).

Chapter 18

J.R.R. Tolkein, *The Hobbit.* (George Allen & Unwin, 1937).

Nicole Gratton and Monique Séguin, *Dreams and Death: The Benefits of Dreams Before, During and After Death.* (Self-published 2011).

Chapter 19

Walter Berry, *The Mercy of the Fallen.* 2021.

Detail of "The Last Judgment," 1535–1541 by Michelangelo Buonarroti, 16th Century, fresco. Vatican City, Vatican Museums. Licensed through AGEfotostock.

William Shakespeare. *The Tempest,* Act 4 scene 1, (Riverside, 1974).

ACKNOWLEDGMENTS

The unsung heroes of this book are the innumerable dreamers who have shared their dreams with me over the years and allowed the world of awe to open as we explored each dream in depth. Thanks to David Jenkins, a true friend and phenomenal dreamworker, for the endless conversations and support he has given to this project.

Deep gratitude goes to Kay Martin for editing and honing the words and ideas, to Deborah Steinberg for an inspired restructuring of the book, and to Julie Simpson and her fine-toothed copyediting combs. Thanks to Susan Shankin for her awe-oriented book design and layout.

I am also grateful for Sarah La Saulle, who opened my eyes to the world of dreams and art and led me to Jeremy Taylor, my first mentor, along with his colleague Mara Fine. Thanks to the scholarly help of Kelly Bulkeley, Robert Hoss, Deirdre Barrett, Geoff Nelson, and Jane Carleton. The inspirations and conversations with Robert Moss, Michael Meade, Robert Bosnak, Clare Johnson, Kelly Sullivan Walden, Iain Edgar, and Robert Waggoner were invaluable. Thanks to the regular members of my dream group: Lucy Blake-Elahi, Barbara Ketchum, Bambi Corso-Steinmeyer, Van Hamilton, Kathy Gray, Sue Hoskins, Stan Hunter, Wendy Jackson, Nicole Marie, Athena Kolinski, Deanna Allen, Philip Berry, Judy Robinson, Delia Puiatti, Kat Winn, Leslie Thurman, Lauren Schneider, Abner Sarraf, and Linda Jacobson. All of them willingly shared their souls, their dreams and their drawings, many of which are in this book.

Lastly, I would like to thank the vivacious Janet Hoskins, my love and partner. She has been my muse and is the thoughtful soul who saw this book burning in me and insisted that I write it.

ABOUT THE AUTHOR

WALTER BERRY is a certified dream worker based in Los Angeles, California. He conducts a weekly dream group, which has been featured in *The New York Times* and *The Los Angeles Times.*

He is one of the authors of *Chicken Soup for the Soul: Dreams and Premonitions* and has written magazine articles for *DreamTime* magazine. A guest lecturer at Harvard University, The California Institute for the Arts, and The California Institute of Integral Studies, he is a regular contributor to Kelly Sullivan Walden's *Ask Doctor Dream* radio show and appears on various radio programs speaking about dreams.

Berry teaches dream workshops internationally and has been a keynote presenter at an International Association for the Study of Dreams conference.

As a professional lighting designer in the motion picture and television field, he designed the lighting (see next page) for the giant outdoor art sculpture on the Sunset Strip in Los Angeles designed by artist Janet Echelman entitled *Dream Catcher*—a representation of what happens to the brain during dreams.

For more information, visit: drawnintothedream.com

Olivia,
War Eagle!

Sherri Graves Smith
Christmas 2013

This book is dedicated to all Auburn fans! I extend lots of love to four Auburn fans in particular: Angela Williams, Ashley Stough, and Max and Drew Cowan.

Hugs,
Sherri

www.mascotbooks.com

For more information, please contact:
Mascot Books
560 Herndon Parkway #120
Herndon, VA 20170
info@mascotbooks.com

CPSIA Code: PRT1013A
ISBN-10: 1620864436
ISBN-13: 9781620864432

Printed in the United States

COUNTING WITH Aubie™

Sherri Graves Smith

illustrated by

D. T. Walsh

01

**Auburn has 1 mascot,
Aubie the Tiger.
He cheers for Auburn
and is our victorious fighter.**

There are 2 sides to the coin
the ref tosses in the air.
The winning team chooses
defense or offense – that's fair.

3 points are scored
when a field goal is kicked.
When we do it right,
our rivals are licked.

Each game has 4 quarters,
sixty minutes in all.
That's a long time
to play with a ball.

AUBURN
VISITOR
QUARTER
56
4
0
01

TIGERWALK®

Count the 5 band members
marching down the hill.
Tiger Walk's an Auburn tradition
and we do it still.

**A touchdown gives us 6 points
and with the kick it's 7.
Our fans scream so loud
they can be heard in the heavens!**

WAR
EAGLE

Count the 8 letters
in our War Eagle call.
We yell it out
when the Tigers get the ball.

Count 9 fans
wearing Auburn caps.
After the game,
it's time for a nap.

WAR EAGLE

WAR EAGLE
WAR EAGLE
WAR EAGLE
WAR EAGLE
WAR EAGLE
WAR EAGLE
WAR EAGLE
WAR EAGLE
WAR EAGLE
WAR EAGLE

Shout “WAR EAGLE”
with me 10 TIMES!
Now, say it once more
with gusto and pride!

About the Author

Photo © Sara Hanna Photography - www.SaraHanna.com. The photo was taken at the Swan Coach House.

Sherri Graves Smith is a lifelong avid reader and loves watching college football. At an early age, Sherri's parents instilled in her a great love of reading books which she still enjoys doing every day. Sherri volunteered to tutor and read to children because of the positive difference reading has made in her life. This led her to start writing children's books. In writing this book, Sherri wanted to make reading fun, bring in some Auburn tradition, and share in the joy and the experience of passing on the love of books to another generation. She hopes that you enjoyed reading her book as much as she enjoyed writing it!

Bonus Coloring Book!

56
4
0
01

3 1 0
3

1